AF492339

The Detective Book Club

1942 - 2000

A Checklist of 3-in-1 Mystery Omnibuses From Walter J. Black, Inc.

pagesofpages.com
Waterville, Maine 2024

Introduction

Overview

In 1940 Frank Gruber, a young writer living in New York, was trying to break into the book market. He had been writing for *Black Mask* and other pulp magazines, and turned to westerns in an attempt to sell to book publishers. A western, however, was only good for from $250 to $500 a title, so he decided to try his hand at writing mysteries. His first,*The French Key,* was quite successful.

> *[though a friend] I met Walter J. Black, who had a book club for classics. It was called the classics club. I talked to him a number of times and he kept sounding me out about mysteries, but never revealed the reason. Suddenly he announced The Detective Book Club, a mail order operation. This has become, through the years, a very successful thing and a great many of my mysteries have been selections of the club. The first book of mine that Black took on was The Mighty Blockhead. At that time Black paid one thousand dollars flat royalties to the author, of which the original publisher, however, got half[1].*

Gruber goes on to discuss the economics of writing mystery novels.

> *Things were adding up, though. Five hundred from the paperback companies, five hundred from the book club, seven or eight hundred from the original hardcover editions, a couple of hundred from the Grosset & Dunlap seventy-five-cent hardcover editions, one thousand to fifteen hundred dollars for first serial rights; a mystery novel was beginning to earn respectable money.*

The book club did indeed become "a very successful thing". Over the course of probably 60 years the club went on to reprint more than 2700 titles. Its volumes provide a comprehensive selection of mainstream mystery-thriller-suspense titles published throughout the rest of the 20th century and the very beginning of the 21st century. It published Erle Stanley Gardner (in 81 volumes), Hugh Pentecost (50 volumes); George Simenon (40 volumes); Agatha Christie (21 volumes). Frank Gruber (15 volumes); Robert Parker (7 volumes). And on and on, including writers not quite mainstream, such as Friedrich Durrenmatt, Russell Greenan and Patricia Highsmith.

The club began distribution in April of 1942. Walter J. Black, Inc. had been selling books by mail order and through department stores since the 1920's, and was looking to branch out. Branch out they did: the book club survived into the 21st century, initially sending out one volume a month containing three recent mysteries. In the 1970's they added a supplemental distribution scheme, marketed as The Inner Circle, which received initially one, and later two, additional three-in-one volumes very other month, There was also a Reader's Service Plan available, where two regular monthly

---

[1]Gruber, Frank. *The Pulp Jungle.* Los Angeles: Sherbourne Press. [c.1967]. p.170

Introduction

volumes were combined for shipment every other month, with a reduction in postage and handling charges. The frequency of distribution in the their last decade is uncertain, but there are 25 volumes that include books with a copyright date as late as 1999 and another 25 volumes containing at least one title with a 1998 copyright date. There are a couple of volumes where the latest copyright date is 2000; given 53 volumes that could not have been issued prior to 1998, it is very likely the club was active at least throuth 2000, and probably distributing more than 12 volumes each year.

The club also produced numerous promotional volumes containing one ortwo mystery novels.   Single-volume reprints seem particular common in the 1950's. Double-volumes, often with reprints of Erle Stanley Gardner (and his most popular pseudonym, A. A. Fair) are also common. This checklist lists only the 3-in-1 omnibus volumes, whether a regular distribution or a promotional volume. With at least one exception (Ross MacDonald's *Lew Archer, Private Investigator*) the promotional volumes are made up of novels already issued by the club. There is nothing in appearance to distinguish a promotional volume from a regular volume; promotional volumes are identifiable because they contain novels that appear separately in multiple other club volumes. There are around 25 promotional volumes in this listing, but because of their ad hoc nature there were probably many more.

Dating

The book club volumes contain no dating information other than the copyright dates for each of the novels being reprinted. The main source of specific dating information for volumes issued though October 1983 is Michael L. Cook's *Murder By Mail. Inside the Mystery Book Clubs.*[2] This book is now out of print. Cook had access to company records, and was able to identify the month of distribution for each regular issue, as well as distinguish between regular book club issues and volumes issued for the Inner Circle club. Physically there is nothing in the volumes to distinguish between the two sources.

There are a few gaps during the period covered by Cook's listing. No volumes are identified for April and May, 1946; February 1947; or May and June 1948. There are several pairs of months where two volumes were given: August and September 1954; August and September 1955. From January though April 1983 no volumes were issued at all due to their printer suddenly going out of business.

After October 1983 the volume dating becomes an arbitrary assignment based on the copyright dates of the novels included in each omnibus. Volumes are assigned to years based on the copyright dates of the novels each volume contains; the most recent copyright date becomes the year assigned to a volume. It is very unlikely that this is correct for volumes issued in a January or a February of the years from 1984 though to the end. No volume has been found containing a copyright date after 2000, so 2000 is

[2]"Revised and Updated Edition" Bowling Green University Popular Press, c.1983

Introduction

the final year used in this listing.

In 1990 the city of publication listed on title pages was changed from Roslyn, NY to Port Washington, NY.

Beginning with those volumes we have assigned to 1993 the city of publication was moved again, to Woodbury, NY, and the imprint changed from "Published for the Detective Book Club by Walter J. Black, Inc." to simply "The Detective Book Club". It is very likely that the club had ceased operations in 1992 (there are just 4 volumes containing titles with copyright dates reaching 1992), and was restarted in 1994 or 1995. There is a brief mention in *Publishers Weekly*[3] of "the Detective Book Club, recently resurrected by Platinum Press in Woodbury" .

Book Club First Editions?

The club reprinted recent mysteries. In this checklist the publisher of the edition being reprinted, and its year of publication, are listed after each title. Occasionally a book that was published two years previously will be included, and sometimes titles will be included when the original publisher is reissuing books in hardcover, but in general they did not mine publishers' backlists. Sometimes, however, the club seemed to publish concurrently with the trade publisher; and in a few cases they published the first US edition of a title.

The main example of first American editions from the book club are the books by the English writer Roy Vickers. Someone in the selection committee of the Detective Book Club must have been a Vickers fan; of the 12 Vickers titles that appear from the club, 5 were first US publications.

Several titles were published only by the Detective Book Club, including *The Famous McGarry Stories* by Matt Taylor (1958), and *Columbo and the Samurai Sword* by Bill Magee and Craig Schenck (1980).

The Big Blackout by Don Tracy (1959) preceded a paperback original from Pocket Books, as did *The Black Gold Murders* by John B. Ethan (1959). *Murder On Trial* by Michael Underwood was issued by the club in December, 1957; its official US publication date was February, 1958.

A possibly more interesting (because more collectible) example is Agatha Christie's *Blood Will Tell*, issued by the club in January 1952. The official Dodd, Mead publication date (as *Mrs. McGinty's Dead*) was February 1952[4]. The British publication date was March 1952 so a case could be made that the Detective Book Club printing is its true first edition.

Citation Example

[3]October 20, 1997, Volume 244, Issue 43 p.49
[4]*Publishers Weekly* December 28, 1951. p.9.

Introduction

1978.01 *January*
4586710
MacDonald, John D. *One Fearful Yellow Eye.* **1977 Lippincott**
Ferrars, E.X. *The Pretty Pink Shroud.* **1977 Doubleday.**
Wetering, Janwillem van de. *The Japanese Corpse.* **1977**
Houghton Mifflin.

The citations are ordered by year, and by month when month is known. Promotional volumes appear at the end of the year to which they are assigned.

The number at the beginning - 1978.01 above - is used in the indexes to reference a specific volume. These numbers are only useful within the context of this checklist. In the above example, "1978" identifies the year to which the volume is assigned. "01" in this case corresponds to the month, but that will only occasionally be true; it breaks down completely when multiple volumes are issued in any month. When no month is known then order within a year becomes arbitrary (other than for those promotional volumes listed at the end of listings for the year). In a few cases a change in publisher or location or cover design allows a year's volumes to be partially ordered. There are rare cases where a month of issue after 1983 can be independently determined.

The number at the right on the top line is the WorldCat id. WorldCat (www.worldcat.org) is a consolidated database of library catalogs from around the world; A WorldCat id has been identified for nearly every citation in this listing, as part of the verification process. It can be used to retrieve a catalog entry for each of the volumes; often these carry additional details, such as pagination.

The remainder of the listing consists of the three titles included in the volume. Each line contains the author, title, and then the year and publisher of the regular edition being reprinted. Occasionally the club's title will differ from that of the original publisher. Note also that date and publisher are not necessarily that of the first American edition; sometimes the club would pick up re-issues. John D. MacDonald is a good example of that practice; some of his books were paperback originals. *A Deadly Shade of Gold* was published by Fawcett paperbacks in 1965; issued in hardcover by Lippincott in 1974 and by the Club in January of 1975.

Publisher names change a good deal over time; occasionally they are given in somewhat abbreviated form, but where space allows the full name of the publisher has been preserved. Elizabeth Daly, in these listings, was published four times by Farrar & Rinehart. Farrar left (to form Farrar & Straus) and Day's remaining seven titles appeared from Rinehart. Rinehart eventually merged into Holt, Rinehart & Winston. All three forms of Rinehart appear many times in these listings.

Book Design

Introduction

Volumes were originally published in a tan binding with dust jacket. The jackets used a three-panel design, one for each of the three novels present. Author and title are listed, and a sketch presumed to represent a scene from the book. The typography varies from standard to script-type fonts. Colors varied from month to month.

In 1952 the sketch was replaced with a picture of the original hardcover volume (occasionally imagined rather than an actual representation), at a bit of an angle so that part of the spine is visible and one gets a sense of the size of each book being included.

In 1959 the jacket was dropped. The jacket's design was used for pictorial paper-over-board covers.

Around 1993 (see the section *Dating* above) the club's imprint was changed from "Water J. Black for the Detective Book Club / Roslyn. NY" to "The Detective Book Club / Woodbury NY". This probably corresponds to the club going defunct for some period of time, and then being resurrected by The Platinum Press of Woodbury.

In 1996 the jacket design was modified, dropping the representation of the original books, leaving only the author and title in each of the three panels.

The last few volumes assigned to 1999 or 2000 have a new cover design, dropping the three panel design: there is a solid frame around the front, with a top label "Detective Book Club Triple Mysteries", and the three reprints identified in a single panel in the middle.

Numbers

The original price of the club volumes was $1.89 each, and that price was maintained for a surprisingly long time. By 1958 the price was only $2.29. By 1963 the price was $2.89. In 1968 the price was $3.39. In 1975 the price - after very considerable inflation - was just $3.89; in 1977 it was $4.39.

Some indication of the size of the club's membership can be given by the club's reported newspaper advertising budget: $406,579 in 1951, $263,248 in 1952[5] (a year when newspaper ad spending was generally down). It would take more than 18,000 members buying all 12 volumes for a year to gross an amount of revenue equal to the 1951 newspaper ad expenditure; and of course there are production costs, reprint rights, other advertising costs, and general overhead to consider. As a point of comparison, Random House, a large and commercially aggressive publisher, spent $189,145. Other book clubs did have larger expenditures, the largest being the Literary Guild: $767,268 in 1951, $525,614 in 1952: more or less twice that of the Detective Book Club.

In an interview published in 1988[6], total membership was described as a "company secret", but was more than 50,000. Walter Black (grandson of the founder)

---

[5]*Publishers Weekly* Vol 164, July 18, 1953. p194.
[6]*Newsday* Nassau and Suffolk Edition, Long Island. 26 Dec 1988. p.6.

Introduction

said that they bought non-exclusive rights to books for from between $15,000 and $55,000. "A book may get 5,000 to 6,000 copies sold in trade. If we buy the rights, we can get 10 times the volume in sales".

A Final Word

There is some uncertainty about the last years of the Detective Book Club. Because it was a book club it did not receive the kind of attention that regular trade publishers did and do. The phrase "A selection of the Detective Book Club" appears many times in the pages of *Publishers Weekly,* but the club otherwise received very little attention. It was a major source of ad revenue for newspapers and periodicals; it pioneered various forms of direct advertising such as postcard inserts in paperbacks and magazines, but in its final years it received very little notice.

The identification of titles after 1983 is based on personal research, not on company records. In spite of the very large number of volumes identified through the end of the 1990's it is very likely that this listing is incomplete.

The Detective Book Club 1942-2000

1942

1942.01   *April*   657071495
  Gardner, Erle Stanley. *The Case Of The Empty Tin.* 1941 Morrow.
  Christie, Agatha. *Evil Under The Sun.* 1941 Dodd, Mead.
  Lockridge, Frances and Richard. *A Pinch Of Poison.* 1941 Lippincott.
1942.02   *May*   1840815
  Eberhart, Mignon G. *With This Ring.* 1941 Random House.
  Gruber, Frank. *The Mighty Blockhead.* 1942 Farrar & Rinehart.
  Gardner, Erle Stanley. *The D.A. Cooks A Goose.* 1942 Morrow.
1942.03   *June*   3547545
  Christie, Agatha. *The Body in the Library.* 1942 Dodd, Mead.
  Fair, A A. *Double or Quits.* 1941 Morrow.
  Mason, Van Wyck. *The Rio Casino Intrigue.* 1941 Reynal and Hitchcock.
1942.04   *July*   425972835
  Freeman, R Austin. *The Unconscious Witness.* 1942 Dodd, Mead.
  Lockridge, Frances and Richard. *Death On The Aisle.* 1942 Lippincott.
  Holding, Elisabeth Sanxay. *Lady Killer.* 1942 Duell, Sloan and Pearce.
1942.05   *August*   5366058
  Stout, Rex. *Black Orchids.* 1942 Farrar & Rinehart.
  Wilde, Percival. *Tinsley's Bones.* 1942 Random House.
  Taylor, Phoebe Atwood. *The Six Iron Spiders.* 1942 Norton.
1942.06   *September*   1051660741
  Reilly, Helen. *Name Your Poison.* 1942 Random House.
  Oursler, Will. *Folio On Florence White.* 1942 Simon & Schuster.
  Irish, William. *Phantom Lady.* 1942 Lippincott.
1942.07   *October*   6320953
  Gardner, Erle Stanley. *The Case Of The Drowning Duck.* 1942 Morrow.
  Crofts, Freemont Wills. *Fear Comes To Chalfont.* 1942 Dodd, Mead.
  Gilbert, Anthony. *Mystery In The Woodshed.* 1942 Smith and Durrell.
1942.08   *November*   1869470
  Knight, Clifford. *The Affair of the Splintered Heart.* 1942 Dodd, Mead.
  Campbell, Alice. *Ringed With Fire.* 1942 Random House.
  Fitzsimmons, Cortland. *Death Rings a Bell.* 1942 Lippincott.
1942.09   *December*   220695866
  Lockridge, Frances and Richard. *Hanged For A Sheep.* 1942 Lippincott.
  Fair, A A. *Bats Fly At Dusk.* 1942 Morrow.
  McCloy, Helen. *Cue For Murder.* 1942 Morrow.

1943

1943.01   *January*   5135864
  Crane, Frances. *The Yellow Violet.* 1942 Lippincott.
  Gruber, Frank. *The Gift Horse.* 1942 Farrar & Rinehart.
  Rutland, Harriet. *Blue Murder.* 1942 Smith & Durrell.

1943

1943.02   *February*   8119229
Eberhart, Mignon G. *Wolf In Man's Clothing.* 1941 Random House.
Abbot, Anthony. *The Shudders.* 1943 Farrar & Rinehart.
Shriber, Ione Sandberg. *A Body For Bill.* 1942 Farrar & Rinehart.

1943.03   *March*   8207974
Gardner, Erle Stanley. *The Case Of The Smoking Chimney.* 1942 Morrow.
Wolffe, Katherine. *The Attic Room.* 1942 Morrow.
Dickson, Carter. *She Died A Lady.* 1943 Morrow.

1943.04   *April*   425971426
Daly, Elizabeth. *Nothing Can Rescue Me.* 1943 Farrar & Rinehart.
Halliday, Brett. *Murder Wears A Mummer's Mask.* 1943 Dodd, Mead.
Nolan, Jeannette Covert. *Final Appearance.* 1943 Duell, Sloan And Pearce.

1943.05   *May*   10668881
Knight, Clifford. *Affair Of The Jade Monkey.* 1943 Dodd, Mead.
Walling, R A J. *A Corpse by Any Other Name.* 1943 Morrow.
Wylie, Philip. *Corpses At Indian Stones.* 1943 Farrar & Rinehart.

1943.06   *June*   864741644
Gardner, Erle Stanley. *The Case Of The Buried Clock.* 1943 Morrow.
Mace, Merlda. *Headlong For Murder.* 1943 Crestwood Pub.
Sanders, Daphne. *To Catch a Thief.* 1943 Dial Press.

1943.07   *July*   8210933
McCloy, Helen. *Do Not Disturb.* 1943 Morrow.
Grafton, C W. *The Rat Began To Gnaw The Rope.* 1943 Farrar & Rinehart.
Jackson, Giles. *Court Of Shadows.* 1943 Dial Press.

1943.08   *August*   3025114
Lockridge, Frances and Richard. *Death Takes a Bow.* 1943 Lippincott.
Goldman, Lawrence. *Fall Guy For Murder.* 1943 Dutton.
Cores, Lucy. *Painted for the Kill.* 1943 Duell, Sloan and Pearce.

1943.09   *September*   425971424
Daly, Elizabeth. *Evidence of Things Seen.* 1943 Farrar & Rinehart.
Cheyney, Peter. *Dark Duet.* 1943 Dodd, Mead.
Shane, Susannah. *A Lady in a Million.* 1943 Dodd, Mead.

1943.10   *October*   425971414
Crane, Frances. *The Pink Umbrella.* 1943 Lippincott.
Fair, A A. *Cats Prowl At Night.* 1943 Morrow.
Gilbert, Anthony. *The Woman In Red.* 1943 Smith and Durrell.

1943.11   *November*   425971466
Gardner, Erle Stanley. *The Case Of The Drowsy Mosquito.* 1943 Morrow.
Mace, Merlda. *Motto For Murder.* 1943 Crestwood / Black Cat Detective Series.
Knight, Clifford. *The Affair Of The Fainting Butler.* 1943, Dodd, Mead.

1943

1943.12   *December*   9423505
Halliday, Brett. *Blood on the Black Market.* 1943 Dodd, Mead.
Cunningham, A B. *The Great Yant Mystery.* 1943 Dutton.
Hughes, Dorothy B. *The Blackbirder.* 1943 Duell Sloan & Pearce.

1944

1944.01   *January*   6188424
Lord, Garland. *Murder with Love.* 1943 Green Publishing / Big Green Detective.
Stafford, Muriel. *X Marks the Dot.* 1943 Duell. Sloan and Pearce.
Cheyney, Peter. *The Stars are Dark.* 1943 Dodd, Mead.
1944.02   *February*   6320811
Gardner, Erle Stanley. *The D.A. Calls A Turn.* 1944 Morrow.
Crane, Frances. *The Applegreen Cat.* 1943 Lippincott.
Shriber, Ione Sandberg. *Invitation To Murder.* 1943 Farrar & Rinehart.
1944.03   *March*   3637432
McCloy, Helen. *The Goblin Market.* 1943 Morrow.
Irish, William. *Deadline at Dawn.* 1944 Lippincott.
Lockridge, Frances and Richard. *Killing the Goose.* 1944 Lippincott.
1944.04   *April*   425971431
Dickson, Carter. *He Wouldn't Kill Patience.* 1944 Hampton / Morrow.
Roden, H W. *You Only Hang Once.* 1944 Morrow.
Millar, Margaret. *Fire Will Freeze.* 1944 Random House.
1944.05   *May*   587334574
Daly, Elizabeth. *Arrow Pointing Nowhere.* 1944 Farrar & Rinehart.
Fischer, Bruno. *The Hornet's Nest.* 1944 Morrow.
McDougald, Roman. *The Deaths Of Lora Karen.* 1944 Simon & Schuster.
1944.06   *June*   425971485
Hughes, Dorothy B. *The Delicate Ape.* 1944 Duell, Sloan and Pearce.
Homes, Geoffrey. *Six Silver Handles.* 1944 Morrow.
Knotts, Raymond. *And the Deep Blue Sea.* 1944 arrar & Rinehart.
1944.07   *July*   3636601
Lariar, Lawrence. *The Man With the Lumpy Nose.* 1944 Dodd, Mead.
Gardner, Erle Stanley. *The Case Of The Crooked Candle.* 1944 Morrow.
Abbey, Kieran. *Beyond the Dark.* 1944 Scribner.
1944.08   *August*   3495487
Walling, R A J. *The Corpse Without A Clue.* 1944 Morrow.
Woolrich, Cornell. *The Black Path Of Fear.* 1944 Doubleday.
O'Neil, Kerry. *Death Strikes At Heron House.* 1944 Farrar & Rinehart.
1944.09   *September*   425971421
Daly, Elizabeth. *The Book Of The Dead.* 1944 Farrar & Rinehar.
Bramhall, Marion. *Button Button.* 1944 Doubleday.
Vickers, Roy. *A Date With Danger.* 1944 Vanguard Press.

1944

1944.10 *October*   6183171
 Carr, John Dickson. *Till Death Do Us Part.* 1944 Harper.
 Knight, Kathleen Moore. *Intrigue For Empire.* 1944 Duubleday.
 Fair, A A. *Give 'Em The Ax.* 1944 Morrow.
1944.11 *November*   6106485
 Thayer, Lee. *Five Bullets.* 1944 Dodd, Mead.
 Crane, Frances. *The Amethyst Spectacles.* 1944 Random House.
 Knight, Clifford. *The Affair Of The Dead Stranger.* 1944 Dodd, Mead.
1944.12 *December*   871347990
 Gardner, Erle Stanley. *The Case Of The Black-Eyed Blonde.* 1944 Morrow.
 Christie, Agatha. *Death Comes as the End.* 1944 Dodd, Mead.
 Stout, Rex. *Not Quite Dead Enough.* 1944 Farrar & Rinehart.

1945

1945.01 *January*   4361379
 Roden, H W. *Too Busy to Die.* 1944 Morrow.
 Rowe, Anne. *Too Much Poison.* 1944 M S Mill.
 Sanders, George. *Crime on my Hands.* 1944 Simon & Schuster.
1945.02 *February*   81569624
 Lawrence, Hilda. *Blood Upon The Snow.* 1944 Simon & Schuster.
 Cheyney, Peter. *They Never Say When.* 1945 Dodd, Mead.
 Shriber, Ione Sandberg. *Pattern For Murder.* 1944 Farrar & Rinehart.
1945.03 *March*   1149423751
 Crane, Frances. *The Indigo Necklace.* 1945 Random House.
 Footner, Hulbert. *Orchids To Murder.* 1945 Harper.
 Gilbert, Anthony. *Death At The Door.* 1945 Smith & Durrell.
1945.04 *April*   5384862
 Knight, Kathleen Moore. *Stream Sinister.* 1945 Doubleday.
 Reilly, Helen. *Murder On Angler's Island.* 1945 Random House.
 Lockridge, Frances and Richard. *Payoff For The Banker.* 1945 Lippincott.
1945.05 *May*   1036736377
 Halliday, Brett. *Murder Is My Business.* 1945 Dodd, Mead.
 Holbrook, Marion. *Crime Wind.* 1945 Dodd, Mead.
 Millhauser, Bertram. *Whatever Goes Up.* 1945 Doubleday.
1945.06 *June*   6074442
 Martin, A E. *The Outsiders.* 1945 Simon & Schuster.
 Rowe, Anne. *Fatal Purchase.* 1945 M S Mill.
 Roden, H W. *One Angel Less.* 1945 Morrow.
1945.07 *July*   1029272530
 Gardner, Erle Stanley. *The Case Of The Golddigger's Purse.* 1945 Morrow.
 Marsh, Ngaio. *Died in the Wool.* 1945 Little, Brown.
 Allingham, Margery. *Pearls Before Swine.* 1945 Doubleday.

1945

1945.08   *August*   323169
  Kendrick, Baynard. *Out Of Control.* 1945 Morrow.
  Rhode, John. *Too Many Suspects.* 1945 Dodd, Mead.
  Bayer, Oliver Weld. *An Eye For An Eye.* 1945 Doubleday.
1945.09   *September*   1112389257
  Queen, Ellery. *The Murderer is a Fox.* 1945 Little, Brown.
  Hughes, Dorothy B. *Dread Journey.* 1945 Duell, Sloan and Pearce.
  Dickson, Carter. *The Curse of the Bronze Lamp.* 1945 Morrow.
1945.10   *October*   18604251
  Rogers, Samuel. *You'll Be Sorry!.* 1945 Harper.
  Fenisong, Ruth. *The Lost Caesar.* 1945 Doubleday.
  Vickers, Roy. *Four Past Four.* 1945 Jefferson House.
1945.11   *November*   18734289
  Knight, Kathleen Moore. *Port Of Seven Strangers.* 1945 Doubleday.
  Cheyney, Peter. *Sinister Errand.* 1945 Dodd Mead.
  Rowe, Anne. *Up To The Hilt.* 1945 M S Mill.
1945.12   *December*   6186260
  Lariar, Lawrence. *The Girl With the Frightened Eyes.* 1945 Dodd Mead.
  Gardner, Erle Stanley. *The Case Of The Half-Wakened Wife.* 1945 M S Mill.
  Alan, Marjorie. *Dark Prophecy.* 1945 M S Mill.

1946

1946.01   *January*   425970829
  McCloy, Helen. *The One That Got Away.* 1945 Morrow.
  Huggins, Roy. *The Double Take.* 1946 Morrow.
  Coles, Manning. *The Fifth Man.* Doubleday 1946.
1946.02   *February*   864741737
  Gardner, Erle Stanley. *The D.A. Breaks A Seal.* 1946 Morrow.
  Lockridge, Frances and Richard. *Murder Within Murder.* 1946 Lippincott.
  Lawrence, Hilda. *The Pavilion.* 1946 Simon and Schuster.
1946.03   *March*   1652919
  Kelsey, Vera. *Whisper Murder!.* 1946 Doubleday.
  Gilbert, Anthony. *Death Lifts The Latch.* 1946 Smith and Durrell.
  Daly, Elizabeth. *Somewhere In The House.* 1946 Rinehart.
1946.04   *June*   3853621
  Holding, Elisabeth Sanxay. *The Innocent Mrs. Duff.* 1946 Simon and Schuster.
  Martin, A E. *Death In The Limelight.* 1946 Simon and Schuster.
  Knight, Kathleen Moore. *The Trouble At Turkey Hill.* 1946 Doubleday.
1946.05   *July*   933904880
  Carr, John Dickson. *He Who Whispers.* 1946 Harper.
  Armstrong, Charlotte. *The Unsuspected.* 1946 Coward-McCann.
  Fair, A A. *Crows Can't Count.* 1946 Morrow.

1946

1946.06   *August*   6189697
Dent, Lester. *Dead at the Take-Off.* 1946 Doubleday.
Hays, Sue Brown. *Go Down, Death.* 1946 Scribner.
Sale, Richard. *Benefit Performance.* 1946 Simon and Schuster.
1946.07   *September*   1148058441
Eberhart, Mignon G. *Five Passengers From Lisbon.* 1946 Random House.
Roden, H W. *Wake For A Lady.* 1946 Morrow.
Caspary, Vera. *The Murder In The Stork Club.* The Murder In The Stork Clu.
1946.08   *October*   964200615
Gardner, Erle Stanley. *The Case Of The Backward Mule.* 1942 Morrow.
Ford, Leslie. *Honolulu Story.* 1946 Scribner.
Dickson, Carter. *My Late Wives.* 1946 Morrow.
1946.09   *November*   6838918
Crane, Frances. *The Cinnamon Murder.* 1946 Random House.
Dewey, Thomas B. *As Good As Dead.* 1945 Jefferson House.
Daly, Elizabeth. *The Wrong Way Down.* 1946 Rinehart.
1946.10   *December*   1146427258
Eberhart, Mignon G. *The White Dress.* 1945 Random House.
Stout, Rex. *The Silent Speaker.* 1946 Viking.
Christie, Agatha. *The Hollow.* 1946 Dodd Mead.

1947

1947.01   *January*   10241469
Dent, Lester. *Lady To Kill.* 1946 Doubleday.
Taylor, Phoebe Atwood. *Punch With Care.* 1946 Norton.
Gardner, Erle Stanley. *The Case Of The Borrowed Brunette.* 1946 Morrow.
1947.02   *March*   425972840
Gilbert, Anthony. *By Hook or Crook.* 1947 A.S. Barnes.
Page, Marco. *The Shadowy Third.* 1946 Dodd Mead.
Vickers, Roy. *The Whispering Death.* 1947 Jefferson House.
1947.03   *April*   11156280
Carr, John Dickson. *The Sleeping Sphinx.* 1947 Collier.
Gruber, Frank. *Beagle Scented Murder.* 1946 Rinehart.
Lawrence, Hilda. *Death of a Doll.* 1947 Simon and Schuster.
1947.04   *May*   6074956
Gardner, Erle Stanley. *Two Clues.* 1947 Morrow.
Ross, Z H. *Overdue For Death.* 1947 Bobbs-Merrill.
Tucker, Wilson. *The Chinese Doll.* 1946 Rinehart.
1947.05   *June*   41803750
Eberhart, Mignon G. *Another Woman's House.* 1947 Random House.
Colter, Eli. *Cheer For The Dead.* 1947 M S Mill.
Linklater, J Lane. *Shadow For A Lady.* 1947 M S Mill.

1947

1947.06   *July*   7587770
  Gardner, Erle Stanley. *The Case Of The Fan-Dancer's Horse.* 1947 Morrow.
  Reilly, Helen. *The Silver Leopard.* 1946 Random House.
  Block, Libbie. *Bedeviled.* 1947 Doubleday.
1947.07   *August*   35050177
  Ford, Leslie. *The Woman In Black.* 1947 Scribner.
  Richart, Mary. *Murder In the Town.* 1947 Farrar, Straus.
  Roos, Kelley. *Ghost Of A Chance.* 1947 A. A. Wyn.
1947.08   *September*   1020410291
  Reilly, Helen. *The Farmhouse.* 1947 Random House.
  Fair, A A. *Fools Die on Friday.* 1947 Morrow.
  Cheyney, Peter. *Dark Interlude.* 1947 Dodd, Mead.
1947.09   *October*   11541485
  Huggins, Roy. *Too Late For Tears.* 1947 Morrow.
  Crane, Frances. *Murder On The Purple Water.* 1947 Random House.
  Gruber, Frank. *The Whispering Master.* 1947 Rinehart.
1947.10   *November*   220682009
  Gardner, Erle Stanley. *The Case Of The Lazy Lover.* 1947 Morrow.
  Lockridge, Frances and Richard. *Untidy Murder.* 1947 Lippincott.
  Coles, Manning. *Let the Tiger Die.* 1947 Doubleday.
1947.11   *December*   1020410291
  Linklater, J Lane. *Black Opal.* 1947 M S Mill.
  Gallagher, Gale. *I Found Him Dead.* 1947 Coward McCann.
  Crispin, Edmund. *Dead and Dumb.* 1947 Lippincott.
1947.12   *promotional*   6292568
  Gardner, Erle Stanley. *The Case Of The Borrowed Brunette.* 1946 Morrow.
  Gardner, Erle Stanley. *The Case Of The Half-Wakened Wife.* 1945 M S Mill.
  Gardner, Erle Stanley. *The Case Of The Black-Eyed Blonde.* 1944 Morrow.

1948

1948.01   *January*   1028860141
  Holding, Elisabeth Sanxay. *The Blank Wall.* 1947 Simon & Schuster.
  Gilbert, Anthony. *Death in the Wrong Room.* 1947 Barnes.
  Leonard, Charles. *Search for a Scientist.* 1947 Doubleday.
1948.02   *February*   9130833
  Stout, Rex. *Too Many Women.* 1947 Viking Press.
  Daly, Elizabeth. *Night Walk.* 1947 Rinehart.
  Dewey, Thomas B. *Draw The Curtain Close.* 1947 Jefferson House.
1948.03   *March*   5004734
  Christie, Agatha. *There is a Tide.* 1948 Dodd, Mead.
  Treat, Lawrence. *T as in Trapped.* 1947 Morrow.
  Amos, Alan. *Borderline Murder.* 1947 Doubleday.

1948

1948.04   *April*   6013100
King, Rufus. *Lethal Lady.* 1947 Doubleday.
Goodis, David. *Nightfall.* 1947 J. Messner.
Goldthwaite, Eaton K. *Root Of Evil.* 1948 Duell, Sloan & Pearce.

1948.05   *July*   6013100
Cheyney, Peter. *Dance Without Music.* 1948 Dodd, Mead.
Gardner, Erle Stanley. *The Case Of The Lonely Heiress.* 1948 Morrow.
Disney, Dorothy Cameron. *Explosion.* 1948 Random House.

1948.06   *August*   1344543
Gilbert, Anthony. *The Missing Widow.* 1948 A. S. Barnes.
Gruber, Frank. *The Scarlet Feather.* 1948 Rinehart.
Lockridge, Richard and Frances. *I Want to Go Home.* 1948 Lippincott.

1948.07   *September*   1147989306
Daly, Elizabeth. *The Book of the Lion.* 1948 Rinehart.
Mason, Sara Elizabeth. *The Whip.* 1948 Morrow.
Foley, Rae. *No Tears for the Dead.* 1948 Dodd, Mead.

1948.08   *October*   988743
Ford, Leslie. *The Devil's Stronghold.* 1948 Scribner.
Woolrich, Cornell. *Rendezvous In Black.* 1948 Rinehart.
Gardner, Erle Stanley. *The Case Of The Vagabond Virgin.* 1948 Morrow.

1948.09   *November*   24194471
Gardner, Erle Stanley. *The D.A. Takes a Chance.* 1948 Morrow.
McCloy, Helen. *She Walks Alone.* 1948 Random House.
Curtiss, Ursula. *Voice Out of Darkness.* 1948 Dodd, Mead.

1948.10   *December*   978145773
Rice, Craig. *The Fourth Postman.* 1948 Simon & Schuster.
Coles, Manning. *Among Those Absent.* 1948 Doubleday.
Gruber, Frank. *The Lock and the Key.* 1948 Rinehart.

1949

1949.01   *January*   1013306485
Lockridge, Frances and Richard. *Murder is Served.* 1948 Lippincott.
Christie, Agatha. *The Witness for the Prosecution.* and Three Blind Mice.
Knight, Clifford. *Dark Abyss.* 1949 Dutton.

1949.02   *February*   7544017
Crane, Frances. *Black Cypress.* 1948 Random House.
Fair, A A. *Bedrooms Have Windows.* 1949 Morrow.
Coxe, George Harmon. *The Hollow Needle.* 1948 Knopf.

1949.03   *March*   988245971
Cheyney, Peter. *Dark Wanton.* 1949 Dodd, Mead.
DuBois, Theodora. *The Face Of Hate.* 1948 Doubleday.
Gardner, Erle Stanley. *The Case Of The Dubious Bridegroom.* 1949 Morrow.

1949

1949.04   *April*   3219557
Allingham, Margery. *More Work for the Undertaker.* 1949 Doubleday.
Lockridge, Richard and Frances. *Spin Your Web Lady.* 1949 Lippincott.
Gilbert, Anthony. *The Innocent Bottle.* 1949 Barnes.
1949.05   *May*   11540923
Knight, Kathleen Moore. *Dying Echo.* 1949 Doubleday.
Lawrence, Hilda. *Duet of Death.* 1947 Simon & Schuster.
Brean, Herbert. *The Darker the Night.* 1949 Morrow.
1949.06   *June*   9126671
Coxe, George Harmon. *Lady Killer.* 1949 Knopf.
Foley, Rae. *Girl From Nowhere.* 1949 Dodd, Mead.
Lorac, E C R. *Place For A Poisoner.* 1949 Doubleday.
1949.07   *July*   7024879
Reilly, Helen. *Staircase Four.* 1949 Random House.
Bonett, John and Emery. *Dead Lion.* 1949 Doubleday.
Clark, Philip. *The Dark River.* 1949 Simon & Schuster.
1949.08   *August*   5634289
Disney, Dorothy Cameron. *The Hangman's Tree.* 1949 Random House.
Hagen, Miriam-Ann. *Dig Me Later.* 1949 Doubleday.
Gruber, Frank. *The Leather Duke.* 1949 Rinehart.
1949.09   *September*   178683
Eberhart, Mignon G. *House of Storm.* 1949 Random House.
Gilbert, Michael. *He Didn't Mind Danger.* 1948 Harper.
Treat, Lawrence. *Trial and Terror.* 1949 Morrow.
1949.10   *October*   3219457
Allingham, Margery. *Deadly Duo.* 1949 Doubleday.
Tucker, Wilson. *The Stalking Man.* 1949 Rinehart.
Scherf, Margaret. *The Gun in Daniel Websters Bust.* 1949 Doubleday.
1949.11   *November*   5957153
Daly, Elizabeth. *And Dangerous To Know.* 1949 Rinehart.
Cheyney, Peter. *The Man Nobody Saw.* 1949 Dodd, Mead.
Crane, Frances. *The Flying Red horse.* 1949 Random.
1949.12   *December*   6350380
Gardner, Erle Stanley. *The D.A. Breaks An Egg.* 1949 Morrow.
Rohmer, Sax. *Hangover House.* 1949 Random House.
Powell, Richard. *Shark River.* 1949 Simon & Schuster.

1950

1950.01   *January*   43772329
Campbell, Alice. *Veiled Murder.* 1949 Random House.
Gardner, Erle Stanley. *The Case Of The Negligent Nymph.* 1949 Morrow.
Palmer, Stuart. *Four Lost Ladies.* 1949 Morrow.

1950

1950.02	*February*	1013352293

Reeve, Christopher. *Lady, Be Careful.* 1950 M S Mill.
Foley, Rae. *Bones of Contention.* 1950 Dodd, Mead.
Bunce, Frank. *So Young a Body.* 1950 Simon & Schuster.

1950.03	*March*	6876469

Du Bois, Theodora. *It's Raining Violence.* 1949 Doubleday.
Cheyney, Peter. *One of Those Things.* 1950 Dodd Mead.
Iams, Jack. *Do Not Murder Before Christmas.* 1949 Morrow.

1950.04	*April*	1039490448

Knight, Kathleen Moore. *The Bass Derby Murder.* 1949 Doubleday.
Walling, R A J. *The Corpse With The Missing Watch.* 1949 Morrow.
Curtiss, Ursula. *The Second Sickle.* 1950 Dodd, Mead.

1950.05	*May*	79405501

Gilbert, Anthony. *Death Knocks Three Times.* 1949 Random House.
Blizard, Marie. *The Dark Corner.* 1950 M S Mill.
Olsen, D B. *Something About Midnight.* 1950 Doubleday.

1950.06	*June*	7959377

Murray, Max. *The Neat Little Corpse.* 1950 Farrar, Straus.
Dunn, Dorothy. *Murder's Web.* 1950 Harper.
Crispin, Edmund. *Sudden Vengeance.* 1950 Dodd, Mead.

1950.07	*July*	1035611019

Frome, David. *Homicide House.* 1949 Rinehart.
Iams, Jack. *What Rhymes With Murder?.* 1950 Morrow.
Spicer, Bart. *Blues For The Prince.* 1950 Dodd, Mead.

1950.08	*August*	1036892903

Mccloy, Helen. *Through A Glass, Darkly.* 1950 Random House.
Vickers, Roy. *Maid To A Murder.* 1950 M S Mill.
Powell, Richard. *Shell Game.* 1950 Simon & Schuster.

1950.09	*September*	5634340

Daly, Elizabeth. *Death And Letters.* 1950 Rinehart.
Goodis, David. *Of Missing Persons.* 1950 Morrow.
Christie, Agatha. *A Murder Is Announced.* 1950 Dodd, Mead.

1950.10	*October*	43009503

Neville, Margot. *Murder of a Nymph.* 1950 Doubleday.
Eberhart, Mignon G. *Hunt With the Hounds.* 1950 Random House.
Steiguer, Walter De. *Jewels for a Shroud.* Morrow 1950.

1950.11	*November*	988185000

Coles, Manning. *Dangerous by Nature.* 1950 Doubleday.
Swiggett, Howard. *The Hidden And The Hunted.* 1950 Morrow.
Kelland, Clarence Budington. *Stolen Goods.* 1949 Harper.

1950

1950.12 *December*		8189812

Russell, Charlotte M. *Between Us And Evil.* 1950 Doubleday.
Hamilton, Donald. *Murder Twice Told.* 1950 Rinehart.
Cheyney, Peter. *Lady, Beware.* 1950 Dodd Mead.

1951

1951.01   *January*   8134078
Weston, Garnett. *Legacy Of Fear.* 1950 M S Mill.
Brand, Christianna. *Cat And Mouse.* 1950 Knopf.
Gardner, Erle Stanley. *The Case Of The One-Eyed Witness.* 1950 Morrow.

1951.02   *February*   9651601
Coxe, George Harmon. *The Frightened Fiancee.* 1950 Knopf.
Thayer, Lee. *Too Long Endured.* 1950 Dodd, Mead.
Rinehart, Mary Roberts. *Episode Of The Wandering Knife.* 1950 Rinehart.

1951.03   *March*   6876634
Shriber, Ione Sandberg. *Never Say Die.* 1950 Rinehart.
Upfield, Arthur W. *Bachelors Of Broken Hill.* 1950 Doubleday.
Foley, Rae. *The Hundreth Door.* 1950 Dodd, Mead.

1951.04   *April*   6182994
Ford, Leslie. *Murder Is The Pay-Off.* 1951 Scribner.
Cumberland, Marten. *The House In The Forest.* 1950 Doubleday.
O'Finn, Thaddeus. *Happy Holiday.* 1950 Rinehart.

1951.05   *May*   988185432
Reeve, Christopher. *Murder Steps Out.* 1951 M S Mill.
Knight, Kathleen Moore. *The Silent Partner.* 1950 Doubleday.
Palmer, Stuart. *The Green Ace.* 1950 M S Mill.

1951.06   *June*   8223274
Cheyney, Peter. *Dark Bahama.* 1951 Dodd, Mead.
Daly, Elizabeth. *The Book Of The Crime.* 1951 Rinehart.
Irish, William. *Strangler's Serenade.* 1951 Rinehart.

1951.07   *July*   11516298
Ullman, Allan and Fletcher, Lucile. *Night Man.* 1951 Random House.
Gilbert, Anthony. *Murder Comes Home.* 1951 Random House.
Gardner, Erle Stanley. *The Case Of The Fiery Fingers.* 1951 Morrow.

1951.08   *August*   190828169
Vickers, Roy. *The Sole Survivor and The Kynsard Affair.* DBC 1st US.
Scherf, Margaret. *The Corpse With One Shoe.* 1951 Doubleday ??.
Ambler, Eric. *Judgement On Deltchev.* 1951 Knopf.

1951.09   *September*   11514924
McCloy, Helen. *Alias Basil Willing.* 1951 Random House.
Lorac, E C R. *Accident by Design.* 1951 Doubleday.
Blizard, Marie. *The Watch Sinister.* 1951 M S Mill.

1951

| 1951.10 | *October* | 6106379 |

Cheyney, Peter. *Ladies Won't Wait.* 1951 Dodd, Mead.
Bradley, Mary Hastings. *Murder In The Family.* 1951 Longmans, Green.
Kelland, Clarence Budington. *The Great Mail Robbery.* 1950 Harper.

| 1951.11 | *November* | 5651638 |

Nelson, Hugh Lawrence. *Gold In Every Grave.* 1951 Rinehart.
Gilbert, Anthony. *The Wrong Body.* 1951 Random House.
Foley, Rae. *An Ape In Velvet.* 1951 Dodd, Mead.

| 1951.12 | *December* | 1029437621 |

DuBois, Theodora. *Fowl Play.* 1951 Doubleday.
Crispin, Edmund. *The Long Divorce.* 1951 Dodd, Mead.
Gardner, Erle Stanley. *The Case Of The Angry Mourner.* 1951 Morrow.

1952

| 1952.01 | *January* | 4381695 |

Reilly, Helen. *Lament For The Bride.* 1951 Random House.
Olsen, D B. *The Cat And The Capricorn.* 1951 Doubleday.
Christie, Agatha. *Blood Will Tell.* 1952 Dodd, Mead.

| 1952.02 | *February* | 4381745 |

Palmer, Stuart. *Nipped In The Bud.* 1951 M S Mills.
Garve, Andrew. *By-Line For Murder.* 1951 Harper.
Amos, Alan. *Panic In Paradise.* 1951 Doubleday.

| 1952.03 | *March* | 4044800 |

Fair, A A. *Top Of The Heap.* 1952 Morrow.
Coles, Manning. *Night Train To Paris.* 1952 Doubleday.
Christie, Agatha. *The Under Dog And Other Stories.* 1951 Dodd, Mead.

| 1952.04 | *April* | 20009364 |

Ford, Leslie. *The Bahamas Murder Case.* 1952 Scribners.
Lorac, E C R. *I Could Murder Her.* 1951 Popular Library.
Murray, Max. *Good Luck To The Corpse.* 1951 Farrar Straus and Young.

| 1952.05 | *May* | 6898802 |

Fenisong, Ruth. *Dead Yesterday.* 1951 Doubleday.
Vickers, Roy. *Murder in Two Flats.* 1952 M S Mill.
Benson, Ben. *Stamped for Murder.* 1952 M S Mill.

| 1952.06 | *June* | 6738917 |

Reilly, Helen. *The Double Man.* 1952 Random House.
Cheyney, Peter. *The Urgent Hangman.* 1952 Dodd, Mead.
Foley, Rae. *Wake The Sleeping Wolf.* 1952 Dodd, Mead.

| 1952.07 | *July* | 8223235 |

Knight, Kathleen Moore. *Death Goes to a Reunion.* 1952 Doubleday.
Garve, Andrew. *Murder Through the Looking Glass.* 1951 Harper.
Ballard, Helen Mabry. *To the Tune of Murder.* 1952 M S Mill.

1952

1952.08 *August*   9623841
 Gardner, Erle Stanley. *The Case Of The Moth-Eaten Mink.* 1952 Morrow.
 Knight, Clifford. *Death And The Little Brother.* 1952 Dutton.
 O'Farrell, William. *Grow Young And Die.* 1952 Doubleday.
1952.09 *September*   317422053
 Kelland, Clarence Budington. *The Key Man.* 1952 Harper.
 Fleming, Joan. *The Man Who Looked Back.* 1951 Doubleday.
 Carey, Bernice. *The Missing Heiress.* 1952 Doubleday.
1952.10 *October*   8248483
 Eberhart, Mignon G. *Dead Men's Plans.* 1952 Random House.
 Eby, Lois and Fleming, John. *Death Begs The Question.* 1952 Abelard.
 Carnac, Carol. *It's Her Own Funeral.* 1952 Doubleday.
1952.11 *November*   5620132
 Murray, Max. *The Doctor and the Corpse.* 1952 Farrar, Straus And Young.
 Knight, Kathleen Moore. *Valse Macabre.* 1952 Doubleday.
 Gilbert, Anthony. *A Case for Mr. Crook.* 1952 Random House.
1952.12 *December*   474891795
 Irish, William. *Eyes That Watch You.* 1952 Rinehart.
 Bird, Brandon. *Downbeat For A Dirge.* 1952 Dodd, Mead.
 Erskine, Margaret. *Look Behind You, Lady.* 1952 Doubleday.

1953

1953.01 *January*   4027774
 Gardner, Erle Stanley. *The Case Of The Grinning Gorilla.* 1952 Morrow.
 Sherwood, John. *Ambush For Anatol.* 1952 Doubleday.
 Nelson, Hugh Lawrence. *The Sleep Is Deep.* 1952 Rinehart.
1953.02 *February*   7599519
 Foley, Rae. *The Man In The Shadow.* 1953 Dodd, Mead.
 Millar, Margaret. *Vanish In An Instant.* 1952 Random House.
 MacDonald, Philip. *Something To Hide.* 1952 Doubleday.
1953.03 *March*   488935663
 Christie, Agatha. *Funerals Are Fatal.* 1953 Dodd, Mead.
 Little, Constance and Gwyneth. *The Black Iris.* 1953 Doubleday.
 Tyre, Nedra. *Death Of An Intruder.* 1953 Knopf.
1953.04 *April*   5620149
 Knight, Kathleen Moore. *Akin To Murder.* 1953 Doubleday.
 Curtiss, Ursula. *The Iron Cobweb.* 1953 Dodd, Mead.
 Holding, Elisabeth Sanxay. *Widow's Mite.* 1953 Simon & Schuster.
1953.05 *May*   18604202
 Strange, John Stephen. *Let The Dead Past.* 1953 Doubleday.
 Dean, Amber. *Collectors Item.* 1953 Doubleday.
 Vickers, Roy. *The Department Of Dead Ends.* 1947 Spivak.

1953

1953.06   *June*   5620101
Wentworth, Patricia. *Out of the Past.* 1953 Lippincott.
Griswold, George. *A Checkmate for the Colonel.* 1953 Dutton.
Holden, Genevieve. *Killer Loose!.* 1953 Doubleday.

1953.07   *July*   317079091
Gardner, Erle Stanley. *The Case Of The Hesitant Hostess.* 1953 Morrow.
Johns, Veronica Parker. *Murder by the Day.* 1953 Doubleday.
Nelson, Hugh Lawrence. *The Fence.* 1953 Rinehart.

1953.08   *August*   894327041
Eberhart, Mignon G. *The Unknown Quantity.* 1953 Random House.
Davis, Frederick C. *Drag The Dark.* 1953 Doubleday.
Huston, H C. *With Murder For Some.* 1953 Macmillan.

1953.09   *September*   5620093
Upfield, Arthur W. *Murder Must Wait.* 1953 Doubleday.
Sterling, Stewart. *The Big Ear.* 1953 Dutton.
Grew, William. *Doubles In Death.* 1953 Doubleday.

1953.10   *October*   2691003
Fair, A A. *Some Women Won't Wait.* 1953 Morrow.
Rhode, John. *The Mysterious Suspect.* 1953 Dodd, Mead.
Bagby, George. *A Big Hand for the Corpse.* 1953 Doubleday.

1953.11   *November*   989877167
Knight, Kathleen Moore. *Three Of Diamonds.* 1953 Doubleday.
Derby, Mark. *The Big Water.* 1953 Viking.
Rinehart, Mary Roberts. *The Frightened Wife.* 1953 Rinehart.

1953.12   *December*   4017768
Simenon, Georges. *No Vacation for Maigret.* 1953 Doubleday.
Creasey, John. *Figure in the Dusk.* 1952 Harper.
Franklin, Max. *Justice Has No Sword.* 1953 Rinehart.

1954

1954.01   *January*   761238952
Gardner, Erle Stanley. *The Case Of The Green-Eyed Sister.* 1953 Morrow.
Neville, Margot. *Murder of the Well-Beloved.* 1953 Doubleday.
Bagby, George. *Dead Drunk.* 1953 Doubleday.

1954.02   *February*   41773640
Nelson, Hugh Lawrence. *Kill With Care.* 1953 Rinehart.
Gilbert, Anthony. *Black Death.* 1953 Random House.
Crane, Frances. *Murder In Bright Red.* 1953 Random House.

1954.03   *March*   4027759
Gardner, Erle Stanley. *The Case Of The Fugitive Nurse.* 1954 Morrow.
Hymers, John. *Utter Death.* Utter Deat.
Sheridan, Juanita. *The Waikiki Widow.* 1953 Doubleday.

1954

1954.04	*April*	1978525

Eberhart, Mignon G. *Man Missing.* 1954 Random House.
Wilmer, Dale. *Dead Fall.* 1954 Bouregy & Curl.
Bremner, Marjorie. *Murder Most Familiar.* Murder Most Familia.

1954.05	*May*	5398824

Gruber, Frank. *The Lonesome Badger.* 1954 Rinehart.
Holden, Genevieve. *Sound An Alarm.* 1954 Doubleday.
Vickers, Roy. *Murder Will Out.* Murder Will Ou.

1954.06	*June*	1971844

Palmer, Stuart. *Cold Poison.* 1954 M S Mill.
Erskine, Margaret. *Dead by Now.* 1954 Doubleday.
Hitchens, Dolores. *Beat Back The Tide.* 1954 Doubleday.

1954.07	*July*	5620114

McConnaughey, James. *Three For The Money.* 1954 William Sloane.
Candy, Edward. *Which Doctor?.* 1953 Rinehart.
Knight, Kathleen Moore. *High Rendezvous.* 1954 Doubleday.

1954.08	*August*	5340792

Gardner, Erle Stanley. *The Case Of The Runaway Corpse.* 1954 Morrow.
Potts, Jean. *Go, Lovely Rose.* 1954 Scribner.
Carr, John Dickson. *The Third Bullet and Other Stories.* 1954 Harper.

1954.09	*August*	987967087

Bird, Brandon. *Hawk Watch.* 1954 Dodd, Mead.
Gilbert, Anthony. *Death Won't Wait.* 1954 Random House.
Blizard, Marie. *Conspiracy of Silence.* 1954 M S Mill.

1954.10	*September*	5398764

Armstrong, Charlotte. *The Better To Eat You.* 1954 Coward McCann.
Estes, Carroll Cox. *The Moon Gate.* 1954 Doubleday.
Piper, Peter. *The Corpse That Came Back.* 1954 Random House.

1954.11	*September*	5436691

Reilly, Helen. *Tell Her It's Murder.* 1954 Random House.
Ames, Delano. *Coffin For Christopher.* 1954 Ives Washburn.
O'Sullivan, J B. *Don't Hang Me Too High.* 1954 M S Mill.

1954.12	*October*	988221785

Ford, Leslie. *Invitation To Murder.* 1954 Scribner.
Bagby, George. *The Body In The Basket.* 1954 Doubleday.
Innes, Michael. *Dead Man's Shoes.* 1954 Dodd, Mead.

1954.13	*November*	5436438

McCloy, Helen. *He Never Came Back.* 1954 Random House.
Thayer, Lee. *Dead Reckoning.* 1954 Dodd Mead.
Wentworth, Patricia. *The Benevent Treasure.* 1954 Lippincott.

1954

1954.14 *December* 5436513
Gruber, Frank. *The Limping Goose.* 1954 Rinehart.
Crane, Frances. *The Coral Princess Murders.* 1954 Random House.
McGerr, Pat. *Fatal In My Fashion.* 1954 Doubleday.

1955

1955.01 *January* 84193352
Gardner, Erle Stanley. *The Case Of The Restless Redhead.* 1954 Morrow.
Davis, Frederick C. *Another Morgue Heard From.* 1954 Doubleday.
Vickers, Roy. *Six Murders in the Suburbs.* DBC 1st US.
1955.02 *February* 988234761
Disney, Doris Miles. *The Last Straw.* 1954 Doubleday.
Roberts, Lee. *The Pale Door.* 1955 Dodd, Mead.
Erskine, Margaret. *The Dead Don't Speak.* 1955 Doubleday ?.
1955.03 *March* 949852558
Gardner, Erle Stanley. *The Case Of The Glamorous Ghost.* 1955 Morrow.
Foley, Rae. *Death And Mr. Potter.* 1955 Dodd, Mead.
Coles, Manning. *The Man In The Green Hat.* 1955 Doubleday.
1955.04 *April* 4471954
Christie, Agatha. *So Many Steps to Death.* 1955 Dodd, Mead.
Simenon, Georges. *Maigret in New York.* 1955 Doubleday.
Crane, Frances. *Death in Lilac Time.* 1955 Random House.
1955.05 *May* 988272031
Knight, Kathleen Moore. *The Robineau Look.* 1955 Doubleday.
Canning, Victor. *Twist Of The Knife.* 1955 William Sloane.
Carleton, Marjorie. *Vanished.* 1955 Morrow.
1955.06 *June* 5625504
Allingham, Margery. *The Estate Of The Beckoning Lady.* 1955 Doubleday.
Masterson, Whit. *Dead, She Was Beautiful.* 1955 Dodd, Mead.
Nolan, Jeannette Covert. *Sudden Squall.* 1955 Ives Washburn.
1955.07 *July* 5622259
Gardner, Erle Stanley. *The Case Of The Sun Bather's Diary.* 1955 Morrow.
Gill, Josephine Eckert. *The House That Died.* 1955 Doubleday.
Griswold, George. *The Pinned Man.* 1955 Little, Brown.
1955.08 *August* 7246201
Ransome, Stephen. *The Frazer Acquittal.* 1955 Doubleday.
Albrand, Martha. *The Mask Of Alexander.* 1954 Random House.
Hansen, Robert P. *Walk A Wicked Mile.* 1955 M S Mill.
1955.09 *August* 5625528
Kelland, Clarence Budington. *Murder Makes An Entrance.* 1955 Harper.
Wentworth, Patricia. *Poison In The Pen.* 1954 Lippincott.
Ballinger, Bill S. *The Tooth And The Nail.* 1955 Harper.

1955

1955.10   *September*   5690331
Ford, Leslie. *Murder Comes To Eden.* 1955 Scribner.
Durrenmatt, Friedrich. *The Judge And His Hangman.* 1955 Harper.
Gilbert, Anthony. *A Question Of Murder.* 1955 Random House.
1955.11   *September*   5625555
Bennett, Ken. *Passport For A Renegade.* 1955 Doubleday.
Potts, Jean. *Dark Destination.* 1955 Scribners ?.
Masterson, Whit. *All Through The Night.* 1955 Dodd, Mead.
1955.12   *October*   5620070
Bagby, George. *Shadow on the Window.* 1955 Doubleday.
Thayer, Lee. *Who Benefits?.* 1955 Dodd, Mead.
White, Lionel. *Flight Into Terror.* 1955 Dutton.
1955.13   *November*   5625577
Gardner, Erle Stanley. *The Case Of The Nervous Accomplice.* 1955 Morrow.
Frost, Barbara. *Innocent Bystander.* 1955 Coward-McCann.
Disney, Doris Miles. *Trick Or Treat.* 1955 Doubleday.
1955.14   *December*   1029260751
Reilly, Helen. *Compartment K.* 1955 Random House.
Davis, Frederick C. *Night Drop.* 1955 Doubleday.
Vickers, Roy. *Double Image.* DBC 1st US.

1956

1956.01   *January*   5620190
Simenon, Georges. *Inspector Maigret And The Dead Girl.* 1955 Doubleday.
McCloy, Helen. *Long Body.* 1955 Random House.
Ferrars, E X. *Enough To Kill A Horse.* 1955 Doubleday.
1956.02   *February*   780880860 (?)
Gardner, Erle Stanley. *The Case Of The Terrified Typist.* 1956 Morrow.
Amos, Alan. *They're Going To Kill Me.* 1955 Doubleday.
Sherry, Edna. *Backfire.* 1956 Dodd, Mead.
1956.03   *March*   8024115
Lowe, Kenneth. *No Tears For Shirley Minton.* 1955 Doubleday.
Alexander, David. *Shoot A Sitting Duck.* 1955 Random House.
Armstrong, Anthony. *A Room At The Hotel Ambre.* 1956 Doubleday.
1956.04   *April*   5625624
Eberhart, Mignon G. *Postmark Murder.* 1955 Random House.
Simenon, Georges. *Inspector Maigret And The Burglar's Wife.* 1956 Doubleday.
Rutledge, Nancy. *Wanted For Murder.* 1956 Random House.
1956.05   *May*   6032330
Kelland, Clarence Budington. *Death Keeps A Secret.* 1956 Harper.
Alexander, David. *Die, Little Goose.* 1956 Random House.
Borgenicht, Miriam. *Don't Look Back.* 1956 Doubleday.

1956

1956.06   *June*   6032301
Gardner, Erle Stanley. *The Case Of The Demure Defendant.* 1956 Morrow.
Creasey, John. *The Beauty Queen Killer.* 1956 Harper.
Hansen, Robert P. *Murder is Where You Find It.* 1956 M S Mill.

1956.07   *July*   5625473
Halliday, Brett. *The Blonde Cried Murder.* 1956 Dodd, Mead.
Gilbert, Anthony. *And Death Came Too.* 1956 Random House.
Berckman, Evelyn. *The Strange Bedfellow.* 1956 Dodd, Mead.

1956.08   *August*   5620058
Tucker, Wilson. *The Man In My Grave.* 1956 Rinehart.
Canning, Victor. *Burden of Proof.* 1956 William Sloane.
Nielsen, Helen. *Borrow The Night.* 1956 Morrow.

1956.09   *September*   5620223
Ransome, Stephen. *The Men In Her Death.* 1956 Doubleday.
Garve, Andrew. *The End Of The Track.* 1956 Harper.
Olsen, D B. *Death Walks On Cat Feet.* 1956 Doubleday.

1956.10   *October*   5686140
Crane, Frances. *Horror on the Ruby X.* 1956 Random House.
Ferrars, E X. *We Haven't Seen Her Lately.* 1956 Doubleday.
Webb, Jack. *The Bad Blonde.* 1956 Rinehart.

1956.11   *November*   5686126
Gardner, Erle Stanley. *The Case Of The Gilded Lady.* 1956 Morrow.
Nielsen, Helen. *The Crime is Murder.* 1956 Morrow.
Gilbert, Anthony. *Riddle of a Lady.* 1956 Random House.

1956.12   *December*   5855530
Christie, Agatha. *Dead Man's Folly.* 1956 Dodd, Mead.
Gardiner, Dorothy. *What Crime Is It?.* 1956 Dodd, Mead.
Quentin, Patrick. *Man In The Net.* 1956 Simon & Schuster.

1957

1957.01   *January*   5592812
Gardner, Erle Stanley. *The Case Of The Lucky Loser.* 1957 Morrow.
Disney, Doris Miles. *Unappointed Rounds.* 1956 Doubleday.
Hunt, Kyle. *Kill Once, Kill Twice.* 1956 Simon & Schuster.

1957.02   *February*   5855706
Fair, A A. *Beware The Curves.* 1956 Morrow.
Foley, Rae. *The Last Gamble.* 1956 Dodd, Mead.
Hansen, Robert P. *Mark Three For Murder.* 1957 M S Mill.

1957.03   *March*   7959302
McCloy, Helen. *Two-Thirds Of A Ghost.* 1956 Random House.
Ferrars, E X. *Kill Or Cure.* 1956 Doubleday.
Hardy, William. *Malice Domestic.* 1957 Dodd, Mead.

1957

1957.04 *April*   962864079
 Reilly, Helen. *The Canvas Dagger.* 1956 Random House.
 Foley, Rae. *Run For Your Life.* 1957 Dodd, Mead.
 Alexander, David. *The Murder Of Whistler's Brother.* 1956 Random House.
1957.05 *May*   5620142
 Fair, A A. *You Can Die Laughing.* 1957 Morrow.
 Thayer, Lee. *Guilt Is Where You Find It.* 1957 Dodd, Mead.
 Kendrick, Baynard. *Reservations For Death.* 1957 Morrow.
1957.06 *June*   5855464
 Ford, Leslie. *The Girl From The Mimosa Club.* 1957 Scribner.
 Masterson, Whit. *A Shadow In The Wild.* 1957 Dodd, Mead.
 Disney, Doris Miles. *Method In Madness.* 1957 Dodd, Mead.
1957.07 *July*   5688786
 Gardner, Erle Stanley. *The Case Of The Screaming Woman.* 1957 Morrow.
 Carnac, Carol. *The Late Miss Trimming.* 1957 Doubleday.
 Davis, Dorothy Salisbury. *Death Of An Old Sinner.* 1957 Scribner.
1957.08 *August*   7063183
 Kelland, Clarence Budington. *The Nameless Corpse.* 1957 Harper.
 Rutledge, Nancy. *The Frightened Murderer.* 1957 Random House.
 Gordons, The. *The Big Frame.* 1957 Doubleday.
1957.09 *September*   5592850
 Alexander, David. *Hush-A-Bye Murder.* 1957 Random House.
 Fenwick, Elizabeth. *Poor Harriet.* 1957 Harper.
 Coles, Manning. *Death Of An Ambassador.* 1957 Doubleday.
1957.10 *October*   5651484
 Potts, Jean. *The Man With The Cane.* 1957 Scribner.
 Fair, A A. *Some Slips Don't Show.* 1957 Morrow.
 Scherf, Margaret. *Judicial Body.* 1957 Doubleday.
1957.11 *November*   1029287897
 Gardner, Erle Stanley. *The Case Of The Daring Decoy.* 1957 Morrow.
 Ferrars, E X. *Count The Cost.* 1957 Doubleday.
 Roberts, Lee. *Once A Widow.* 1957 Dodd, Mead.
1957.12 *December*   5592943
 Gordons, The. *Captive.* 1957 Doubleday.
 Underwood, Michael. *Murder On Trial.* 1958 Ives Washburn.
 Curtiss, Ursula. *The Stairway.* 1957 Dodd, Mead.

1958

1958.01 *January*   11695556
 Gardner, Erle Stanley. *The Case Of The Long-Legged Models.* 1958 Morrow.
 Bingham, John. *Murder Off The Record.* 1957 Dodd. Mead.
 Disney, Doris Miles. *My Neighbor's Wife.* 1957 Doubleday.

1958

1958.02	*February*	4994688

Eberhart, Mignon G. *Another Man's Murder.* 1957 Random House.
Hansen, Robert P. *Back To The Wall.* 1957 M S Mill.
Alexander, David. *Death Of Humpty Dumpty.* 1957 Random House.

1958.03	*March*	1035759437

White, Lionel. *Invitation to Violence.* 1958 Dutton.
Siegel, Doris. *How Still My Love.* 1957 M S Mill.
Amos, Alan. *Fatal Harvest.* 1957 Doubleday.

1958.04	*April*	5872145

Bagby, George. *The Three-Time Losers.* 1958 Doubleday.
Gilbert, Anthony. *Death Against The Clock.* 1958 Random House.
Foley, Rae. *Escape To Fear.* 1958 Dodd, Mead.

1958.05	*May*	4123834

Gardner, Erle Stanley. *The Case Of The Foot-Loose Doll.* 1958 Morrow.
Thayer, Lee. *Still No Answer.* 1958 Dodd, Mead.
Taylor, Matt. *The Famous McGarry Stories.* DBC 1st.

1958.06	*June*	2960678

Marsh, Ngaio. *Singing In The Shrouds.* 1958 Little, Brown.
Matheson, Richard. *A Stir Of Echoes.* 1958 Lippincott.
Sibley, Celestine. *The Malignant Heart.* 1958 Doubleday.

1958.07	*July*	5592922

Fair, A A. *The Count Of Nine.* 1958 Morrow.
York, Jeremy. *Seeds Of Murder.* 1958 Scribner.
Drachman, Theodore S, M.D.. *Something For The Birds.* 1958 Crown.

1958.08	*August*	2919727

Simenon, Georges. *None of Maigret's Business.* 1958 Doubleday.
Crane, Frances. *The Man in Gray.* 1958 Random House.
Herber, William. *Death Paints a Portrait.* 1958 Lippincott.

1958.09	*September*	5592681

Dean, Spencer. *Dishonor Among Thieves.* 1958 Doubleday.
Eberhart, Mignon G. *Deadly is the Diamond.* 1958 Random House.
Hawkins, John and Ward. *Death Watch.* 1958 Dodd, Mead.

1958.10	*October*	5872027

Mathews, D L. *Reach Of Fear.* 1958 Rinehart.
Ferrars, E X. *Depart This Life.* 1958 Doubleday.
Hardy, William. *A Little Sin.* 1958 Dodd, Mead.

1958.11	*November*	5852097

Gardner, Erle Stanley. *The Case Of The Calendar Girl.* 1958 Morrow.
Woolrich, Cornell. *Violence.* 1958 Dodd, Mead.
York, Jeremy. *Sight Of Death.* Scribner 1956.

1958

1958.12 *December*	41781747

Reilly, Helen. *Ding Dong Bell.* 1958 Random House.
Pentecost, Hugh. *The Obituary Club.* 1958 Dodd, Mead.
Hansen, Robert P. *Deadly Purpose.* 1958 M S Mill.

1959

1959.01	*January*	5905020
Gardner, Erle Stanley. *The Case Of The Deadly Toy.* 1958.
Vickers, Roy. *Seven Chose Murder.* DBC 1st?.
Dean, Spencer. *The Merchant Of Murder.* 1959.

1959.02	*February*	5592741
Martin, Robert. *Killer Among Us.* 1958 Dodd, Mead.
Waugh, Hillary. *The Girl Who Cried Wolf.* 1958 Doubleday.
Roos, Kelley. *Requiem For A Blonde.* 1948 Dodd, Mead.

1959.03	*March*	5872050
Fair, A A. *Pass The Gravy.* 1959 Morrow.
Thielen, Bernard. *Open Season.* 1958 Mystery House.
Fenwick, Elizabeth. *A Long Way Down.* 1959 Harper.

1959.04	*April*	6588651
Walsh, Thomas. *Dangerous Passenger.* 1959 Little, Brown.
York, Jeremy. *My Brother's Killer.* 1958 Scribner.
Nielsen, Helen. *The Fifth Caller.* 1959 Morrow.

1959.05	*May*	5872114
Christie, Agatha. *Ordeal by Innocence.* 1958 Dodd, Mead.
Mathews, D L. *The Fatal Amateur.* 1959 Rinehart.
Kelland, Clarence Budington. *Where There's Smoke.* 1958 Harper.

1959.06	*June*	5904970
Knight, Kathleen Moore. *Beauty Is A Beast.* 1959 Doubleday.
Nisot, E H. *The Sleepless Men.* 1959 Doubleday.
Tracy, Don. *The Big Blackout.* DBC 1st.

1959.07	*July*	178486
Gardner, Erle Stanley. *The Case Of The Mythical Monkeys.* 1959 Morrow.
Cornish, Constance. *Dead Of Winter.* 1959 Simon & Schuster.
Masterson, Whit. *The Dark Fantastic.* 1959 Dodd, Mead.

1959.08	*August*	5872089
Eberhart, Mignon G. *Melora.* 1959 Random House.
Ethan, John B. *The Black Gold Murders.* DBC 1st.
Gilbert, Anthony. *Prelude To Murder.* 1959 Random House.

1959.09	*September*	5872125
Millar, Margaret. *The Listening Walls.* 1959 Random House.
Vickers, Roy. *The Girl Who Wouldn't Talk.* DBC 1st US.
Martin, Robert. *A Key To The Morgue.* 1959 Dodd, Mead.

1959

1959.10   *October*   1137030549
Carr, John Dickson. *Scandal At High Chimneys.* 1959 Harper.
Disney, Doris Miles. *Did She Fall Or Was She Pushed.* 1959 Doubleday.
Thayer, Lee. *Two Ways To Die.* 1959 Dodd, Mead.

1959.11   *November*   4579468
Gardner, Erle Stanley. *The Case Of The Singing Skirt.* 1959 Morrow.
Crane, Frances. *The Buttercup Case.* 1959 Random House.
Kendrick, Baynard. *Hot Red Money.* 1959 Dodd, Mead.

1959.12   *December*   276886668
Reilly, Helen. *Not Me Inspector.* 1959 Random House.
Creasey, John. *Hit and Run.* 1959 Scribners.
Spicer, Bart. *Exit Running.* 1959 Dodd, Mead.

1960

1960.01   *January*   1197975643
Gardner, Erle Stanley. *The Case Of The Waylaid Wolf.* 1959 Morrow.
Foley, Rae. *Dangerous To Me.* 1959 Dodd, Mead.
Gilbert, Anthony. *Death Casts A Long Shadow.* 1959 Random House.

1960.02   *February*   780884346
Pentecost, Hugh. *The Lonely Target.* 1959 Dodd, Mead.
Offord, Lenore Glen. *Walking Shadow.* 1959 Simon & Schuster.
Hansen, Robert P. *There's Always A Payoff.* 1959 M S Mill.

1960.03   *March*   1196281586
Coles, Manning. *Concrete Crime.* 1960 Doubleday.
Disney, Doris Miles. *No Next Of Kin.* 1959 Doubleday.
Wees, F S. *The Country Of The Strangers.* 1960 Doubleday.

1960.04   *April*   933777654
Masterson, Whit. *A Hammer In His Hand.* 1960 Dodd, Mead.
York, Jeremy. *Come Here And Die.* 1959 Scribner.
Ransome, Stephen. *Warning Bell.* 1960 Doubleday.

1960.05   *May*   4090393
Marsh, Ngaio. *False Scent.* 1959 Little, Brown.
Hitchens, Bert and Dolores. *The Man Who Followed Women.* 1959 Doubleday.
Gordons, The. *Tiger On My Back.* 1960 Doubleday.

1960.06   *June*   5398628
Dewey, Thomas B. *The Girl Who Wasn't There.* 1960 Simon & Schuster.
Haggard, William. *Venetian Blind.* 1959 Ives Washburn.
Dean, Amber. *Bullet Proof.* 1960 Doubleday.

1960.07   *July*   178677
Gardner, Erle Stanley. *The Case Of The Duplicate Daughter.* 1959 Morrow.
Garve, Andrew. *The Golden Deed.* 1960 Harper.
Ross, Ivan T. *Murder Out Of School.* 1960 Simon & Schuster.

1960

1960.08   *August*   780880018
Eberhart, Mignon G. *Jury Of One*. 1960 Random House.
Williams, Brad. *A Borderline Case*. 1960 M S Mill.
Kendrick, Baynard. *The Aluminum Turtle*. 1960 Dodd, Mead.
1960.09   *September*   6051492
Reilly, Helen. *Follow Me*. 1960 Random House.
Holton, Leonard. *A Pact With Satan*. 1960 Dodd, Mead.
McGovern, James. *The Berlin Couriers*. 1960 Abelard Schuman.
1960.10   *October*   5398714
Upfield, Arthur W. *The Valley Of Smugglers*. 1960 Doubleday.
Farrell, Henry. *Whatever Happened To Baby Jane?*. 1960 Rinehart.
Waugh, Hillary. *Road Block*. 1960 Doubleday.
1960.11   *November*   6074694
Fair, A A. *Kept Women Can't Quit*. 1960 Morrow.
Vance, John Holbrook. *The Man In The Cage*. 1960 Random House.
Thayer, Lee. *Dead On Arrival*. 1960 Dodd, Mead.
1960.12   *December*   4580441
Alexander, David. *Pennies From Hell*. 1960 Lippincott.
Creasey, John. *Murder: One Two Three*. 1960 Scribner.
Crane, Frances. *Death-Wish Green*. 1960 Random House.

1961

1961.01   *January*   780880838
Gardner, Erle Stanley. *The Case Of The Shapely Shadow*. 1960 Morrow.
Gilbert, Anthony. *Out For The Kill*. 1960 Random House.
Knight, Kathleen Moore. *Invitation To Vengeance*. 1960 Doubleday.
1961.02   *February*   3219489
Macdonald, Ross. *The Ferguson Affair*. 1960 Knopf.
Dean, Spencer. *Murder After A Fashion*. 1960 Doubleday.
Nielsen, Helen. *Sing Me A Murder* 1960 Morrow.
1961.03   *March*   6051387
Millar, Margaret. *A Stranger In My Grave*. 1960 Random House.
Ransome, Stephen. *Some Must Watch*. 1961 Doubleday.
Rydell, Forbes. *If She Should Die*. 1961 Doubleday.
1961.04   *April*   6178590
Pentecost, Hugh. *The Deadly Friend*. 1961 Dodd, Mead.
Proctor, Maurice. *Devil's Due*. 1960 Harper.
Foley, Rae. *It's Murder, Mr Potter*. 1961 Dodd, Mead.
1961.05   *May*   4471890
Gardner, Erle Stanley. *The Case Of The Spurious Spinster*. 1961 Morrow.
Dean, Amber. *Encounter with Evil*. 1961 Doublwday.
Creasey, John. *The Killing Strike*. 1961 Scribner.

1961

1961.06   *June*   6074549
    Simenon, Georges. *Maigret Rents a Room.* 1961 Doubleday.
    Sherry, Edna. *Call the Witness.* 1961 Dodd, Mead.
    Huntsberry, William E. *Oscar Mooney's Head.* 1961 Holt, Rinehart & Winston.
1961.07   *July*   6074799
    Fair, A A. *Bachelors Get Lonely.* 1961 Morrow.
    Farrell, Henry. *Death On The Sixth Day.* 1961 Holt, Rinehart & Winston.
    Withers, E L. *Heir Apparent.* 1961 Doubleday.
1961.08   *August*   6019018
    Fleming, Ian. *Thunderball.* 1961 Vking Press.
    Philips, Judson. *Murder Clear, Track Fast.* 1961 Dodd, Mead.
    Holden, Genevieve. *Deadlier Than The Male.* 1961 Doubleday.
1961.09   *September*   6051549
    Eberhart, Mignon G. *The Cup, The Blade Or The Gun.* 1961 Random House.
    Coles, Manning. *Search For A Sultan.* 1961 Doubleday.
    James, Breni. *Night Of The Kill.* 1961 Simon & Schuster.
1961.10   *October*   6074636
    Mathews, D L. *A Very Welcome Death.* 1961 Holt, Rinehart & Winston.
    Webb, Jack. *One For My Dame.* 1961 Holt, Rinehart & Winston.
    Kirk, Russell. *The Old House Of Fear.* 1961 Fleet Publishing.
1961.11   *November*   6074761
    Gardner, Erle Stanley. *The Case Of The Bigamous Spouse.* 1960 Morrow.
    Keith, Carlton. *Missing, Presumed Dead.* 1961 Doubleday.
    Pentecost, Hugh. *Choice Of Violence.* 1961 Dodd, Mead.
1961.12   *December*   6051435
    Kelland, Clarence Budington. *The Sinister Strangers.* 1961 Dodd, Mead.
    Christie, Agatha. *Double Sin and Other Stories.* 1961 Dodd, Mead.
    Holton, Leonard. *The Secret Of The Doubting Saint.* 1961 Dodd, Mead.

1962

1962.01   *January*   6106298
    Gardner, Erle Stanley. *The Case Of The Reluctant Model.* 1961 Morrow.
    Reilly, Helen. *Certain Sleep.* 1961 Random House.
    Walsh, Thomas. *The Eye of the Needle.* 1961 Simon & Schuster.
1962.02   *February*   2415216
    White, Lionel. *A Grave Undertaking.* 1961 Dutton.
    Gilbert, Anthony. *After The Verdict.* 1961 Random House.
    Blanc, Suzanne. *The Green Stone.* 1961 Harper.
1962.03   *March*   6074851
    Fair, A A. *Shills Can't Cash Chips.* 1961 Morrow.
    Disney, Doris Miles. *Should Auld Acquaintance.* 1962 Doubleday.
    Creasey, John. *Murder, London - New York.* 1961 Scribner.

1962

1962.04   *April*   6074930
  Gruber, Frank. *Brothers of Silence.* 1962 Dutton.
  Thayer, Lee. *And One Cried Murder.* 1962 Dodd, Mead.
  Ross, Ivan T. *Old Students Never Die.* 1962 Doublday.

1962.05   *May*   6051702
  Kelland, Clarence Budington. *The Artless Heiress.* 1962 Dodd Mead.
  McLarty, Nancy. *Chain of Death.* 1962 Doubleday.
  Ransome, Stephen. *Without A Trace.* 1962 Doubleday.

1962.06   *June*   6019125
  Bohle, Edgar. *The Wife That Died Twice.* 1962 Random House.
  York, Jeremy. *Thicker Than Water.* 1962 Doubleday.
  Lanham, Edwin. *Passage to Danger.* 1962 Harcourt, Brace.

1962.07   *July*   7859524
  Gardner, Erle Stanley. *The Case Of The Blonde Bonanza.* 1962 Morrow.
  Chaber, M F. *Jade for a Lady.* 1962 Holt, Rinehart & Winston.
  Pentecost, Hugh. *The Cannibal Who Overate.* 1962 Dodd, Mead.

1962.08   *August*   890496266
  Creasey, John. *Death of a Racehorse.* 1959 Scribner.
  Egan, Lesley. *The Borrowed Alibi.* 1962 Harper.
  Stein, Marc. *Home and Murder.* 1962 Doubleday.

1962.09   *September*   5437191
  Fair, A A. *Try Anything Once.* 1962 Morrow.
  Sherry, Edna. *Girl Missing.* 1962 Dodd, Mead.
  Mason, Van Wyck. *Trouble in Burma.* 1962 Doubleday.

1962.10   *October*   1035617259
  Millar, Margaret. *How Like An Angel.* 1962 Random House.
  Garve, Andrew. *Prisoner's Friend.* 1962 Harper.
  Brown, Fredric. *The Five-Day Nightmare.* 1962 Dutton.

1962.11   *November*   811772630
  Christie, Agatha. *The Pale Horse.* 1962 Dodd, Mead.
  Williams, Brad. *The Well-Dressed Skeleton.* 1962 M S Mill.
  Malcolm-Smith, George. *The Lady Finger.* 1962 Doubleday.

1962.12   *December*   780880013
  Eberhart, Mignon G. *Enemy in the House.* 1962 Random House.
  Philips, Judson. *A Dead Ending.* 1962 Dodd, Mead.
  Foley, Rae. *Repent at Leisure.* 1962 Dodd, Mead.

1963

1963.01   *January*   5505441
  Gardner, Erle Stanley. *The Case Of The Ice-Cold Hands.* 1962 Morrow.
  Reilly, Helen. *The Day She Died.* 1962 Random House.
  Walsh, Thomas. *A Thief in the Night.* 1962 Simon & Schuster.

1963

1963.02   *February*   5396068
Disney, Doris Miles. *Find the Woman.* 1962 Doubleday.
Gilbert, Anthony. *Uncertain Death.* 1962 Random House.
Egan, Lesley. *Against the Evidence.* 1962 Harper.

1963.03   *March*   5398352
Gardner, Erle Stanley. *The Case Of The Mischievous Doll.* 1963 Morrow.
Haggard, William. *The Unquiet Sleep.* 1962 Ives Washburn.
Pentecost, Hugh. *The Tarnished Angel.* 1963 Dodd, Mead.

1963.04   *April*   5436571
Holton, Leonard. *Deliver Us From Wolves.* 1963 Dodd, Mead.
Allingham, Margery. *The China Governess.* 1962 Doubleday.
Unekis, Richard. *The Chase.* 1962 Walker.

1963.05   *May*   78604868
Fair, A A. *Fish or Cut Bait.* 1963 Morrow.
Dean, Amber. *Deadly Contact.* 1963 Doubleday.
Ransome, Stephen. *The Night, The Woman.* 1963 Dodd, Mead.

1963.06   *June*   8231522
Masterson, Whit. *The Man on a Nylon String.* 1963 Dodd, Mead.
Foley, Rae. *Back Door to Death.* 1963 Dodd, Mead.
Fish, Robert L. *Isle of Snakes.* 1963 Simon & Schuster.

1963.07   *July*   8146059
Curtiss, Ursula. *The Wasp.* 1963 Dodd, Mead.
Ross, Ivan T. *The Man Who Would Do Anything.* 1963 Doubleday.
Madden, E S. *Craig's Spur.* 1961 Vanguard.

1963.08   *August*   7959283
Gilbert, Michael. *After The Fine Weather.* 1963 Harper.
Gardiner, Dorothy. *Lion In Wait.* 1963 Doubleday.
Peters, Bryan. *The Big H.* 1963 Holt, Rinehart & Winston.

1963.09   *September*   5398245
Gardner, Erle Stanley. *The Case Of The Step-Daughter's Secret.* 1963 Morrow.
Gilbert, Anthony. *No Dust In The Attic.* 1963 Random House.
Caldwell, Taylor. *The Late Clara Beame.* 1963 Doubleday.

1963.10   *October*   5437261
Gruber, Frank. *Bridge Of Sand.* 1963 Dutton.
Harris, John Norman. *The Weird World Of Wes Beattie.* 1963 Harper.
Gordons, The. *Undercover Cat.* 1963 Doubleday.

1963.11   *November*   5398483
Eberhart, Mignon G. *Run Scared.* 1963 Random House.
Heyes, Douglas. *The 12th Of Never.* 1963 Random House.
Egan, Lesley. *Run To Evil.* 1963 Harper.

1963

1963.12   *December*   4451348
Mason, Van Wyck. *Zanzibar Intrigue*. 1963 Doubleday.
Creasey, John. *The Scene Of The Crime*. 1961 Scribner.
Disney, Doris Miles. *Here Lies....* 1963 Doubleday.

1964

1964.01   *January*   1657242
Gardner, Erle Stanley. *The Case Of The Amorous Aunt*. 1963 Morrow.
Pike, Robert L. *Mute Witness*. 1963 Doubleday.
Waugh, Hillary. *Prisoner's Plea*. 1963 Doubleday.
1964.02   *February*   174489
Dewey, Thomas B. *A Sad Song Singing*. 1963 Simon & Schuster.
Haggard, William. *The High Wire*. 1963 Ives Washburn.
Broun, Daniel. *Egypt's Choice*. 1963 Holt, Rinehart & Winston.
1964.03   *March*   780880698
Gardner, Erle Stanley. *The Case Of The Daring Divorce*. 1964 Morrow.
Fish, Robert L. *The Shrunken Head*. 1963 Simon & Schuster.
Lockridge, Frances and Richard. *Quest of the Bogeyman*. 1964 Lippincott.
1964.04   *April*   5436635
Holton, Leonard. *Flowers by Request*. 1964 Dodd, Mead.
Gilbert, Anthony. *Ring for a Noose*. 1963 Random House.
Foley, Rae. *Fatal Lady*. 1964 Dodd, Mead.
1964.05   *May*   8142290
Fair, A A. *Up For Grabs*. 1964 Morrow.
Disney, Doris Miles. *The Hospitality Of The House*. 1964 Doubleday.
Ross, Ivan T. *Teacher's Blood*. Doubleday 1964.
1964.06   *June*   7431176
Simenon, Georges. *Maigret's Dead Man*. 1964 Doubleday.
Pentecost, Hugh. *Only the Rich Die Young*. 1964 Dodd, Mead.
Blanc, Suzanne. *The Yellow Villa*. 1964 Doubleday.
1964.07   *July*   2652095
Walsh, Thomas. *To Hide A Rogue*. 1964 Simon & Schuster.
Creasey, John. *Policeman's Dread*. 1964 Scribner.
Nielsen, Helen. *Verdict Suspended*. 1964 Morrow.
1964.08   *August*   1430988
Ransome, Stephen. *Meet In Darkness*. 1964 Dodd, Mead.
DuBois, Theodora. *Shannon Terror*. 1964 Ives Washburn.
White, Lionel. *The Ransomed Madonna*. 1964 Dutton.
1964.09   *September*   7959175
Gardner, Erle Stanley. *The Case Of The Phantom Fortune*. 1964 Morrow.
Curtiss, Ursula. *Out Of The Dark*. 1964 Dod, Mead.
Pike, Robert L. *The Quarry*. 1964 Dodd, Mead.

1964

1964.10   *October*   989877159
Gruber, Frank. *The Greek Affair.* 1964 Dutton.
Haggard, William. *The Antagonists.* 1964 Ives Washburn.
Cores, Lucy. *The Misty Curtain.* 1964 Harper.
1964.11   *November*   2652112
Christie, Agatha. *The Clocks.* 1964 Dodd, Mead.
Wayland, Patrick. *Counterstroke.* 1964 Doubleday.
McBain, Ed. *Ax.* 1963 Simon & Schuster.
1964.12   *December*   989876909
Philips, Judson. *The Laughter Trap.* 1964 Dodd, Mead.
Disney, Doris Miles. *The Departure Of Mr. Gaudette.* 1964 Doubleday.
Chaber, M E. *Six Who Ran.* 1964 Holt, Rinehart & Winston.

1965

1965.01   *January*   2650903
Gardner, Erle Stanley. *The Case Of The Horrified Heir.* 1964 Morrow.
McGerr, Patricia. *Is There a Traitor in the House?.* 1964 Doubleday.
Pentecost, Hugh. *The Shape of Fear.* 1964 Dodd, Mead.
1965.02   *February*   744557621
Eberhart, Mignon G. *Call After Midnight.* 1964 Random House.
Creasey, John. *Hang the Little Man.* 1963 Scribner.
Ransome, Stephen. *One-Man Jury.* 1964 Dodd, Mead.
1965.03   *March*   852551324
Gardner, Erle Stanley. *The Case Of The Troubled Trustee.* 1965 Morrow.
Richards, Clay. *The Gentle Assassin.* 1964 Bobbs-Merrill.
Archer, Frank. *The Malabang Pearl.* 1964 Doubleday.
1965.04   *April*   8123985
Walsh, Thomas. *The Tenth Point.* 1964 Simon & Schuster.
Coles, Manning. *A Knife For The Juggler.* 1964 Doubleday.
Foley, Rae. *Suffer A Witch.* 1965 Dodd, Mead.
1965.05   *May*   1687046
Fair, A A. *Cut Thin to Win.* 1965 Morrow.
Philips, Judson. *The Black Glass City.* 1965 Dodd, Mead.
Fish, Robert L. *The Diamond Bubble.* 1965 Simon & Schuster.
1965.06   *June*   9183125
Waugh, Hillary. *End Of A Party.* 1965 Doubleday.
Gilbert, Anthony. *The Fingerprint.* 1965 Random House.
Hitchens, Dolores. *The Bank With The Bamboo Door.* 1965 Simon & Schuster.
1965.07   *July*   8092997
Pentecost, Hugh. *The Sniper.* 1965 Dodd, Mead.
Keith, Carlton. *The Hiding Place.* 1965 Doubleday.
Ransome, Stephen. *Alias His Wife.* 1965 Dodd, Mead.

1965

1965.08 *August*		8164504

Roos, Kelley. *Necessary Evil.* 1965 Dodd, Mead.
Creasey, John. *Look Three Ways At Murder.* 1965 Scribner.
Scherf, Margaret. *Corpse with the Flannel Nightgown.* 1965 Doubleday.

1965.09 *September*		5506184

Gardner, Erle Stanley. *The Case Of The Beautiful Beggar.* 1965 Morrow.
Bagby, George. *Mysteriouser an Mysteriouser.* 1965 Doubleday.
Wayland, Patrick. *The Waiting Game.* 1965 Doubleday.

1965.10 *October*		8122108

Forbes, Stanton. *Relative To Death.* 1965 Doubleday.
Sherry, Edna. *Strictly A Loser.* 1965 Doublday.
Peters, Ellis. *Who Lies Here?.* 1965 Morrow.

1965.11 *November*		5391496

Eberhart, Mignon G. *R.S.V.P. Murder.* 1965 Random House.
Philips, Judson. *The Twisted People.* 1965 Dodd, Mead.
Malcolm-Smith, George. *Come Out, Come Out.* 1965 Doubleday.

1965.12 *December*		7851263

White, Lionel. *The House on K Street.* 1965 Dutton.
Allingham, Margery. *The Mind Readers.* 1965 Morrow.
Pike, Robert L. *Police Blotter.* 1965 Doubleday.

1966

1966.01 *January*		8146168

Mason, Van Wyck. *Maracaibo Mission.* 1965 Doubleday.
Haggard, William. *The Powder Barrel.* 1965 Ives Washburn.
Masterson, Whit. *711 - Officer Needs Help.* 1965 Dodd, Mead.

1966.02 *February*		8138212

Gruber, Frank. *Little Hercules.* 1965 Dutton.
Foley, Rae. *Call It Accident.* 1965 Dodd, Mead.
Ransome, Stephen. *The Sin File.* 1965 Dodd, Mead.

1966.03 *March*		8181848

Fish, Robert L. *Brazilian Sleigh Ride.* 1965 Simon & Schuster.
Creasey, John. *Murder, London-Australia.* 1965 Scribner.
Roos, Kelley. *Grave Danger.* 1965 Dodd, Mead.

1966.04 *April*		8159143

Pentecost, Hugh. *Hide Her From Every Eye.* 1966 Dodd, Mead.
Gilbert, Anthony. *The Voice.* 1965 Random House.
Waugh, Hillary. *Girl On The Run.* 1965 Doubleday.

1966.05 *May*		6189683

Fair, A A. *Widows Wear Weeds.* 1966 Morrow.
Gilman, Dorothy. *The Unexpected Mrs. Pollifax.* 1966 Doubleday.
Walsh, Thomas. *The Resurrection Man.* 1966 Simon & Schuster.

1966

1966.06 *June*		20191251

Armstrong, Charlotte. *Dream Of Fair Woman.* 1966 Coward, McCann.
Hubbard, P M. *The Holm Oaks.* 1966 Atheneum.
Thayer, Lee. *Dusty Death.* 1966 Dodd, Mead.

1966.07 *July* — 9183005

Ransome, Stephen. *The Hidden Hour.* 1966 Dodd, Mead.
Nielsen, Helen. *After Midnight.* 1966 Morrow.
Cavanaugh, Arthur. *The Children Are Gone.* 1966 Simon & Schuster.

1966.08 *August* — 7728580

Foley, Rae. *Wild Night.* 1966 Dodd, Mead.
Knox, Bill. *Devilweed.* 1966 Doubleday.
Ballinger, Bill S. *The Heir Hunters.* 1966 Harper.

1966.09 *September* — 8204945

Gardner, Erle Stanley. *The Case Of The Worried Waitress.* 1966 Morrow.
Albrand, Martha. *The Door Fell Shut.* 1966 New American Library.
Kane, Henry. *The Midnight Man.* 1966 Macmillan.

1966.10 *October* — 34409009

Pentecost, Hugh. *The Evil That Men Do.* 1966 Dodd, Mead.
Braun, Lilian Jackson. *The Cat Who Could Read Backwards.* 1966 Dutton.
Ferrars, E X. *No Peace For The Wicked.* 1966 Doubleday.

1966.11 *November* — 8196683

Dewey, Thomas B. *Deadline.* 1966 Simon & Schuster.
Gilbert, Anthony. *Passenger To Nowhere.* 1966 Random House.
Roos, Kelley. *One False Move.* 1966 Dodd, Mead.

1966.12 *December* — 8136763

Gruber, Frank. *Run, Fool, Run.* 1966 Dutton.
Wees, F S. *Faceless Enemy.* 1966 Doubleday.
Holton, Leonard. *Out Of The Depths.* 1966 Dodd, Mead.

1967

1967.01 *January* — 898930843

Christie, Agatha. *At Bertram's Hotel.* 1965 Dodd, Mead.
Forbes, Stanton. *A Business Of Bodies.* 1966 Doubleday.
Kane, Henry. *Conceal And Disguise.* 1966 Macmillan.

1967.02 *February* — 8092936

Waugh, Hillary. *Pure Poison.* 1966 Doubleday.
Curtiss, Ursula. *Danger: Hospital Zone.* 1966 Dodd, Mead.
Bagby, George. *Dirty Pool.* 1966 Doubleday.

1967.03 *March* — 3219812

Eberhart, Mignon G. *Witness At Large.* 1966 Random House.
Fish, Robert L. *Always Kill A Stranger.* 1967 Putnam.
Foley, Rae. *Scared To Death.* 1966 Dodd, Mead.

1967

1967.04   *April*   3219534
Walsh, Thomas. *The Face Of The Enemy.* 1966 Simon & Schuster.
Hitchens, Dolores. *The Man Who Cried All The Way Home.* 1966 Simon & Schuster.
White, Lionel. *The Crimshaw Memorandum.* 1967 Dutton.

1967.05   *May*   3218145
Fair, A A. *Traps Need Fresh Bait.* 1967 Morrow.
Blanc, Suzanne. *The Rose Window.* 1967 Doubleday.
Delving, Michael. *Smiling the Boy Fell Dead.* 1966 Scribner.

1967.06   *June*   3221428
Gruber, Frank. *The Twilight Man.* 1967 Dutton.
Nielsen, Helen. *A Killer in the Street.* 1967 Morrow.
Haggard, William. *The Power House.* 1966 Ives Washburn.

1967.07   *July*   5396226
Gardner, Erle Stanley. *The Case Of The Queenly Contestant.* 1967 Morrow.
Foley, Rae. *Fear of a Stranger.* 1967 Dodd, Mead.
Stein, Aaron Marc. *Deadly Delight.* 1967 Doubleday.

1967.08   *August*   83043937
Gilbert, Anthony. *The Looking Glass Murder.* 1966 Random House.
Disney, Doris Miles. *Night of Clear Choice.* 1967 Doubleday.
Stark, Richard. *The Damsel.* 1967 Macmillan.

1967.09   *September*   3219397
Pentecost, Hugh. *The Golden Trap.* 1967 Dodd, Mead.
Johnston, Velda. *Along a Dark Path.* 1967 Dodd, Mead.
Kruger, Paul. *Weave a Wicked Web.* 1967 Simon & Schuster.

1967.10   *October*   680159506
Dewey, Thomas B. *Death and Taxes.* 1967 Putnam.
Hubbard, P M. *The Tower.* 1967 Atheneum.
Fish, Robert L. *The Hochman Miniatures.* 1966 New American Library.

1967.11   *November*   3219353
Masterson, Whit. *Play Like You're Dead.* 1967 Dodd, Mead.
Hebden, Mark. *The Eyewitness.* 1966 Harcourt, Brace & World.
Foley, Rae. *The Shelton Conspiracy.* 1967 Dodd, Mead.

1967.12   *December*   3219822
Philips, Judson. *Thursday's Folly.* 1967 Dodd, Mead.
Gilbert, Anthony. *The Visitor.* 1967 Random House.
Taylor, H Baldwin. *The Trouble With Tycoons.* 1967 Doubleday.

1968

1968.01   *January*   4608289
Eberhart, Mignon G. *The Woman On The Roof.* 1967 Random House.
Chaber, M E. *A Man In The Middle.* 1967 Holt, Rinehart & Winston.
Roos, Kelley. *Who Saw Maggie Brown?.* 1967 Dodd, Mead.

1968

1968.02   *February*   4618007
Collins, Michael. *Act Of Fear.* 1967 Dodd, Mead.
Bagby, George. *Corpse Candle.* 1967 Doubleday.
Knox, Bill. *Blacklight.* 1967 Doubleday.
1968.03   *March*   6659555
Pentecost, Hugh. *Dead Woman Of The Year.* 1967 Dodd, Mead.
Disney, Doris Miles. *Money For The Taking.* 1968 Doubleday.
Hewens, Frank E. *The Murder Of The Dainty-Footed Model.* 1968 Macmillan.
1968.04   *April*   5178450
Gruber, Frank. *The Gold Gap.* 1968 Dutton.
Garve, Andrew. *A Very Quiet Place.* 1967 Harper.
Letton, Jennette. *Incident at Hendon.* 1967 Macrae Smith.
1968.05   *May*   2651096
Christie, Agatha. *Endless Night.* 1967 Dodd, Mead.
Fish, Robert L. *The Bridge That Went Nowhere.* 1968 Putnam.
Scherf, Margaret. *The Banker's Bones.* 1968 Doubleday.
1968.06   *June*   4608309
Haggard, William. *The Conspirators.* 1968 Walker.
Potts, Jean. *The Trash Stealer.* 1967 Scribner.
MacLeod, Robert. *The Iron Sanctuary.* 1968 Holt, Rinehart & Winston.
1968.07   *July*   8160485
Simenon, Georges. *Maigret and the Headless Corpse.* 1967 Harcourt, Brace & World.
Foley, Rae. *Malice Domestic.* 1968 Dodd, Mead.
McGurk, Slater. *The Big Dig.* 1968 Macmillan.
1968.08   *August*   8125502
Kane, Henry. *Laughter In The Alehouse.* 1968 Macmillan.
Allingham, Margery. *Cargo Of Eagles.* 1968 Morrow.
Wilcox, Collin. *The Third Figure.* 1968 Dodd, Mead.
1968.09   *September*   928174733
Gardner, Erle Stanley. *The Case Of The Careless Cupid.* 1968 Morrow.
Forbes, Stanton. *If Two of Them are Dead.* 1968 Doubleday.
Roos, Kelley. *To Save His Life.* 1968 Dodd, Mead.
1968.10   *October*   5341041
McBain, Ed. *Fuzz.* 1968 Doubleday.
Keith, Carlton. *A Taste Of Sangria.* 1968 Doubleday.
Chaber, M E. *Wild Midnight Falls.* 1968 Holt, Rinehart & Winston.
1968.11   *November*   1036612075
Simenon, Georges. *Maigret's Pickpocket.* 1967 Harcourt, Brace & World.
Peters, Elizabeth. *The Jackal's Head.* 1968 Meredith.
Wells, Tobias. *Murder Most Fouled Up.* 1968 Doubleday.

1968

1968.12 *December*   8115671
 Palmer, Stuart. *Rook Takes Knight.* 1968 Random House.
 Curtiss, Ursula. *Don't Open That Door.* 1968 Dodd, Mead.
 Holton, Leonard. *A Touch Of Jonah.* 1968 Dodd, Mead.

1969

1969.01 *January*   5340696
 Coxe, George Harmon. *An Easy Way To Go.* 1968 Knopf.
 Carvic, Heron. *Picture Miss Seeton.* 1968 Harper.
 Johnston, Velda. *A Howling In The Woods.* 1968 Dodd, Mead.
1969.02 *February*   6140835
 Gilbert, Anthony. *Murder Anonymous.* 1968 Random House.
 Travis, Gretchen. *Too Old to Die.* 1968 Putnam.
 Stark, Richard. *The Dame.* 1969 Macmillan.
1969.03 *March*   6179321
 Eberhart, Mignon G. *Message from Hong Kong.* 1969 Random House.
 Knox, Bill. *Figurehead.* 1968 Doubleday.
 Philips, Judson. *Hot Summer Killing.* 1968 Dodd, Mead.
1969.04 *April*   746151576
 Haggard, William. *A Cool Day for Killing.* 1968 Walker.
 Potts, Jean. *The Little Lie.* 1968 Scribner.
 Stern, Richard Martin. *Merry Go Round.* 1968 Scribner.
1969.05 *May*   3598386
 Simenon, Georges. *Maigret in Vichy.* 1968 Harcourt, Brace & World.
 Gordons, The. *Night Before the Wedding.* 1969 Doubleday.
 Bagby, George. *Honest Reliable Corpse.* 1969 Doubleday.
1969.06 *June*   6161212
 Gruber, Frank. *The Etruscan Bull.* 1969 Dutton.
 Collins, Michael. *The Brass Rainbow.* 1968 Dodd, Mead.
 Pentecost, Hugh. *The Girl With Six Fingers.* 1969 Dodd, Mead.
1969.07 *July*   6161175
 Fish, Robert L. *The Xavier Affair.* 1969 Putnam.
 Letton, Jennette. *Allegra's Child.* 1969 MacRae Smith.
 Baxt, George. *I, Said the Demon!.* 1969 Random House.
1969.08 *August*   928177072
 Wells, Tobias. *Die Quickly, Dear Mother.* 1969 Doubleday.
 Foley, Rae. *No Hiding Place.* 1969 Dodd, Mead.
 Gilbert, Anthony. *Missing From Her Home.* 1969 Random House.
1969.09 *September*   6165858
 Pentecost, Hugh. *Girl Watcher's Funeral.* 1969 Dodd, Mead.
 Peters, Elizabeth. *The Camelot Caper.* 1969 Meredith.
 Vance, John Holbrook. *The Deadly Isles.* 1969 Bobbs-Merrill.

The Detective Book Club 1942-2000

1969

| 1969.10 | *October* | 6122318 |

Masterson, Whit. *The Last One Kills.* 1969 Dodd, Mead.
Siller, Hilda Van. *The Watchers.* 1969 Doubleday.
Reagan, Thomas B. *The Caper.* 1969 Putnam.

| 1969.11 | *November* | 7246103 |

McBain, Ed. *Shotgun.* 1969 Doubeday.
Angus, Sylvia. *Death Of A Hittite.* 1969 Macmillan.
Stark, Richard. *The Blackbird.* 1969 Macmillan.

| 1969.12 | *December* | 6156833 |

Palmer, Start & Fletcher, Flora. *Hildegarde Withers Makes The Scene.* 1969 Random Hou
Ashe, Gordon. *A Clutch Of Coppers.* 1969 Holt, Rinehart & Winston.
Fisher, Steve. *Saxon's Ghost.* 1969 Sherbourne Press.

1970

| 1970.01 | *January* | 6074896 |

Gardner, Erle Stanley. *The Case Of The Fabulous Fake.* 1969 Morrow.
Foley, Rae. *Girl on a High Wire.* 1969 Dodd, Mead.
Dewey, Thomas B. *The Love-Death Thing.* 1969 Simon & Schuster.

| 1970.02 | *February* | 3583181 |

Wells, Tobias. *The Young Can Die Protesting.* 1969 Doubleday.
Johnston, Velda. *I Came to a Castle.* 1969 Dodd, Mead.
Maling, Arthur. *Decoy.* 1969 Harper.

| 1970.03 | *March* | 3583267 |

Christie, Agatha. *Hallowe'en Party.* 1969 Dodd, Mead.
Forbes, Stanton. *The Name's Death, Remember Me?.* 1969 Doubleday.
Holton, Leonard. *A Problem in Angels.* 1970 Dodd, Mead.

| 1970.04 | *April* | 6184020 |

Lockridge, Richard. *Troubled Journey.* 1970 Lippincott.
Osborne, Helena. *The Yellow Gold of Tiryns.* 1969 Coward McCann.
Coxe, George Harmon. *Double Identity.* 1970 Knopf.

| 1970.05 | *May* | 6165885 |

Fair, A A. *All Grass Isn't Green.* 1970 Morrow.
Armstrong, Charlotte. *The Protege.* 1970 Putnam.
Gruber, Frank. *The Spanish Prisoner.* 1969 Doubleday.

| 1970.06 | *June* | 3598434 |

Knox, Bill. *Blueback.* 1969 Doubleday.
Johnston, Velda. *The Phantom Cottage.* 1970 Dodd, Mead.
Brown, J E. *Incident at 125th Street.* 1970 Doubleday.

| 1970.07 | *July* | 3595855 |

McBain, Ed. *Jigsaw.* 1970 Doubleday.
Bagley, Desmond. *The Spoilers.* 1970 Doubleday.
Forbes, Stanton. *She Was Only the Sheriff's Daughter.* 1970 Doubleday.

1970

1970.08	*August*	6126930

Gilman, Dorothy. *The Amazing Mrs. Pollifax.* 1970 Doubleday.
Stein, Aaron Marc. *Alp Murder.* 1970 Doubleday.
Carvic, Heron. *Miss Seeton Draws The Line.* 1970 Harper.

1970.09	*September*	6140901

Pike, Robert L. *Reardon.* 1970 Doubleday.
Stadley, Pat. *Autumn Of A Hunter.* 1970 Random House.
Roos, Kelley. *What Did Hattie See?.* 1950 Dodd, Mead.

1970.10	*October*	6151978

Wells, Tobias. *Dinky Died.* 1970 Doubleday.
Hillerman, Tony. *The Blessing Way.* 1970 Harper.
Peters, Elizabeth. *The Dead Sea Cipher.* 1970 Dodd, Mead.

1970.11	*November*	6114562

Westlake, Donald E. *The Hot Rock.* 1970 Simon & Schuster.
Millar, Margaret. *Beyond This Point Are Monsters.* 1970 Random House.
Garve, Andrew. *Boomerang.* 1970 Harper.

1970.12	*December*	6126944

Masterson, Whit. *The Death of Me Yet.* 1970 Dodd, Mead.
Hubbard, P M. *High Tide.* 1970 Atheneum.
Delving, Michael. *Die Like a Man.* 1970 Scribner.

1971

1971.01	*January*	962864727

Eberhart, Mignon G. *El Rancho Rio.* 1970 Random House.
Gilbert, Anthony. *Mr. Crook Lifts The Mask.* 1970 Random House.
Harper, David. *Hijacked.* 1970 Dodd, Mead.

1971.02	*February*	3598531

Dewey, Thomas B. *The Taurus Trip.* 1970 Simon & Schuster.
Reagan, Thomas B. *Blood Money.* 1970 Putnam.
Stern, Richard Martin. *Manuscript for Murder.* 1970 Scribner.

1971.03	*March*	3581137

Charteris, Leslie. *The Saint in Pursuit.* 1970 Doubleday.
Foley, Rae. *A Calculated Risk.* 1970 Dodd, Mead.
Maling, Arthur. *Go-Between.* 1970 Harper.

1971.04	*April*	10476557

Roos, Kelley. *Suddenly One Night.* 1970 Dodd, Mead.
Johnston, Velda. *The Light in the Swamp.* 1970 Dodd, Mead.
Carson, Robert. *The Golden Years Caper.* 1970 Little, Brown.

1971.05	*May*	3979659

Gardner, Erle Stanley. *The Case Of The Crimson Kiss.* 1970 Morrow.
Johnston, Velda. *The People on the Hill.* 1971 Dodd, Mead.
Reagan, Thomas B. *The Inside-Out Heist.* 1970 Putnam.

1971

1971.06	*June*	3979795

Pentecost, Hugh. *A Plague Of Violence.* 1970 Dodd, Mead.
Disney, Doris Miles. *Do Not Fold, Spindle Or Mutilate.* 1970 Doubleday.
Fish, Robert L. *The Green Hell Treasure.* 1971 Putnam.

1971.07	*July*	6136191

Macdonald, Ross. *The Underground Man.* knopf 1971.
Forbes, Stanton. *The Sad, Sudden Death Of My Fair Lady.* 1971 Doubleday.
Chaber, M E. *The Bonded Dead.* 1971 Holt, Rinehart & Winston.

1971.08	*August*	2197378

McBain, Ed. *Hail, Hail, The Gang's All Here.* 1971 Doubleday.
Ashe, Gordon. *The Kidnapped Child.* 1971 Holt, Rinehart & Winston.
Foley, Rae. *This Woman Wanted.* 1971 Dodd, Mead.

1971.09	*September*	3595783

Queen, Ellery. *A Fine And Private Place.* 1971 World.
Curtiss, Ursula. *Letter Of Intent.* 1971 Dodd, Mead.
Westlake, Donald E. *I Gave At The Office.* 1971 Simon & Schuster.

1971.10	*September/October Inner Circle*	7853337

Stark, Richard. *Lemons Never Lie.* 1971 World.
Disney, Doris Miles. *Three's A Crowd.* 1971 Doubleday.
Gilbert, Anthony. *Tenant For The Tomb.* 1971 Random House.

1971.11	*October*	6165825

Pentecost, Hugh. *The Deadly Joke.* 1971 Dodd, Mead.
Carvic, Heron. *Witch Miss Seaton.* 1971 Harper.
Masterson, Whit. *The Gravy Train.* 1971 Dodd, Mead.

1971.12	*November*	5987201

Garve, Andrew. *The Late Bill Smith.* 1971 Harper.
Hitchens, Dolores. *The Baxter Letters.* 1971 Putnam.
McMahon, Thomas Patrick. *Jink.* 1971 Simon & Schuster.

1971.13	*November/December Inner Circle*	8138040

Maling, Arthur. *Loophole.* 1971 Harper.
Fish, Robert L. *Rub-A-Dub-Dub.* 1971 Simon & Schuster.
Foley, Rae. *Ominous Star.* 1971 Dodd, Mead.

1971.14	*December*	3595751

Tryon, Thomas. *The Other.* 1971 Knopf.
Keating, H R F. *Inspector Ghote Breaks An Egg.* 1971 Doubleday.
Johnston, Velda. *The Face In The Shadows.* 1971 Dodd, Mead.

1971.15	*promotional*

Gardner, Erle Stanley. *The Case of the Careless Cupid.* 1968 Morrow.
Queen, Ellery. *A Fine And Private Place.* 1971 World.
Ashe, Gordon. *The Kidnaped Child.* 1971 Holt, RInehart & Winston.

1972

1972.01   *January*   1029261378
Gardner, Erle Stanley. *The Case Of The Crying Swallow.* 1971 Morrow.
Wells, Tobias. *The Foo Dog.* 1971 Doubleday.
Christie, Agatha. *Nemesis.* 1971 Dodd, Mead.
1972.02   *February*   904231597
Stark, Richard. *Slayground.* 1971 Random House.
Disney, Doris Miles. *The Chandler Policy.* 1971 Putnam.
Williams, Brad and Erlich, J W. *A Conflict Of Interest.* 1971 Holt, Rinehart & Winston.
1972.03   *March*   1986569
Eberhart, Mignon G. *Two Little Rich Girls.* 1971 Random House.
Hillerman, Tony. *The Fly On The Wall.* 1971 Harper.
Knox, Bill. *Seafire.* 1971 Doubleday.
1972.04   *March/April Inner Circle*   8172495
Roos, Kelley. *Bad Trip.* 1971 Dodd, Mead.
Gilman, Dorothy. *The Elusive Mrs. Pollifax.* 1971 Doubleday.
Wilcox, Collin. *Dead Aim.* 1971 Random House.
1972.05   *April*   5916956
Marric, J J. *Gideon's Art.* 1971 Harper.
Craig, John. *If You Want To See Your Wife Again....* 1971 Putnam.
Johnston, Velda. *The Mourning Tree.* 1972 Dodd, Mead.
1972.06   *May*   811865171
Gardner, Erle Stanley. *The Case Of The Irate Witness.* 1972 Morrow.
O'Donnell, Lillian. *The Phone Calls.* 1972 Putnam.
Delving, Michael. *A Shadow Of Himself.* 1972 Scribner.
1972.07   *June*   877179382
Charteris, Leslie. *The Saint And The People Importers.* 1972 Doubleday.
Davis, Mildred. *Three Minutes To Midnight.* 1971 Random House.
Pike, Robert L. *The Gremlin's Grampa.* 1972 Doubleday.
1972.08   *July*   1730680
Simenon, Georges. *Maigret Sets a Trap.* 1972 Harcourt.
Fleming, Joan. *Be a Good Boy.* 1971 Putnam.
Pentecost, Hugh. *Birthday, Deathday.* 1972 Dodd, Mead.
1972.09   *July/August Inner Circle*   827271566
Coxe, George Harmon. *Woman With a Gun.* 1972 Knopf.
Leonard, Constance. *The Other Maritha.* 1972 Dodd, Mead.
Holton, Leonard. *The Mirror of Hell.* 1972 Dodd, Mead.
1972.10   *August*   1855632
Ashe, Gordon. *Wait For Death.* 1972 Holt, Rinehart & Winston.
Foley, Rae. *Sleep Without Morning.* 1972 Dodd, Mead.
Lockridge, Richard. *Death In A Sunny Place.* 1971 Lippincott.

1972

1972.11	*September*	3581224

Scherf, Margaret. *To Cache A Millionaire.* 1972 Doubleday.
Garve, Andrew. *The Case Of Robert Quarry.* 1972 Harper.
Goldstein, Arthur D. *A Person Shouldn't Die Like That.* 1972 Random House.

1972.12	*September/October Inner Circle*	6156818

Garfield, Brian. *Relentless.* 1972 World.
Creasey, John. *Take A Body.* 1972 World.
Mason, Michael. *71 Hours.* 1972 Coward, McCann.

1972.13	*October*	1868517

Forbes, Stanton. *But I Wouldn't Want To Die There.* 1972 Doubleday.
Gilbert, Anthony. *Murder's A Waiting Game.* 1972 Random House.
Ball, John. *Five Pieces Of Jade.* 1972 Harper.

1972.14	*November*	3583213

Creasey, John. *A Splinter Of Glass.* 1972 Scribner.
Stone, Hampton. *The Kid Who Came Home With A Corpse.* 1972 Simon & Schuster.
Kyle, Duncan. *Flight Into Fear.* 1972 St Martins.

1972.15	*November/December Inner Circle*	6126915

Ashe, Gordon. *A Rabble Of Rebels.* 1971 Holt, Rinehart & Winston.
Keating, H R F. *Inspector Ghote Goes By Train.* 1971 Doubleday.
Franklin, Steve. *The Chickens In The Airshaft.* 1972 Doubleday.

1972.16	*December*	3598488

Disney, Doris Miles. *The Day Miss Bessie Lewis Disappeared.* 1972 Doubleday.
McBain, Ed. *Sadie When She Died.* 1972 Doubleday.
Kenrick, Tony. *A Tough One to Lose.* 1972 Bobbs-Merrill.

1972.17	*promotional*

Gardner, Erle Stanley. *The Case Of The Fabulous Fake.* 1969 Morrow.
Queen, Ellery. *A Fine And Private Place.* 1971 World.
Ashe, Gordon. *The Kidnaped Child.* 1971 Holt, RInehart & Winston.

1972.18	*promotional*	751247446

Gardner, Erle Stanley. *The Case Of The Irate Witness.* 1972 Morrow.
Eberhart, Mignon G. *Two Little Rich Girls.* 1971 Random House.
Marric, J J. *Gideon's Art.* 1971 Harper.

1973

1973.01	*January*	3611609

Gardner, Erle Stanley. *The Case Of The Fenced-In Woman.* 1972 Morrow.
Foley, Rae. *The First Mrs. Winston.* 1972 Dodd, Mead.
Marric, J J. *Gideon's Men.* 1972 Harper.

1973.02	*January/February Inner Circle*	5970691

Creasey, John. *Lame Dog Murder.* 1972 World.
Green, William M. *Avery's Fortune.* 1972 Bobbs-Merrill.
Harrison, Harry. *Montezuma's Revenge.* 1972 Doubleday.

1973

1973.03   *February*   5399741
     Garfield, Brian. *Death Wish.* 1972 McKay.
     Fremlin, Celia. *Appointment With Yesterday.* 1972 Lippincott.
     Pentecost, Hugh. *The Champagne Killer.* 1972 Dodd.

1973.04   *March*   5436374
     Masterson, Whit. *Why She Cries, I Do Not Know.* 1972 Dodd, Mead.
     George, Theodore. *The Deadly Homecoming.* 1972 Dodd, Mead.
     Haggard, William. *The Protectors.* 1972 Walkter.

1973.05   *March/April Inner Circle*   5872172
     Wells, Tobias. *A Die In The Country.* 1972 Doubleday.
     Angus, Sylvia. *Arson And Old Lace.* 1972 World.
     Driscoll, Peter. *The Wilby Conspiracy.* 1972 Lippincott.

1973.06   *April*   5399732
     Coxe, George Harmon. *The Silent Witness.* 1973 Knopf.
     Potts, Jean. *The Troublemaker.* 1972 Scribner.
     Creasey, John. *Inspector West Takes Charge.* 1972 Scribner.

1973.07   *May*   7493340
     Gardner, Erle Stanley. *The Case Of The Postponed Murder.* 1973 Morrow.
     Fleming, Joan. *Alas Poor Father.* 1973 Putnam.
     Stein, Aaron Marc. *The Finger.* 1973 Doubleday.

1973.08   *May/June Inner Circle*   6136124
     Williams, Brad and Erlich, J W. *A Matter Of Confidence.* 1973 Holt, Rinehart & Winston.
     Gatenby, Rosemary. *Hanged For A Sheep.* 1973 Dodd, Mead.
     Baker, Ivon. *Grave Doubt.* 1972 McKay Washburn.

1973.09   *June*   1830519
     Francis, Dick. *Smokescreen.* 1972 Harper.
     McCloy, Helen. *A Change of Heart.* 1973 Dodd, Mead.
     Lewis, Roy. *A Wolf by the Ears.* 1972 World.

1973.10   *July*   1835042
     Simenon, Georges. *Maigret and the Informer.* 1973 Jarcourt Brace Jovanovich.
     Cleary, Jon. *Ransom.* 1973 Morrow.
     Disney, Doris Miles. *Only Couples Need Apply.* 1973 Doubleday.

1973.11   *July/August Inner Circle*   5399761
     Knox, Bill. *Stormtide.* 1972 Doubleday.
     Ashe, Gordon. *The Croaker.* 1972 Holt, Rinehart & Winston.
     Constantine, K C. *The Rocksburg Railroad Murders.* 1972 Saturday Review Press.

1973.12   *August*   1855886
     Pentecost, Hugh. *Walking Dead Man.* 1973 Dodd, Mead.
     Creasey, John. *The Theft of the Magna Carta.* 1973 Scribner.
     Stern, Richard Martin. *Death in the Snow.* 1973 Scribner.

1973

1973.13	*September*	3581240

Eberhart, Mignon G. *Murder In Waiting.* 1973 Random Housr.
Miles, John. *The Night Hunters.* 1973 Bobbs-Merrill.
Keating, H R F. *Inspector Ghote Trusts The Heart.* 1973 Doubleday.

1973.14	*September/October Inner Circle*	4239175

Innes, Hammond. *The Golden Soak.* 1973 Knopf.
Woodhouse, Martin. *Blue Bone.* 1973 Coward, McCann & Geoghegan.
Pronzini, Bill. *Undercurrent.* 1973 Random House.

1973.15	*October*	1870131

Masterson, Whit. *The Undertaker Wind.* 1973 Dodd, Mead.
Ashe, Gordon. *A Life For A Death.* 1973 Holt, Rinehart & Winston.
Gilman, Dorothy. *A Palm For Mrs. Pollifax.* 1973 Doubleday.

1973.16	*November*	1036832192

Foley, Rae. *Reckless Lady.* 1973 Dodd, Mead.
Eden, Matthew. *Conquest Before Autumn.* 1973 Abelard-Schuman.
Chaber, M E. *Born to be Hanged.* 1973 Holt, Rinehart & Winston.

1973.17	*November/December Inner Circle*	8159528

John, Owen. *Sabotage.* 1973 Dutton.
Blazer, J S. *Deal Me Out.* 1973 Bobbs-Merrill.
Dean, Amber. *Be Home By Eleven.* 1973 Putnam.

1973.18	*December*	3595961

Rothblatt, H B and Fish, Robert L. *A Handy Death.* 1973 Simon & Schuster.
Peters, Elizabeth. *Borrower Of The Night.* 1973 Dodd, Mead.
Haggard, William. *The Notch On The Knife.* 1973 Walker.

1973.19	*promotional*	4618091

Queen, Ellery. *A Fine And Private Place.* 1971 World.
Gardner, Erle Stanley. *The Case Of The Postponed Murder.* 1973 Morrow.
Christie, Agatha. *Nemesis.* 1971 Dodd, Mead.

1973.20	*promotional*	3816676

Eberhart, Mignon G. *Two Little Rich Girls.* 1971 Random House.
Francis, Dick. *Smokescreen.* 1972 Harper.
Simenon, Georges. *Maigret and the Informer.* 1973 Harcourt Brace Jovanovich.

1974

1974.01	*January*	1834334

MacDonald, John D. *The Turquoise Lament.* 1973 Lippincott.
Johnston, Velda. *The White Pavilion.* 1973 Dodd, Mead.
Marric, J J. *Gideon's Press.* 1973 Harper.

1974.02	*January/February Inner Circle*	6161255

Davis, Dorothy Salisbury. *The Little Brothers.* 1973 Scribner.
Moyes, Patricia. *The Curious Affair Of The Third Dog.* 1973 Holt, Rinehart & Winston.
Sjowall, Maj & Wahloo, Per. *The Locked Room.* 1973 Pantheon.

1974

1974.03   *February*   7493442
Holton, Leonard. *The Devil to Play.* 1974 Dodd, Mead.
Creasey, John. *Inspector West at Home.* 1973 Scribner.
Wells, Tobias. *Brenda's Murder.* 1973 Doubleday.

1974.04   *March*   4600144
Simenon, Georges. *Maigret and the Bum.* 1973 Harcourt Brace Jovanovich.
Waters, T A. *The Lost Victim.* 1973 Random House.
Hebden, Mark. *The Dark Side of the Island.* 1973 Harcourt Brace Jovanovich.

1974.05   *March/April Inner Circle*   5620209
Cleary, Jon. *Peter's Pence.* 1974 Morrow.
Fleming, Joan. *You Won't Let Me Finnish.* 1973 Putnam.
Blankenship, William D. *The Leavenworth Irregulars.* 1974 Bobbs-Merrill.

1974.06   *April*   1028667605
Pentecost, Hugh. *The Beautiful Dead.* 1973 Dodd, Mead.
Braddon, Russell. *The Thirteenth Trick.* 1973 Norton.
Ferguson, Austin. *Jet Stream.* 1973 Morrow.

1974.07   *May*   1834959
Francis, Dick. *Slay-Ride.* 1974 Harper.
Wren, M K. *Curiosity Didn't Kill The Cat.* 1973 Doubleday.
Garve, Andrew. *The Lester Affair.* 1974 Harper.

1974.08   *May/June Inner Circle*   5872161
Driscoll, Peter. *In Connection With Kilshaw.* 1974 Lippincott.
Pentecost, Hugh. *Bargain With Death.* 1974 Dodd, Mead.
Highsmith, Patricia. *Ripley's Game.* 1974 Knopf.

1974.09   *June*   1730727
Ashe, Gordon. *Murder With Mushrooms.* 1974 Holt, Rinehart & Winston.
Pike, Robert L. *Bank Job.* 1974 Doubleday.
Gilbert, Anthony. *A Nice Little Killing.* 1973 Random House.

1974.10   *July*   5872188
Simenon, Georges. *Maigret Loses His Temper.* 1974 Harcourt Brace Jovanovich.
Johnston, Velda. *I Came to the Highlands.* 1974 Dodd, Mead.
Garfield, Brian. *The Threepersons Hunt.* 1974 M Evans.

1974.11   *July/August Inner Circle*   4947940
Masterson, Whit. *The Man With Two Clocks.* 1974 Dodd, Mead.
Philips, Judson. *The Power Killers.* 1974 Dodd, Mead.
Huff, T E. *Meet A Dark Stranger.* 1974 Hawthorne.

1974.12   *August*   3577457
Coxe, George Harmon. *The Inside Man.* 1974 Knopf.
Foley, Rae. *One O'Clock At The Gotham.* 1974 Dodd, Mead.
Disney, Doris Miles. *Don't Go Into The Woods Today.* 1974 Doubleday.

1974

1974.13   *September*   1874093
Simenon, Georges. *The Venice Train.* 1974 Harcourt Brace Jovanovich.
Fish, Robert L. *The Wager.* 1974 Putnam.
Marsh, Ngaio. *Black As He's Painted.* 1974 Little, Brown.
1974.14   *September/October Inner Circle*   5019922
Canning, Victor. *The Painted Tent.* 1974 Morrow.
Slesar, Henry. *The Thing At The Door.* 1974 Random House.
Underwood, Michael. *A Pinch Of Snuff.* 1974 Macmillan.
1974.15   *October*   5039591
Westlake, Donald E. *Jimmy The Kid.* 1974 Mysterious Press.
Foley, Rae. *The Brownstone House.* 1974 Dodd, Mead.
Westheimer, David. *The Olmec Head.* 1974 Little, Brown.
1974.16   *November*   3581250
Pentecost, Hugh. *The Judas Freak.* 1974 Dodd, Mead.
White, Alan. *The Long Fuse.* 1974 Harcourt, Brace, Jovanovich.
Keating, H R F. *Bats Fly Up for Inspector Ghote.* 1974 Doubleday.
1974.17   *November/December Inner Circle*   5011764
Knox, Bill. *Whitewater.* 1974 Doubleday.
Goldstein, Arthur D. *You're Never Too Old To Die.* 1974 Random House.
Ball, John. *Mark One: The Dummy.* 1974 Little, Brown.
1974.18   *December*   4588632
Deighton, Len. *Spy Story.* 1974 Harcourt Brace Jovanovich.
Ferrars, E X. *Hanged Man's House.* 1974 Doubleday.
Albrand, Martha. *Zurich/AZ900.* 1974 Holt, Rinehart & Winston.
1974.19   *promotional*   15034378
Simenon, Georges. *Maigret and the Bum.* 1973 Harcourt Brace Jovanovich.
Sjowall, Maj & Wahloo, Per. *The Locked Room.* 1973 Pantheon.
MacDonald, John D. *The Turquoise Lament.* 1973 Lippincott.

1975

1975.01   *January*   1834970
MacDonald, John D. *A Deadly Shade of Gold.* 1974 Lippincott.
Morice, Anne. *Death of a Heavenly Twin.* 1974 St Martins.
Simenon, Georges. *Maigret and the Millionaires.* 1973 Harcourt Brace Jovanovich.
1975.02   *February*   4618026
Eberhart, Mignon G. *Danger Money.* 1974 Random House.
Garfield, Brian. *The Romanov Succession.* 1974 M. Evans.
Peters, Ellis. *The Horn Of Roland.* 1974 Morrow.
1975.03   *March*   311171021
MacDonald, John D. *The Dreadful Lemon Sky.* 1974 Lippincott.
Johnston, Velda. *The House On The Left Bank.* 1975 Dodd, Mead.
Ashe, Gordon. *A Herald Of Doom.* 1973 Holt, Rinehart & Winton.

1975

1975.04	*March/April Inner Circle*	5020801

Kyle, Duncan. *Terror's Cradle.* 1974 St Martins.
Davis, Mildred. *Tell Them What's-Her-Name Called.* 1975 Random House.
Gordons, The. *Catnapped.* 1974 Doubleday.

1975.05	*April*	1855211

Marric, J J. *Gideon's Fog.* 1974 Harper.
Foley, Rae. *The Dark Hill.* 1975 Dodd, Mead.
Haggard, William. *The Kinsmen.* 1974 Walker.

1975.06	*May*	5020499

Garfield, Brian. *Hopscotch.* 1975 M. Evans.
Disney, Doris Miles. *Cry For Help.* 1975 Doubleday.
Hebden, Mark. *A Pride Of Dolphins.* 1974 Harcourt, Brace, Jovanovich.

1975.07	*May/June Inner Circle*	5022135

Priestley, J B. *Salt Is Leaving.* 1975 Harper.
Winter, Abigail. *Whispering Caverns.* 1974 Simon & Schuster.
Templeton, Charles. *The Kidnapping Of The President.* 1974 Simon & Schuster.

1975.08	*June*	5021941

Pentecost, Hugh. *Time of Terror.* 1975 Dodd, Mead.
Fleming, Joan. *How To Live Dangerously.* 1974 Putnam.
Innes, Hammond. *North Star.* 1974 Knopf.

1975.09	*July*	4600211

Simenon, Georges. *Maigret And The Loner.* 1975 Harcourt, Brace & Jovanovich.
Clark, Mary Higgins. *Where Are The Children?.* 1975 Simon & Schuster.
Fish, Robert L. *Trouble In Paradise.* 1975 Doubleday.

1975.10	*July/August Inner Circle*	5855758

Kirk, Michael. *All Other Perils.* 1975 Doubleday.
Mackenzie, Donald. *The Spreewald Collection.* 1975 Houghton Mifflin.
Allbeury, Ted. *Omega-Minus.* 1975 Viking.

1975.11	*August*	3581178

Francis, Dick. *Knockdown.* 1974 Harper.
Hough Jr., John. *The Guardian.* Atlantic Little Brown 1975.
Gilman, Dorothy. *A Nun In The Closet.* 1975 Doubleday.

1975.12	*September*	5904983

MacDonald, John D. *The Deep Blue Good-By.* 1973 Lippincott.
Cleary, Jon. *The Safe House.* 1974 Morrow.
Ferrars, E X. *Alive And Dead.* 1974 Doubleday.

1975.13	*September/October Inner Circle*	5020703

Land, Myrick. *Last Flight.* 1975 Norton.
Carter, Diana. *The Ghost Writer.* 1975 Macmillan.
Sela, Owen. *The Bengali Inheritance.* 1975 Pantheon.

1975

1975.14 *October*   3581276
 Ashe, Gordon. *The Big Call.* 1975 Holt, Rinehart & Winston.
 O'Donnell, Lillian. *The Baby Merchants.* 1975 Putnam.
 Symons, Julian. *A Three-Pipe Problem.* 1975 Harper.
1975.15 *November*   5021817
 Pentecost, Hugh. *Honeymoon With Death.* 1975 Dodd, Mead.
 Wren, M K. *A Multitude Of Sins.* 1975 Doublday.
 Driscoll, Peter. *The White Lie Assignment.* 1975 Lippincott.
1975.16 *November/December Inner Circle*   11738222
 Maling, Arthur. *Bent Man.* 1975 Harper.
 McMullen, Mary. *A Country Kind Of Death.* 1975 Doubleday.
 Underwood, Michael. *The Juror.* 1975 St Martins.
1975.17 *December*   5872044
 Knox, Bill. *Rally to Kill.* 1975 Doubleday.
 Foxx, Jack. *Dead Run.* 1975 Bobbs-Merrill.
 Woods, Sara. *Done to Death.* 1975 Holt, Rinehart & Winston.
1975.18 *promotional*   4586667
 Eberhart, Mignon G. *Danger Money.* 1974 Random House.
 Simenon, Georges. *Maigret And The Loner.* 1975 Harcourt, Brace & Jovanovich.
 Francis, Dick. *Knockdown.* 1974 Harper.
1975.19 *promotional*   10327534
 MacDonald, John D. *A Deadly Shade of Gold.* 1974 Lippincott.
 Eberhart, Mignon G. *Danger Money.* 1974 Random House.
 Simenon, Georges. *Maigret and the Millionaires.* 1973 Harcourt Brace Jovanovich.
1975.20 *promotional*   8683195
 Marric, J J. *Gideon's Fog.* 1974 Harper.
 Ferrars, E X. *Alive And Dead.* 1974 Doubleday.
 Ashe, Gordon. *The Big Call.* 1975 Holt, Rinehart & Winston.

1976

1976.01 *January*   4608490
 Simenon, Georges. *Maigret and the Man on the Bench.* 1975 Harcourt Brace Jovanovich.
 Charteris, Leslie. *Catch the Saint.* 1975 Doubleday.
 Coxe, George Harmon. *No Place for Murder.* 1975 Knopf.
1976.02 *January/February Inner Circle*   5872038
 Rendell, Ruth. *Shake Hands Forever.* 1975 Doubleday.
 Booton, Kage. *The Toy.* 1975 Doubleday.
 Duncan, Robert L. *Dragons At The Gate.* 1975 Morrow.
1976.03 *February*   4608093
 Garfield, Brian. *Death Sentence.* 1975 M. Evans.
 Foley, Rae. *The Barclay Place.* 1975 Dodd, Mead.
 Parker, Robert B. *Mortal Stakes.* 1975 Houghton Mifflin.

1976

| 1976.04 | *March* | 3595902 |

MacDonald, John D. *Nightmare In Pink.* 1973 Lippincott.
Ferrars, E X. *Drowned Rat.* 1975 Doubleday.
Wells, Tobias. *Hark, Hark, The Watchdogs Bark.* 1975 Doubleday.

| 1976.05 | *March/April Inner Circle* | 962863319 |

Goldstein, Arthur D. *Nobody's Sorry He Got Killed.* 1976 Random House.
Potts, Jean. *My Brother's Killer.* 1975 Scribner.
Law, Janice. *The Big Payoff.* 1975 Houghton Mifflin.

| 1976.06 | *March/April Inner Circle* | 5905009 |

Morice, Anne. *Nursery Tea and Poison.* 1975 St Martins.
Fletcher, Lucille. *80 Dollars To Stamford.* 1975 Random House.
Orum, Poul. *The Scapegoat.* 1975 Pantheon.

| 1976.07 | *April* | 3611464 |

Simenon, Georges. *Maigret and the Black Sheep.* 1976 Harcourt, Brace & Jovanovich.
Constantine, K C. *A Fix Life This.* 1975 Saturday Review Press.
Ashe, Gordon. *A Blast of Trumpets.* 1976 Holt, Rinehart & Winston.

| 1976.08 | *May* | 4608411 |

Francis, Dick. *High Stakes.* 1975 Harper.
Disney, Doris Miles. *Winifred.* 1976 Doubleday.
Pentecost, Hugh. *The Fourteen Dilemma.* 1976 Dodd, Mead.

| 1976.09 | *May/June Inner Circle* | 5021434 |

Michaels, Barbara. *The Sea Kings' Daughter.* 1975 Dodd, Mead.
Williams, Alan. *Gentleman Traitor.* 1975 Harcourt Brace Books Jovanovich.
Stratton, Ted. *Tourist Trap.* 1975 Putnam.

| 1976.10 | *June* | 4586787 |

Pike, Robert L. *Deadline: 2 a.m..* 1975 Doubleday.
Carvic, Heron. *Odds On Miss Seeton.* 1975 Harper.
Green, William M. *See How They Run.* 1975 Bobbs-Merrill.

| 1976.11 | *July* | 4608124 |

Johnston, Velda. *The Frenchman.* 1976 Dodd, Mead.
Maling, Arthur. *Ripoff.* 1976 Harper.
Ashe, Gordon. *A Shadow of Death.* 1976 Holt, Rinehart & Winston.

| 1976.12 | *July/August Inner Circle* | 5690376 |

Black, Gavin. *A Big Wind For Summer.* 1975 Harper.
Einstein, Charles. *The Blackjack Hijack.* 1976 Random House.
Seaman, Donald. *The Chameleon Course.* 1976 Coward, Mccann & Geoghegan.

| 1976.13 | *August* | 3581201 |

Philips, Judson. *Backlash.* 1976 Dodd, Mead.
Foley, Rae. *Where Helen Lies.* 1976 Dodd, Mead.
Canning, Victor. *The Kingsford Mark.* 1976 Morrow.

1976

1976.14   *September*   3611517
Simenon, Georges. *Maigret And The Apparition.* 1976 Harcourt Brace Jovanovich.
Morice, Anne. *Death of a Wedding Guest.* 1976 St Martins.
Cleary, Jon. *A Sound of Lightning.* 1976 Morrow.
1976.15   *September/October Inner Circle*   5022319
Simmons, Geoffrey S. *The Z-Papers.* 1976 Arbor House.
Keating, H R F. *A Remarkable Case Of Burglary.* 1975 Doubleday.
Lewin, Michael Z. *Night Cover.* 1976 Knopf.
1976.16   *October*   3581198
O'Donnell, Lillian. *Leisure Dying.* 1976 Putnam.
Underwood, Michael. *Menaces, Menaces.* 1976 St Martins.
Woods, Sara. *My Life Is Done.* 1976 St Martins.
1976.17   *November*   3583143
Eberhart, Mignon G. *Family Fortune.* 1976 Random House.
Pentecost, Hugh. *Die After Dark.* 1976 Dodd, Mead.
Davis, Dorothy Salisbury. *A Death In The Life.* 1976 Scribner.
1976.18   *November/December Inner Circle*   5630128
Winslow, Pauline Glen. *The Brandenburg Hotel.* 1976 St Martins.
Foote-Smith, Elizabeth. *Gentle Albatross.* 1976 Putnam.
Wetering, Janwillem van de. *Tumbleweed.* 1976 Houghton Mifflin.
1976.19   *December*   4588648
Simenon, Georges. *The Hatter's Phantoms.* 1976 Harcourt Brace Jovanovich.
Foley, Rae. *Put Out The Light.* 1976 Dodd, Mead.
Driscoll, Peter. *The Barboza Credentials.* 1976 Lippincott.
1976.20   *promotional*   10536692
Garfield, Brian. *Death Sentence.* 1975 M. Evans.
Eberhart, Mignon G. *Danger Money.* 1974 Random House.
Morice, Anne. *Nursery Tea and Poison.* 1975 St Martins.
1976.21   *promotional*   11460713
MacDonald, John D. *The Deep Blue Good-By.* 1973 Lippincott.
MacDonald, John D. *Nightmare In Pink.* 1973 Lippincott.
MacDonald, John D. *The Dreadful Lemon Sky.* 1974 Lippincott.
1976.22   *promotional*   27855423
Johnston, Velda. *The Frenchman.* 1976 Dodd, Mead.
Francis, Dick. *High Stakes.* 1975 Harper.
Ashe, Gordon. *A Shadow of Death.* 1976 Holt, Rinehart & Winston.
1976.23   *promotional*   6260549
O'Donnell, Lillian. *Leisure Dying.* 1976 Putnam.
Parker, Robert B. *Mortal Stakes.* 1975 Houghton Mifflin.
MacDonald, John D. *The Dreadful Lemon Sky.* 1974 Lippincott.

1976

1976.24   *promotional*   921883964
Simenon, Georges. *Maigret and the Black Sheep.* 1976 Harcourt, Brace & Jovanovich.
O'Donnell, Lillian. *The Baby Merchants.* 1975 Putnam.
Francis, Dick. *High Stakes.* 1975 Harper.

1977

1977.01   *January*   4588504
Deighton, Len. *Catch A Falling Spy.* 1976 Harcourt, Brace & Jovanovich.
Peters, Ellis. *Never Pick Up Hitch-Hikers!.* 1976 Morrow.
Asimov, Isaac. *More Tales Of The Black Widowers.* 1976 Doubleday.
1977.02   *January/February Inner Circle*   5019821
Anderson, J R L. *Death In The Channel.* 1976 Stein & Day.
McMullen, Mary. *Funny, Jonas, You Don't Look Dead.* 1976 Doubleday.
Luard, Nicholas. *The Orion Line.* 1977 Harcourt Brace Jovanovich.
1977.03   *February*   4022282
MacDonald, John D. *Purple Place for Dying.* 1976 Lippincott.
Garve, Andrew. *Home to Roost.* 1976 Crowell.
Sjowall, Maj & Wahloo, Per. *The Terrorists.* 1976 Pantheon.
1977.04   *March*   4471937
Marric, J J. *Gideon's Drive.* 1976 Harper.
Millar, Margaret. *Ask For Me Tomorrow.* 1976 Random House.
Knox, Bill. *Hellspout.* 1976 Doubleday.
1977.05   *March/April Inner Circle*   5022431
Wetering, Janwillem van de. *The Corpse On The Dike.* 1976 Houghton Mifflin.
Mackay, Amanda. *Death Is Academic.* 1976 McKay.
Ashford, Jeffrey. *Slow Down The World.* 1976 Walker.
1977.06   *March/April Inner Circle*   5022231
Scott, Virgil and Koski, Dominic. *Walk-In.* 1976 Simon & Schuster.
Greenan, Russell H. *The Bric-A-Brac Man.* 1976 Random House.
Stein, Aaron Marc. *Lend Me Your Ears.* 1976 Doubleday.
1977.07   *April*   4471900
Gilman, Dorothy. *Mrs. Pollifax On Safari.* 1976 Doubleday.
Ashe, Gordon. *A Plague Of Demons.* 1976 Holt, Rinehart & Winston.
Holton, Leonard. *A Corner Of Paradise.* 1977 St Martins.
1977.08   *May*   5852184
Johnston, Velda. *Deveron Hall.* 1976 Dodd, Mead.
Masterson, Whit. *Hunter Of The Blood.* 1977 Dodd, Mead.
Wren, M K. *Oh, Bury Me Not.* 1976 Doubleday.
1977.09   *May/June Inner Circle*   704520784
Foote-Smith, Elizabeth. *Never Say Die.* 1977 Putnam.
MacKenzie, Donald. *Raven And The Ratcatcher.* 1976 Houghton Mifflin.
Marshall, William. *The Hatchet Man.* 1976 Holt, Rinehart & Winston.

1977

1977.10	*June*	4586741

Westlake, Donald E. *A Travesty.* 1977 M. Evans.
Haggard, William. *Yesterday's Enemy.* 1976 Walker.
Underwood, Michael. *Murder With Malice.* 1977 St Martins.

1977.11	*July*	4637443

Francis, Dick. *In The Frame.* 1977 Harper.
Ferrars, E X. *Blood Flies Upwards.* 1976 Doubleday.
Morice, Anne. *Murder In Mimicry.* 1977 St Martins.

1977.12	*July/August Inner Circle*	5020051

Kirk, Michael. *Dragonship.* 1977 Doubleday.
Thomson, June. *Case Closed.* 1977 Doubleday.
Henissart, Paul. *The Winter Spy.* 1976 Simon & Schuster.

1977.13	*August*	4588481

Johnston, Velda. *The Etruscan Smile.* 1975 Dodd, Mead.
Foley, Rae. *The Slippery Step.* 1977 Dodd, Mead.
Garfield, Brian. *Recoil.* 1977 Morrow.

1977.14	*September*	4588531

Simenon, Georges. *Maigret and the Spinster.* 1977 Harcourt Brace Jovanovich.
Wetering, Janwillem van de. *Death of a Hawker.* 1977 Houghton Mifflin.
Canning, Victor. *The Doomsday Carrier.* 1977 Morrow.

1977.15	*September/October Inner Circle*	6027066

Maling, Arthur. *Schroeder's Game.* 1977 Harper.
Carmichael, Harry. *The Motive.* 1974 Dutton.
Stevenson, Anne. *Coil Of Serpents.* 1977 Putnam.

1977.16	*September/October Inner Circle*	5622240

Duncan, Robert L. *Temple Dogs.* 1977 Morrow.
McMullen, Mary. *A Dangerous Funeral.* 1977 Doubleday.
Hallahan, William H. *Catch Me, Kill Me.* 1977 Bobbs-Merrill.

1977.17	*October*	4588561

O'Donnell, Lillian. *Aftershock.* 1977 Putnam.
Innes, Hammond. *The Big Footprints.* 1977 Random House.
Keating, H R F. *Filmi, Filmi, Inspector Ghote.* 1977 Doubleday.

1977.18	*November*	4618071

Sela, Owen. *An Exchange Of Eagles.* 1977 Pantheon.
Dolson, Hildegarde. *Beauty Sleep.* 1977 Lippincott.
Ball, John. *Police Chief.* 1977 Doubleday.

1977.19	*November/December Inner Circle*	962865261

Byrne, Robert. *The Tunnel.* 1977 Harcourt, Brace & Jovanovich.
Gill, Bartholomew. *McGarr and the Politician's Wife.* 1977 Scribner.
Arrighi, Mel. *Turkish White.* 1977 Harcourt, Brace & Jovanovich.

1977

1977.20   *December*   5085624
Ashe, Gordon. *Elope To Death.* 1977 Holt, Rinehart.
Westlake, Donald E. *Nobody's Perfect.* 1977 M. Evans.
Guthrie Jr., A B. *The Genuine Article.* 1977 Houghton Mifflin.

1977.21   *promotional*   950038054
O'Donnell, Lillian. *Aftershock.* 1977 Putnam.
Macdonald, Ross. *Lew Archer Private Investigator.* 1977 Mysterious Press.
Ball, John. *Police Chief.* 1977 Doubleday.

1977.22   *promotional*   5938395
Sela, Owen. *An Exchange Of Eagles.* 1977 Pantheon.
Simenon, George. *Maigret and the Spinster.* 1977 Harcourt Brace Jovanovich.
Lockridge, Richard. *The Tenth Life.* 1977 Lippincott.

1977.23   *promotional*   27855420
Eberhart, Mignon G. *Family Fortune.* 1976 Random House.
Johnston, Velda. *The Etruscan Smile.* 1975 Dodd, Mead.
MacDonald, John D. *One Fearful Yellow Eye.* 1977 Lippincott.

1977.24   *promotional*   5938395
Ball, John. *Police Chief.* 1977 Doubleday.
Francis, Dick. *In The Frame.* 1977 Harper.
Garfield, Brian. *Recoil.* 1977 Morrow.

1977.25   *promotional*   1036977848
Sjowall, Maj & Wahloo, Per. *The Terrorists.* 1976 Pantheon.
Eberhart, Mignon G. *Family Fortune.* 1976 Random House.
Simenon, Georges. *Maigret And The Apparition.* 1976 Harcourt Brace Jovanovich.

1978

1978.01   *January*   4586710
MacDonald, John D. *One Fearful Yellow Eye.* 1977 Lippincott.
Ferrars, E X. *The Pretty Pink Shroud.* 1977 Doubleday.
Wetering, Janwillem van de. *The Japanese Corpse.* 1977 Houghton Mifflin.

1978.02   *January/February Inner Circle*   5855953
Mackenzie, Donald. *Raven And The Kamikaze.* 1977 Houghton Mifflin.
Law, Janice. *Gemini Trip.* 1977 Houghton Mifflin.
Quinn, Derry. *The Limbo connection.* 1976 St Martins.

1978.03   *February*   1020465108
Lockridge, Richard. *The Tenth Life.* 1977 Lippincott.
Woods, Sara. *A Thief For Two.* 1977 St Martins.
Philips, Judson. *Five Roads To Death.* 1977 Dodd, Mead.

1978.04   *March*   4456502
Eberhart, Mignon G. *Nine O'Clock Tide.* 1977 Random House.
Cunningham, E V. *The Case Of The One-Penny Orange.* 1977 Holt, Rinehart & Winston.
McMullen, Mary. *Death By Bequest.* 1977 Doubleday.

1978

1978.05   *March/April Inner Circle*   5855588
Wolfe, Michael. *The Panama Paradox.* 1977 Harper & Row.
Winslow, Pauline Glen. *The Witch Hill Murder.* 1977 St Martins.
Leather, Edwin. *The Vienna Elephant.* 1977 Dodd, Mead.

1978.06   *March/April Inner Circle*   962888235
Wainwright, John. *Pool Of Tears.* 1977 St Martins.
Haddad, C A. *Operation Apricot.* 1978 Harper.
Whitney, Alec. *Death In Darkness.* 1977 Doubleday.

1978.07   *April*   1030104331
Simenon, Georges. *Maigret and the Hotel Majestic.* 1977 Harcourt.
Wilcox, Collin. *The Watcher.* 1978 Random House.
James, P D. *Death of an Expert Witness.* 1977 Scribner.

1978.08   *May*   5851998
Wetering, Janwillem van de. *The Blond Baboon.* 1978 Houghton Mifflin.
Morice, Anne. *Scared To Death.* 1977 St Martins.
Pentecost, Hugh. *Death After Breakfast.* 1978 Dodd, Mead.

1978.09   *May/June Inner Circle*   5852335
Rendell, Ruth. *A Judgement In Stone.* 1978 Doubleday.
Forrest, Richard. *Death Through The Looking Glass.* 1978 Bobbs-Merrill.
Ashford, Jeffrey. *Hostage To Death.* 1977 Walker.

1978.10   *June*   4584570
Ball, John. *A Killing In The Market.* 1978 Doubleday.
Fleming, Joan. *Every Inch A Lady.* 1977 Putnam.
Knox, Bill. *Witchrock.* 1978 Doubleday.

1978.11   *July*   5855418
Johnston, Velda. *The Hour Before Midnight.* 1978 Dodd, Mead.
Maling, Arthur. *Lucky Devil.* 1978 Harper.
Underwood, Michael. *Crooked Wood.* 1978 St Martins.

1978.12   *July/August Inner Circle*   5852261
Fremlin, Celia. *The Spider-Orchid.* 1978 Doubleday.
Bagley, Desmond. *The Enemy.* 1978 Doubleday.
Winslow, Pauline Glen. *Copper' Gold.* 1978 St Martin.

1978.13   *August*   6018529
Charteris, Leslie. *Send for the Saint.* 1978 Doubleday.
Wren, M K. *Nothing's Certain But Death.* 1978 Doubleday.
Cunningham, E V. *The Case Of The Russian Diplomat.* 1978 Holt, Rinehart, and Winston.

1978.14   *September*   5020883
MacDonald, John D. *The Empty Copper Sea.* 1978 Lippincott.
Peters, Elizabeth. *Street Of The Five Moons.* 1978 Dodd, Mead.
Cleary, Jon. *Vortex.* 1978 Morrow.

1978

1978.15 *September/October Inner Circle*   5938404
Stein, Benjamin. *The Croesus Conspiracy.* 1978 Simon & Schuster.
Quest, Erica. *The Silver Castle.* 1978 Doubleday.
Williams, David. *Treasure Up In Smoke.* 1978 St Martins.
1978.16 *September/October Inner Circle*   5938442
Gill, Bartholomew. *McGarr On The Cliffs Of Moher.* 1978 Scribner.
Brett, Simon. *An Amateur Corpse.* 1978 Scribner.
Allbeury, Ted. *The Man With The President's Mind.* 1978 Simon & Schuster.
1978.17 *October*   5021690
Parker, Robert B. *The Judas Goat.* 1978 Houghton Mifflin.
Ferrars, E X. *Murders Anonymous.* 1978 Doubleday.
Ross, Frank. *Sleeping Dogs.* 1978 Atheneum.
1978.18 *November*   5021590
Morice, Anne. *Murder By Proxy.* 1978 St Martins.
Phillps, Judson. *A Murder Arranged.* 1978 Dodd, Mead.
Garve, Andrew. *Counterstroke.* 1978 Crowell.
1978.19 *November/December Inner Circle*   5938429
Law, Janice. *Under Orion.* 1978 Houghton Mifflin.
LaRosa, Linda J and Tannenbaum, Barry. *The Random Factor.* 1978 Doubleday.
Hilton, John Buxton. *Some Run Crooked.* 1978 St Martins.
1978.20 *December*   226635564
Pentecost, Hugh. *Deadly Trap.* 1978 Dodd, Mead.
Michaels, Barbara. *Wait for What Will Come.* 1978 Dodd Mead.
Dibdin, Michael. *The Last Sherlock Holmes Story.* 1978 Random House.
1978.21 *promotional*   7321213
Cunningham, E V. *The Case Of The Russian Diplomat.* 1978 Holt.
Simenon, Georges. *Maigret and the Hotel Majestic.* 1977 Harcourt.
James, P D. *Death of an Expert Witness.* 1977 Scribner.
1978.22 *promotional*   20408801
Wetering, Janwillem van de. *The Japanese Corpse.* 1977 Houghton Mifflin.
Michaels, Barbara. *Wait for What Will Come.* 1978 Dodd Mead.
Parker, Robert B. *The Judas Goat.* 1975 Houghton Mifflin.
1978.23 *promotional*   1027529290
Dibdin, Michael. *The Last Sherlock Holmes Story.* 1978 Random House.
MacDonald, John D. *The Empty Copper Sea.* 1978 Lippincott.
Hallahan, William H. *Catch Me, Kill Me.* 1977 Bobbs-Merrill.
1978.24 *promotional*   9445879
Eberhart, Mignon G. *Nine O'Clock Tide.* 1977 Random House.
James, P D. *Death of an Expert Witness.* 1977 Scribner.
Allbeury, Ted. *The Man With the President's Mind.* 1978 Simon and Schuster.

1979

1979.01   *January*   991975437
Simenon, Georges. *Maigret's Pipe.* 1978 Harcourt Brace Jovanovich.
MacKenzie, Donald. *Raven Settles a Score.* 1978 Houghton Mifflin.
McMullen, Mary. *The Man With Fifty Complaints.* 1978 Doubleday.

1979.02   *January/February Inner Circle*   6024369
Meynell, Lawrence. *The Thirteen Trumpeters.* 1978 Stein & Day.
Drummond, Ivor. *A Stench Of Poppies.* 1978 St Martins.
Anderson, J R L. *A Sprig Of Sea Lavender.* 1979 St Martins.

1979.03   *February*   5938408
Duncan, Robert L. *Fire Storm.* 1978 Morrow.
Ferrars, E X. *Last Will And Testament.* 1978 Doubleday.
Bagby, George. *Guaranteed To Fade.* 1978 Doubleday.

1979.04   *March*   5938439
Eberhart, Mignon G. *The Bayou Road.* 1979 Random House.
Kirk, Michael. *Salvage Job.* 1979 Doubleday.
Hallahan, William H. *Keeper Of The Children.* 1978 Morrow.

1979.05   *March/April Inner Circle*   5938399
Crisp, N J. *The London Deal.* 1978 St Martins.
Ball, John [editor]. *Cop Cade.* 1978 Doubleday.
Angus, Sylvia. *Dead To Rites.* 1978 Crown.

1979.06   *March/April Inner Circle*   6024378
MacLeod, Charlotte. *Rest You Merry.* 1978 Doubleday.
Barry, Nora. *Sherbourne's Folly.* 1978 Doubleday.
Gage, Edwin. *Phoenix No More.* 1978 Harper.

1979.07   *April*   5938411
Johnston, Velda. *The Silver Dolphin.* 1979 Dodd, Mead.
Underwood, Michael. *Anything But The Truth.* 1978 St Martins.
Fish, Robert L. *Pursuit.* 1978 Doubleday.

1979.08   *May*   7431235
Charteris, Leslie. *The Saint In Trouble.* 1978 Doubleday.
McMullen, Mary. *Welcome To The Grave.* 1979 Doubleday.
Driscoll, Peter. *Pangolin.* 1979 Lippincott.

1979.09   *May/June Inner Circle*   7343575
Alding, Peter. *Murder Is Suspected.* 1977 Walker.
Curtiss, Ursula. *The Menace Within.* 1979 Dodd, Mead.
Cromie, Alice. *Lucky To Be Alive?.* 1978 Simon & Schuster.

1979.10   *June*   6560887
Simenon, Georges. *Maigret In Exile.* 1979 Harcourt Brace Jovanovich.
Maling, Arthur. *The Rheingold Route.* 1979 Harper.
Millar, Margaret. *The Murder Of Miranda.* 1979 Random House.

1979

1979.11   *July*   6561003
Creasey, John. *A Sharp Rise in Crime.* 1978 Scribner.
Ehrlich, Max. *Reincarnation in Venice.* 1979 Simon & Schuster.
Stein, Aaron Marc. *The Rolling Heads.* 1979 Doubleday.

1979.12   *July/August Inner Circle*   7325469
Yorke, Margaret. *The Come-On.* 1978 Harper.
Hill, Peter. *The Enthusiast.* 1978 Houghton Mifflin.
Goodrum, Charles. *Carnage of the Realm.* 1979 Crown.

1979.13   *August*   5938436
Fish, Robert L. *A Gross Carriage Of Justice.* 1979 Doubleday.
Ferrars, E X. *In At The Kill.* 1979 Doubleday.
Masterson, Whit. *The Slow Gallows.* 1979 Dodd, Mead.

1979.14   *September*   1084450779
Deighton, Len. *SS-GB.* 1979 Knopf.
Keating, H R F. *Inspector Ghote Draws The Line.* 1979 Doubleday.
Gilbert, Michael. *The Empty House.* 1978 Harper.

1979.15   *September/October Inner Circle*   7349640
Ashford, Jeffrey. *The Anger Of Fear.* 1978 Walker.
Barroll, Clare. *A Strange Place For A Murder.* 1979 Scribner.
Sladek, John. *Invisible Green.* 1977 Walker.

1979.16   *September/October Inner Circle*   962865061
Simon, Roger L. *Peking Duck.* 1979 Simon & Schuster.
Jobson, Hamilton. *To Die A Little.* 1979 St Martins.
Burley, W J. *Wycliffe And The Scapegoat.* 1979 Doubleday.

1979.17   *October*   7321042
Canning, Victor. *Birdcage.* 1978 Morrow.
Bagley, Desmond. *Flyaway.* 1979 Doubleday.
Pentecost, Hugh. *Random Killer.* 1979 Dodd, Mead.

1979.18   *November*   779084138
Peters, Elizabeth. *Summer Of The Dragon.* 1979 Dodd, Mead.
Philips, Judson. *Why Murder?.* 1979 Dodd, Mead.
Knox, Bill. *Live Bait.* 1979 Doubleday.

1979.19   *November/December Inner Circle*   7354764
Radley, Sheila. *Death In The Morning.* 1979 Scribner.
Webster, Noah. *Incident In Iceland.* 1979 Doubleday.
Quest, Erica. *The October Cabaret.* 1979 Doubleday.

1979.20   *November/December Inner Circle*   7431199
Barnard, Robert. *Death Of A Mystery Writer.* 1979 Scribner.
Leather, Edwin. *The Mozart Score.* 1979 Doubleday.
Bruce, Leo. *Death In Albert Park.* 1979 Scribner.

The Detective Book Club 1942-2000

1979

1979.21	*December*	7500702

MacDonald, John D. *The Green Ripper.* 1979 Lippincott.
Charteris, Leslie. *The Saint And The Templar Treasure.* 1979 Doubleday.
Wilcox, Collin. *Power Plays.* 1979 Random House.

1979.22	*promotional*	11709932

Simenon, Georges. *Maigret's Pipe.* 1978 Harcourt Brace Jovanovich.
Johnston, Velda. *The Hour Before Midnight.* 1978 Dodd, Mead.
Ferrars, E X. *Last Will And Testament.* 1978 Doubleday.

1979.23	*promotional*	7782775

Charteris, Leslie. *The Saint In Trouble.* 1978 Doubleday.
Ehrlich, Max. *Reincarnation in Venice.* 1979 Simon & Schuster.
Johnston, Velda. *The Silver Dolphin.* 1979 Dodd, Mead.

1980

1980.01	*January*	702642117

Johnston, Velda. *The People From The Sea.* 1978 Dodd, Mead.
Underwood, Michael. *Smooth Justice.* 1979 St Martins.
Parker, Robert B. *Wilderness.* 1979 Delacourte.

1980.02	*January*	9060114

Forrest, Richard. *Death in the Willows.* 1979 Holt, Rinehart & Winston.
Magee, Bill and Schenck, Craig. *Columbo and the Samurai Sword.* DBC 1st.
Devine, Dominic. *Sunk Without a Trace.* 1979 St Martins.

1980.03	*January/February Inner Circle*	6609693

MacLeod, Charlotte. *The Luck Runs Out.* 1979 Doubleday.
Babson, Marian. *The Lord Mayor of Death.* 1979 Walker.
Jeffries, Roderic. *Murder Begets Murder.* 1979 St Martins.

1980.04	*February*	6609622

Simenon, Georges. *Maigret And The Toy Village.* 1979 Harcourt Brace Jovanovich.
Peters, Ellis. *Rainbow's End.* 1978 Morrow.
Mackenzie, Donald. *Raven After Dark.* 1979 Houghton Mifflin.

1980.05	*March*	7395521

Snow, C P. *A Coat Of Varnish.* 1979 Scribner.
Michaels, Barbara. *The Walker In Shadows.* 1979 Dodd, Mead.
Maling, Arthur. *The Koberg Link.* 1979 Harper.

1980.06	*March/April Inner Circle*	7431219

Wainwright, John. *Duty Elsewhere.* 1979 St Martins.
Stevenson, Anne. *Mask Of Treason.* 1979 Putnam.
Gollin, James. *The Philomel Foundation.* 1980 St Martins.

1980.07	*March/April Inner Circle*	7354747

Gill, Bartholomew. *McGarr At The Dublin Horse Show.* 1979 Scribner.
Anderson, J R L. *Festival.* 1980 St Martins.
Denham, Bertie. *The Man Who Lost His Shadow.* 1979 Scribner.

1980

| 1980.08 | *April* | 11636329 |

Woods, Sara. *Proceed To Judgement.* 1980 St Martins.
Haggard, William. *Visa To Limbo.* 1979 Walker.
Pentecost, Hugh. *The Homicidal Horse.* 1979 Dodd, Mead.

| 1980.09 | *May* | 7407636 |

Johnston, Velda. *A Presence In An Empty Room.* 1980 Dodd, Mead.
Canning, Victor. *The Satan Sampler.* 1980 Morrow.
Gatenby, Rosemary. *The Third Identity.* 1979 Dodd, Mead.

| 1980.10 | *May/June Inner Circle* | 7729123 |

Gill, Bartholomew. *Death Drop.* 1979 Scribner.
Aird, Catherine. *Some Die Eloquent.* 1980 Doubleday.
Drummond, Ivor. *The Diamonds Of Loreta.* 1980 St Martins.

| 1980.11 | *May/June Inner Circle* | 11636184 |

Ball, John. *Then Came Violence.* 1980 Doubleday.
Keech, Scott. *Ciphered.* 1980 Harper.
White, Terence de Vere. *My Name Is Norval.* 1978 Harper.

| 1980.12 | *June* | 7499236 |

Eberhart, Mignon G. *Casa Madrone.* 1980 Random House.
Law, Janice. *The Shadow Of The Palms.* 1980 Houghton Mifflin.
Pronzini, Bill. *Labyrinth.* 1980 St Martins.

| 1980.13 | *July* | 6730919 |

Simenon, Georges. *Maigret's Rival.* 1980 Harcourt.
Ferrars, E X. *Witness Before the Fact.* 1979 Doubleday.
Rendell, Ruth. *The Lake of Darkness.* 1980 Doubleday.

| 1980.14 | *July/August Inner Circle* | 7116215 |

Babson, Marian. *Murder, Murder, Little Star.* 1980 Walker.
Smith, Kay Nolte. *The Watcher.* 1980 Coward McCann.
Sherburne, James. *Death's Pale Horse.* 1980 Houghton.

| 1980.15 | *July/August Inner Circle* | 7116660 |

Curtiss, Ursula. *The Poisoned Orchard.* 1980 Dodd Mead.
Dale, Celia. *The Deception.* 1979 Harper.
Stang, JoAnne. *Shadows On The Sceptered Isle.* 1980 Crown.

| 1980.16 | *August* | 6730545 |

Davis, Dorothy Salisbury. *Scarlet Night.* 1980 Scribner.
Westlake, Donald E. *Castle In The Air.* 1980 Evans.
Underwood, Michael. *Victim Of Circumstance.* 1980 St Martins.

| 1980.17 | *September* | 7003179 |

James, P D. *Innocent Blood.* 1980 Scribner.
Pentecost, Hugh. *Beware Young Lovers.* 1980 Dodd Mead.
Woods, Sara. *They Stay for Death.* 1980 St Martins.

1980

1980.18   *September/October Inner Circle*   7914015
Haddad, C A. *The Academic Factor.* 1980 Harper.
Freemantle, Brian. *Charlie Muffin, USA.* 1980 Doubleday.
Goller, Nicholas. *Tomorrow's Silence.* 1980 St Martins.

1980.19   *September*   8093886
Leather, Sir Edward. *The Duveen Letter.* 1980 Doubleday.
Thomson, June. *Alibi In Time.* 1980 Doubleday.
Strong, Michael. *Danger Feeds My Fear.* 1980 Walker.

1980.20   *October*   7003192
Peters, Elizabeth. *The Love Talker.* 1980 Dodd Mead.
Duncan, Robert L. *Brimstone.* 1980 Morrow.
Highsmith, Patricia. *The Boy Who Followed Ripley.* 1980 Lippincott.

1980.21   *November*   7077938
Truman, Margaret. *Murder in the White House.* 1980 Arbor House.
Bagby, George. *Country and Fatal.* 1980 Doubleday.
Knox, Bill. *Bombship.* 1980 Doubleday.

1980.22   *November*   7087131
Ashford, Jeffrey. *A Recipe For Murder.* 1980 Walker.
Heal, Anthony. *Man In The Middle.* 1980 Scribner.
Barnard, Robert. *Death of A Literary Widow.* 1980 Scribner.

1980.23   *November*   7395580
Banks, Oliver. *The Rembrandt Panel.* 1980 Little, Brown.
Craig, Alisa. *A Pint of Murder.* 1980 Doubleday.
Babson, Marian. *Twelve Deaths of Christmas.* 1980 Walker.

1980.24   *December*   7078053
O'Donnell, Lillian. *Wicked Designs.* 1980 Putnam.
McCloy, Helen. *Burn This.* 1980 Dodd Mead.
Winslow, Pauline Glen. *The Counsellor Heart.* 1980 St Martins.

1981

1981.01   *January*   495987630
Parker, Robert B. *Early Autumn.* 1980 Delacourte.
Philips, Judson. *Death is a Dirty Trick.* 1980 Dodd Mead.
Charteris, Leslie. *Count on the Saint.* 1980 Doubleday.

1981.02   *January/February Inner Circle*   7395669
Forrest, Richard. *The Death At Yew Corner.* 1980 Holt, Rinehart and Winston.
Brett, Simon. *The Dead Side Of The Mike.* 1980 Scribner.
Hillerman, Tony. *People Of Darkness.* 1980 Harper.

1981.03   *January/February Inner Circle*   8093813
Lyall, Gavin. *The Secret Servant.* 1980 Viking.
Burley, W J. *Wycliffe In Paul's Court.* 1980 Doubleday.
Holme, Timothy. *The Neapolitan Streak.* 1980 Coward, McCann & Geoghegan.

1981

1981.04	*February*	962864993

McMullen, Mary. *Something Of The Night.* 1980 Doubleday.
Ferrars, E X. *Frog In The Throat.* 1980 Doubleday.
Wilcox, Collin. *Mankiller.* 1980 Random House.

1981.05	*March*	7654725

Simenon, Georges. *Maigret at the Coroner's.* 1980 Harcourt.
Law, Janice. *Death Under Par.* 1980 Houghton.
Pentecost, Hugh. *Death Mask.* 1980 Dodd Mead.

1981.06	*March/April Inner Circle*	8093900

Kirk, Michael. *Cargo Risk.* 1980 Doubleday.
Bellairs, George. *Devious Murder.* 1980 Walker.
Clarke, Anna. *One Of Us Must Die.* 1978 Doubleday.

1981.07	*March/April Inner Circle*	8093871

DeAndrea, William L. *The Lunatic Fringe.* 1980 Evans.
Radley, Sheila. *The Chief Inspector's Daughter.* 1980 Macmillan.
North, Jessica. *Mask Of The Jaguar.* 1981 Coward McCann.

1981.08	*April*	7654841

Innes, Hammond. *Solomons Seal.* 1980 Knopf.
Michaels, Barbara. *The Wizard's Daughter.* 1980 Dodd.
MacKenzie, Donald. *Raven and the Paperhangers.* 1980 Houghton.

1981.09	*May*	7711190

MacDonald, John D. *Free Fall in Crimson.* 1980 Harper.
Stein, Aaron Marc. *A Nose for It.* 1980 Doubleday.
Wren, M K. *Seasons of Death.* 1981 Doubleday.

1981.10	*May/June Inner Circle*	8093857

Barnard, Robert. *Death In A Cold Climate.* 1981 Scribner.
Craig, Alisa. *The Grub-and-Stakers Move A Mountain.* 1981 Doubleday.
Aird, Catherine. *Passing Strange.* 1981 Doubleday.

1981.11	*May/June Inner Circle*	8093926

Godden, Jon. *In Her Garden.* 1981 Knopf.
Paul, Barbara. *First Gravedigger.* 1980 Doubleday.
Hensley, Joe L. *Outcasts.* 1981 Doubleday.

1981.12	*June*	8056685

Ball, John. *Trouble For Tallon.* 1981 Doubleday.
Canning, Victor. *Fall From Grace.* 1980 Morrow.
Pentecost, Hugh. *Murder In Luxury.* 1981 Dodd.

1981.13	*July*	8159549

Francis, Dick. *Reflex.* 1981 Putnam.
Woods, Sara. *Cry Guilty.* 1981 St Martins.
Keating, H R F. *Go West, Inspector Ghote.* 1981 Doubleday.

1981

| 1981.14 | *July/August Inner Circle* | 7711288 |

Worboys, Anne. *Run, Sara, Run.* 1981 Scribner.
Shaw, Howard. *Killing No Murder.* 1981 Scribner.
Quest, Erica. *Design For Murder.* 1981 Doubleday.

| 1981.15 | *July/August Inner Circle* | 8355389 |

Yorke, Margaret. *The Scent Of Fear.* 1980 St Martins.
Hill, Reginald. *A Killing Kindness.* 1980 Pantheon.
Lemarchand, Elizabeth. *Change For The Worse.* 1981 Walker.

| 1981.16 | *August* | 989391409 |

Eberhart, Mignon G. *Family Affair.* 1981 Random House.
Peters, Ellis. *Monk's-Hood.* 1980 Morrow.
Bagby, George. *A Question Of Quarry.* 1981 Doubleday.

| 1981.17 | *September* | 8093835 |

Peters, Elizabeth. *The Curse Of The Pharaohs.* 1981 Dodd.
Gash, Jonathan. *Spend Game.* 1980 Ticknor & Fields.
Roos, Kelley. *Murder On Martha's Vineyard.* 1981 Walker.

| 1981.18 | *September/October Inner Circle* | 704520733 |

Dewhurst, Eileen. *Drink This.* 1981 Doubleday.
Paul, Barbara. *Your Eyelids Are Growing Heavy.* 1981 Doubleday.
Bell, Josephine. *A Question Of Inheritance.* 1980 Walker.

| 1981.19 | *September/October Inner Circle* | 8093916 |

Brett, John. *Who'd Hire Brett.* 1981 St Martins.
Suyker, Betty. *Death Scene.* 1981 St Martins.
Clarke, Anna. *Letter From The Dead.* 1981 Doubleday.

| 1981.20 | *October* | 8093823 |

Ferrars, E X. *Experiment with Death.* 1981 Doubleday.
Haggard, William. *The Median Line.* 1979 Walker.
Morice, Anne. *The Men in Her Death.* 1981 St Martins.

| 1981.21 | *November* | 1043695030 |

Parker, Robert B. *A Savage Place.* 1981 Delacourte.
Pronzini, Bill. *Hoodwink.* 1981 St Martins.
Stein, Aaron Marc. *A Body For A Buddy.* 1981 Doubleday.

| 1981.22 | *November/December Inner Circle* | 8678445 |

Babson, Marian. *Dangerous To Know.* 1980 Walker.
Grimes, Martha. *The Man With A Load Of Mischief.* 1981 Little, Brown.
Audemars, Pierre. *And One For The Dead.* 1981 Walker.

| 1981.23 | *November/December Inner Circle* | 8678414 |

Brett, Simon. *Situation Tragedy.* 1981 Scribners.
Sherburne, James. *Death's Gray Angel.* 1981 Houghton.
Lewin, Michael Z. *Missing Woman.* 1981 Mysterious Press.

1981

1981.24   *December*   11636269
Philips, Judson. *Murder As The Curtain Rises*. 1981 Dodd.
Winslow, Pauline Glen. *The Rockefeller Gift*. 1981 St Martins.
Knox, Bill. *A Killing In Antiques*. 1981 Doubleday.
1981.25   *promotional*   12739116
Simenon, Georges. *Maigret At The Coroners*. 1980 Harcourt.
Francis, Dick. *Reflex*. 1981 Putnam.
Woods, Sara. *Cry Guilty*. 1981 St Martins.

1982

1982.01   *January*   8882510
Simenon, Georges. *Maigret on the Defensive*. 1981 Harcourt.
Stevenson, Anne. *Turkish Rondo*. 1981 Morrow.
Michaels, Barbara. *Someone in the House*. 1981 Dodd, Mead.
1982.02   *January/February Inner Circle*   9691100
Mackay, Amanda. *Death On The Eno*. 1981 Little, Brown.
Shaw, Howard. *Death Of A Don*. 1981 Scribner.
Layne, Marion Margery. *The Balloon Affair*. 1981 Dodd, Mead.
1982.03   *January/February Inner Circle*   9179272
Ashford, Jeffrey. *The Loss Of The Culion*. 1981 Walker.
Dobyns, Stephen. *Saratoga Swimmer*. 1981 Atheneum.
Cody, Liza. *Dupe*. 1981 Scribner.
1982.04   *February*   8882491
Pentecost, Hugh. *Sow Death, Reap Death*. 1981 Dodd, Mead.
Woods, Sara. *Dearest Enemy*. 1981 Sdt Martins.
Cleary, Jon. *The Golden Sabre*. 1981 Morrow.
1982.05   *March*   9072154
Haggard, William. *The Money Men*. 1981 Walker.
Hillerman, Tony. *The Dark Wind*. 1982 Harper.
Underwood, Michael. *Double Jeopardy*. 1981 St Martins.
1982.06   *March/April Inner Circle*   10000564
Frimmer, Steven. *Dead Matter*. 1981 Holt, Rinehart & Winston.
Clark, Douglas. *Roast Eggs*. 1981 Dodd, Mead.
Mitchell, Gladys. *The Death-Cap Dancers*. 1981 St Martins.
1982.07   *March/April Inner Circle*   10000608
Webster, Noah. *A Problem In Prague*. 1982 Doubleday.
Roy Harley. *A Cracking of Spines*. 1981 St Martins.
DeAndrea, William L. *Killed In The Act*. 1981 Doubeday.
1982.08   *April*   8580006
Bagby, George. *The Sitting Duck*. 1981 Doubleday.
Babson, Marian. *Line Up For Murder*. 1981 Walker.
Barnard, Robert. *Death By Sheer Torture*. 1981 Scribner.

1982

| 1982.09 | *May* | 10327430 |

McMullen, Mary. *Better Off Dead.* 1982 Doubleday.
Canning, Victor. *Memory Boy.* 1981 Morrow.
Gash, Jonathan. *The Vatican Rip.* 1981 Ticknor & Fields.

| 1982.10 | *May/June Inner Circle* | 10804321 |

Bellairs, George. *All Roads To Sospel.* 1981 Walker.
Langton, Jane. *Natural Enemy.* 1982 Ticknor & Fields.
Serafin, David. *Saturday Of Glory.* 1981 St Martins.

| 1982.11 | *May/June Inner Circle* | 10819838 |

Smith, Kay Nolte. *Catching Fire.* 1982 Coward, McCann & Geoghegan.
Crispin, Edmund. *Frequent Hearses.* 1981 Walker.
Ward, Edmund. *The Baltic Emerald.* 1981 St Martins.

| 1982.12 | *June* | 9746329 |

Pronzini, Bill. *Scattershot.* 1982 St Martins.
Peters, Ellis. *Saint Peter's Fair.* 1981 Mysterious Press.
Mackenzie, Donald. *Raven's Revenge.* 1982 Houghton Mifflin.

| 1982.13 | *July* | 9072207 |

Francis, Dick. *Twice Shy.* 1982 Putnam.
Stein, Aaron Marc. *Hangman's Row.* 1982 Doubleday.
Babson, Marian. *Bejewelled Death.* 1982 Walker.

| 1982.14 | *July/August Inner Circle* | 10819889 |

McInerny, Ralph. *Let Us Prey.* 1982 Vanguard.
Mantell, Laurie. *Murder and Chips.* 1980 Walker.
Jeffries, Roderic. *Unseemly End.* 1981 St Martins.

| 1982.15 | *July/August Inner Circle* | 10804347 |

Healey, Ben. *Midnight Ferry to Venice.* 1981 Walker.
Hilton, John Buxton. *Green Frontier.* 1981 St Martins.
Melville, James. *A Sort of Samurai.* 1981 St Martins.

| 1982.16 | *August* | 9072238 |

Underwood, Michael. *Hand Of Fate.* 1982 St Martins.
Peters, Elizabeth. *The Copenhagen Connection.* 1982 St Martins.
Cleary, Jon. *The Faraway Drums.* 1982 Morrow.

| 1982.17 | *September* | 647449447 |

Simenon, Georges. *Maigret Has Doubts.* 1982 Harcourt.
Pentecost, Hugh. *With Intent To Kill.* 1982 Dodd, Mead.
Ferrars, E X. *Thinner Than Water.* 1982 Doubleday.

| 1982.18 | *September/October Inner Circle* | 10488713 |

Sherburne, James. *Death's Clenched Fist.* 1982 Houghton Mifflin.
Thomson, June. *Shadow Of A Doubt.* 1982 Doubleday.
Lewis, Roy. *The Manuscript Murders.* 1982 St Martins.

The Detective Book Club 1942-2000

1982

1982.19	*September/October Inner Circle*	10513431

Clarke, Anna. *Desire To Kill.* 1982 Doubleday.
Davey, Jocelyn. *Murder In Paradise.* 1982 Walker.
Hammond, Gerald. *Fair Game.* 1982 St Martins.

1982.20   *October*   9320054
Eberhart, Mignon G. *Next of Kin.* 1982 Random House.
Woods, Sara. *Enter a Gentlewoman.* 1982 St Martins.
Morice, Anne. *Hollow Vengeance.* 1982 St Martins.

1982.21   *November*   9655897
Haggard, William. *The Mischief Makers.* 1982 Walker.
Bagby, George. *The Golden Creep.* 1982 Doubleday.
Gilbert, Michael. *End-Game.* 1982 Harper.

1982.22   *November/December Inner Circle*   14974879
Dewhurst, Eileen. *Curtain Fall.* 1982 Doubleday.
Crane, Caroline. *The Foretelling.* 1982 Dodd, Mead.
Lovell, Marc. *Spy On The Run.* 1982 Doubleday.

1982.23   *November/December Inner Circle*   11352874
Grimes, Martha. *The Old Fox Deceiv'd.* 1982 Little, Brown.
Dean, S F X. *Such Pretty Toys.* 1982 Walker.
Hebden, Mark. *Pel And The Faceless Corpse.* 1982 Walker.

1982.24   *December*   9655875
Curtiss, Ursula. *Dog In The Manger.* 1982 Dodd, Mead.
Bagley, Desmond. *Windfall.* 1982 Summit.
Peters, Ellis. *The Leper of Saint Giles.* 1982 Morrow.

1983

1983.01   *May*   9904820
Philips, Judson. *Target For Tragedy.* 1982 Dodd, Mead.
Ferrars, E X. *Skeleton In Search Of A Closet.* 1982 Doubleday.
Keating, H R F. *A Rush For The Ultimate.* 1982 Doubleday.

1983.02   *May/June Inner Circle*   11636110
Anderson, J R L. *Death In The City.* 1982 Scribner.
D'Alton, Martina. *Fatal Finish.* 1982 Walker.
Lemarchand, Elizabeth. *Troubled Waters.* 1982 Walker.

1983.03   *May/June Inner Circle*   9904841
Burley, W J. *Wycliffe's Wild Goose Chase.* 1982 Doubleday.
Clemeau, Carol. *The Ariadne Clue.* 1982 Scribner.
Aird, Catherine. *Last Respects.* 1982 Doubleday.

1983.04   *June*   11499608
McMullen, Mary. *Until Death Do Us Part.* 1982 Doubleday.
Barnard, Robert. *Death And The Princess.* 1982 Scribner.
Babson, Marian. *Death Warmed Up.* 1982 Walker.

1983

1983.05   *July*   10589696
James, P D. *The Skull Beneath The Skin.* 1982 Scribner.
Charteris, Leslie. *The Fantastic Saint.* 1982 Doubleday.
Canning, Victor. *Vanishing Point.* 1982 Morrow.

1983.06   *July/August Inner Circle*   11770152
Radley, Sheila. *A Talent For Destruction.* 1982 Scribner.
Tourney, Leonard. *Low Treason.* 1982 Dutton.
Nabb, Magdalen. *Death Of An Englishman.* 1981 Scribner.

1983.07   *July/August Inner Circle*   11486385
Clarke, Anna. *We The Bereaved.* 1982 Doubleday.
Gillespie, Robert B. *Print-Out.* 1983 Dodd, Mead.
Elkins, Aaron J. *Fellowship Of Fear.* 1982 Walker.

1983.08   *August*   10589754
Simenon, Georges. *Maigret And The Nahour Case.* 1982 Harcourt.
Innes, Hammond. *The Black Tide.* 1983 Doubleda.
Westlake, Donald E. *Why Me.* 1983 Viking.

1983.09   *September*   10589723
Barnard, Robert. *The Case Of The Missing Bronte.* 1983 Scribner.
Stein, Aaron Marc. *The Bombing Run.* 1983 Doubleday.
Babson, Marian. *Death Beside The Sea.* 1982 Walker.

1983.10   *September/October Inner Circle*   11636033
Anderson, J R L. *Death in the Greenhouse.* 1983 Scribner.
Lovell, Marc. *Apple Spy In The Sky.* 1983 Doubleday.
Hunter, Alan. *Gently Between The Tides.* 1982 Walker.

1983.11   *September/October Inner Circle*   12145300
DeAndrea, William L. *Killed With A Passion.* 1983 Doubleday.
Dewhurst, Eileen. *Whoever I Am.* 1983 Doubleday.
Holme, Timothy. *A Funeral Of Gondolas.* 1982 Coward, McCann & Geoghegan.

1983.12   *October*   10589739
Peters, Ellis. *The Virgin In The Ice.* 1983 Morrow.
Knox, Bill. *Bloodtide.* 1983 Doubleday.
Gash, Jonathan. *The Sleepers Of Erin.* 1983 Dutton.

1983.13   11464402
Rich, Virginia. *The Baked Bean Supper Murders.* 1983 Dutton.
Hebden, Mark. *Death Set to Music.* 1982 Walker.
Page, Emma. *Last Walk Home.* 1982 Walker.

1983.14   10855620
Francis, Dick. *Banker.* 1983 Putnam.
Pentecost, Hugh. *Murder in High Places.* 1983 Dodd, Mead.
Craig, Alisa. *The Terrible Tide.* 1983 Doubleday.

1983

1983.15	11028819

Harriss, Will. *The Bay Psalm Book Murder.* 1983 Walker.
Nabb, Magdalen. *Death of a Dutchman.* 1983 Scribner.
Taylor, L A. *Footnote to Murder.* 1983 Walker.

1983.16	12145290

Kirk, Michael. *Mayday From Malaga.* 1983 Doubleday.
Elkins, Aaron J. *The Dark Place.* 1983 Mysterious Press.
Warner, Mignon. *Devil's Knell.* 1983 Doubleday.

1983.17	10855594

Gilman, Dorothy. *Mrs. Pollifax On The China Station.* 1983 Doubleday.
Brett, Simon. *Murder In The Title.* 1983 Scribner.
Maling, Arthur. *A Taste Of Treason.* 1983 Harper.

1983.18	11240036

Gordons, The. *Race for the Golden Tide.* 1983 Doubleday.
Charteris, Leslie. *Salvage for the Saint.* 1983 Doubleday.
Bagley, Desmond. *Bahama Crisis.* 1983 Summit.

1984

1984.01	11894615

Asimov, Isaac. *Banquets of the Black Widowers.* 1984 Doubleday.
Stuart, Ian. *The Garb of Truth.* 1984 Doubleday.
Peel, Colin D. *Firestorm.* 1984 Doubleday.

1984.02	11239998

Pentecost, Hugh. *The Copycat Killers.* 1983 Dodd, Mead.
Gilbert, Michael. *The Black Seraphim.* 1984 Harper.
Mackenzie, Donald. *Raven's Longest Night.* 1983 Doubleday.

1984.03	11511689

Peters, Ellis. *The Devil's Novice.* 1984 Morrow.
DeAndrea, William L. *Killed On The Ice.* 1984 Doubleday.
Anthony, Evelyn. *The Company Of Saints.* 1984 Putnam.

1984.04	11837379

Peters, Elizabeth. *Die For Love.* 1984 Congdon & Weed.
Pentecost, Hugh. *The Substitute Victim.* 1984 Dodd, Mead.
Morice, Anne. *Getting Away With Murder?.* 1984 St Martins.

1984.05	11896074

Knox, Bill. *The Hanging Tree.* 1984 Doubleday.
Ferrars, E X. *Something Wicked.* 1983 Doubleday.
Quill, Monica. *And Then There Was Nun.* 1984 Vanguard.

1984.06	12144851

Aird, Catherine. *Harm's Way.* 1984 Doubleday.
Martin, Lee. *Too Sane a Murder.* 1984 St Martins.
Maron, Margaret. *Death of a Butterfly.* 1984 Doubleday.

1984

1984.07   11894697
    Dewhurst, Eileen. *The House that Jack Built.* 1984 Doubleday.
    Dunlap, Susan. *As a Favor.* 1984 St Martins.
    Cohen, Anthea. *Angel of Vengeance.* 1984 Doubleday.
1984.08   11240017
    Pentecost, Hugh. *Murder Out of Wedlock.* 1983 Dodd, Mead.
    Babson, Marian. *A Fool for Murder.* 1983 Walker.
    Wren, M K. *Wake Up, Darlin' Corey.* 1984 Doubleday.
1984.09   11837430
    Garfield, Brian. *Necessity.* 1984 St Martins.
    Fremlin, Celia. *A Lovely Day To Die.* 1984 Doubleday.
    Ferrars, E X. *Root Of All Evil.* 1984 Doubleday.
1984.10   12145316
    Taylor, L A. *Only Half a Hoax.* 1983 Walker.
    Inchbald, Peter. *Short Break in Venice.* 1983 Doubleday.
    Gosling, Paula. *Woman in Red.* 1984 Doubleday.
1984.11   928177373
    Pentecost, Hugh. *The Price Of Silence.* 1984 Dodd, Mead.
    Langton, Jane. *Emily Dickinson Is Dead.* 1984 St Martins.
    Webster, Noah. *A Legacy From Tenerife.* 1984 Doubleday.
1984.12   11511650
    Pentecost, Hugh. *Remember To Kill Me.* 1984 Doubleday.
    Michaels, Barbara. *The Grey Beginning.* 1984 Congdon & Weed.
    Woods, Sara. *The Bloody Book Of Law.* 1984 St Martins.
1984.13   928177372
    Keating, H R F. *The Sheriff Of Bombay.* 1984 Doubleday.
    Winslow, Pauline Glen. *I, Martha Adams.* 1982 Arlington Books.
    Stein, Aaron Marc. *The Garbage Collector.* 1984 Doubleday.
1984.14   12145332
    Lewis, Roy. *Where Agents Fear to Tread.* 1984 St Martins.
    Taylor, Andrew. *Waiting for the End of the World.* 1984 Dodd, Mead.
    Smith, Alison. *Someone Else's Grave.* 1984 St Martins.
1984.15   11894418
    Burley, W J. *Wycliffe and the Beales.* 1984 Doubleday.
    Dentinger, Jane. *First Hit of the Season.* 1984 Doubleday.
    Price, Anthony. *Gunner Kelly.* 1984 Doubleday.

1985

1985.01   13194144
    Cohen, Anthea. *Angel of Death.* 1985 Doubleday.
    Melville, James. *Death of a Daimyo.* 1984 St Martins.
    Resnicow, Herbert. *The Gold Frame.* 1984 St Martins.

1985

1985.02   14079352

    Maron, Margaret. *Bloody Kin.* 1985 Doubleday.
    Lewis, Roy. *A Blurred Reality.* 1985 St Martins.
    McCormick, Claire. *Murder in Cowboy Bronze.* 1985 Walker.

1985.03   13015784

    Peters, Ellis. *Dead Man's Ransom.* 1984 Morrow.
    Kaminsky, Stuart M. *Down For The Count.* 1985 St Martins.
    Van De Wetering, Janwillem. *Inspector Saito's Small Satori.* 1985 Putnam.

1985.04   14079323

    Thomson, June. *A Dying Fall.* 1985 Doubleday.
    Gollin, James. *The Verona Passamezzo.* 1985 Doubleday.
    Lemarchand, Elizabeth. *The Affacombe Affair.* 1985 Walker.

1985.05   12443348

    Hillerman, Tony. *The Ghostway.* 1984 Harper.
    Woods, Sara. *An Obscure Grave.* 1985 St Martins.
    MacKenzie, Donald. *Raven's Shadow.* 1984 Doubleday.

1985.06   12443601

    Marric, J J. *Gideon's Force.* 1985 Stein & Day.
    Underwood, Michael. *The Hidden Man.* 1985 St Martins.
    Forrest, Richard. *Death Under the Lilacs.* 1985 St Martins.

1985.07   13195121

    Paretsky, Sara. *Killing Orders.* 1984 Morrow.
    Togawa, Masako. *The Master Key.* 1984 Dodd.
    Dunlap, Susan. *The Bohemian Connection.* 1985 St Martins.

1985.08   12544677

    Gilbert, Michael. *The Long Journey Home.* 1985 Harper.
    Crane, Caroline. *Someone At The Door.* 1985 Dodd, Mead.
    Craig, Alisa. *The Grub-And-Stakers Quilt A Bee.* 1985 Doubleday.

1985.09   14119643

    Greenwood, John. *The Missing Mr. Mosley.* 1985 Walker.
    Mayo, J K. *The Hunting Season.* 1985 Holt, Rinehart & Winston.
    Meek, M R D. *Hang The Consequences.* 1985 Scribner.

1985.10   13194616

    Lewis, Roy. *Most Cunning Workmen.* 1985 St Martins.
    Finer, Alex. *Deepwater.* 1985 Doubleday.
    McCollum, Robert. *And Then They Die.* 1985 St Martins.

1985.11   13109625

    Gilman, Dorothy. *Mrs. Pollifax And The Hong Kong Buddha.* 1985 Doubleday.
    Morice, Anne. *Dead On Cue.* 1985 St Martins.
    Pronzini, Bill. *Bones.* 1985 St Martins.

1985

1985.12   12144863
    Peters, Elizabeth. *The Mummy Case.* 1985 Congdon & Weed.
    Babson, Marian. *The Cruise of a Deathtime.* 1984 Walker.
    Clarke, Anna. *The Last Judgement.* 1985 Doubleday.

1985.13   12544583
    Pentecost, Hugh. *Murder Round The Clock.* 1985 Dodd, Mead.
    Gash, Jonathan. *Pearlhanger.* 1985 St Martins.
    Babson, Marian. *Death Swap.* 1984 Walker.

1985.14   13109573
    Pentecost, Hugh. *Murder Sweet and Sour.* 1985 Dodd, Mead.
    Ferrars, E X. *The Crime and the Crystal.* 1985 Doubleday.
    Curtiss, Ursula. *The House on Plymouth Street and Other Stories.* 1985 Dodd, Mead.

1985.15   12144874
    Woods, Sara. *Murder's Out Of Tune.* 1984 St Martins.
    MacLeod, Charlotte. *The Curse Of The Giant Hogweed.* 1985 Doubleday.
    Ashford, Jeffrey. *A Sense Of Loyalty.* 1983 Walker.

1985.16   13540263
    Pentecost, Hugh. *The Party Killer.* 1985 Dodd, Mead.
    Cleary, Jon. *City of Fading Light.* 1985 Morrow.
    Pronzini, Bill. *Graveyard Plots.* 1985 St Martins.

1985.17   13015833
    Francis, Dick. *Proof.* 1985 Putnam.
    Canning, Victor. *Birds Of A Feather.* 1985 Morrow.
    Babson, Marian. *A Trail Of Ashes.* 1984 Walker.

1985.18   13281978
    Woods, Sara. *Put Out the Light.* 1985 St Martins.
    Melville, James. *The Death Ceremony.* 1985 St Martins.
    Elkins, Aaron J. *Murder In The Queen's Armes.* 1985 Mysterious Press.

1985.19   13194298
    Melville, James. *Sayonara, Sweet Amaryllis.* 1983 St Martins.
    Roberts, Willo Davis. *The Annalise Experiment.* 1985 Doubleday.
    Hinxman, Margaret. *The Night They Murdered Chelsea.* 1985 Dodd, Mead.

1985.20   14119593
    Taylor, L A. *Shed Light on Death.* 1985 Walker.
    Hervey, Evelyn. *The Man of Gold.* 1983 Doubleday.
    Serafin, David. *The Body in Cadiz Bay.* 1985 St Martins.

1985.21   13194927
    Warner, Mignon. *Speak No Evil.* 1985 Doubleday.
    Jeffers, H Paul. *Murder on Mike.* 1984 St Martins.
    Peel, Colin. *Snowtrap.* 1985 Doubleday.

1985

1985.22   13783706
Lovell, Marc. *The Spy Who Got His Feet Wet.* 1985 Doubleday.
Maron, Margaret. *Death in Blue Folders.* 1985 Doubleday.
Williams, David. *Wedding Treasure.* 1985 St Martins.
1985.23   13281884
Knox, Bill. *Wavecrest.* 1985 Doubleday.
Dunlap, Susan. *Not Exactly A Brahmin.* 1985 St Martins.
Duncan, Robert L. *In The Enemy Camp.* 1985 Delacorte.

1986

1986.01   15073304
Jeffries, Roderic. *Almost Murder.* 1986 St Martins.
Ballard, Mignon F. *Raven Rock.* 1986 Dodd, Mead.
Stuart, Ian. *Pictures in the Dark.* 1986 Doubleday.
1986.02   15068835
McMullen, Mary. *The Bad-News Man.* 1986 Doubleday.
Knox, Bill. *The Crossfire Killings.* 1986 Doubleday.
Keating, H R F. *Mrs. Craggs: Crimes Cleaned Up.* 1985 St Martins.
1986.03   13540207
Michaels, Barbara. *Be Buried In The Rain.* 1985 Atheneum.
Ball, John. *Singapore.* 1986 Dodd, Mead.
Marric, J J. *Gideon's Law.* 1986 Stein & Day.
1986.04   15069163
Underwood, Michael. *Death at Deepwood Grange.* 1986 St Martins.
Frommer, Sara Hoskinson. *Murder in C Major.* 1986 St Martins.
Brett, Simon. *Dead Giveaway.* 1985 Scribner.
1986.05   15645916
Pentecost, Hugh. *Death by FIre.* 1986 Dodd, Mead.
Clarke, Anna. *The Mystery Lady.* 1986 Doubleday.
Muller, Marcia and Pronzini, Bill. *Beyond the Grave.* 1986 Carroll & Graf.
1986.06   16827264
Werry, Richard R. *A Delicately Personal Matter.* 1986 Dodd, Mead.
Fraser, Anthea. *A Shroud for Delilah.* 1986 Doubleday.
Wheat, Carolyn. *Where Nobody Dies.* 1986 St Martins.
1986.07   13845139
Gillespie, Robert B. *The Empress of Coney Island.* 1986 Dodd, Mead.
Miles, Graham. *Evil Mark.* 1985 St Martins.
Breen, Jon L. *Triple Crown.* 1986 Walker.
1986.08   15073242
Radley, Sheila. *Fate Worse than Death.* 1986 Scribner.
Henderson, M R. *By Reason Of.* 1986 Doubleday.
Hilton, John Buxton. *Moondrop to Murder.* 1986 St Martins.

1986

1986.09   14199920
   Westlake, Donald E. *Good Behavior.* 1985 Mysterious Press.
   Kirk, Michael. *A Cut In Diamonds.* 1986 Doubleday.
   Peters, Ellis. *An Excellent Mystery.* 1985 Morrow.
1986.10   15069249
   Ferrars, E X. *I Met Murder.* 1986 Doubleday.
   Singer, Shelley. *Full House.* 1986 St Martins.
   Ashford, Jeffrey. *An Ideal Crime.* 1986 Walker.
1986.11   16827494
   Lemarchand, Elizabeth. *Light Through Glass.* 1986 Walker.
   Martin, Lee. *A Conspiracy of Strangers.* 1986 St Martins.
   Burley, W J. *Wycliffe and the Quiet Virgin.* 1986 Doubleday.
1986.12   15646084
   Pronzini, Bill and Muller, Marcia. *The Lighthouse.* 1986 St Martins.
   Morice, Anne. *Publish and Be Killed.* 1986 St Martins.
   Marshall, William. *Manila Bay.* 1986 Viking.
1986.13   16826927
   Gray, Malcolm. *Look Back on Murder.* 1985 Doubleday.
   Papazoglou, Orania. *Death's Savage Passion.* 1986 Doubleday.
   Biggle Jr., Lloyd. *The Quallsford Inheritance.* 1986 St Martins.
1986.14   16827172
   Taylor, L A. *Love of Money.* 1986 Walker.
   Webb, Martha G. *Even Cops' Daughters.* 1986 Walker.
   Greenwood, L B. *Sherlock Holmes and the Case Of The Raleigh Legacy.* 1986 Atheneum
1986.15   13942041
   Woods, Sara. *Most Deadly Hate.* 1986 St Martins.
   Crane, Caroline. *Circus Day.* 1986 Dodd.
   Lovell, Marc. *The Spy Who Barked In The Night.* 1986 Doubleday.
1986.16   16827033
   Beck, K K. *Murder in a Mummy Case.* 1986 Walker.
   Gosling, Paula. *Wychford Murders.* 1986 Doubleday.
   Nevins, Francis M. *120-Hour Clock.* 1986 Walker.
1986.17   14200075
   Pentecost, Hugh. *Nightmare Time.* 1986 Dodd Mead.
   Marric, J J. *Gideon's Way.* 1986 Stein & Day.
   Peters, Elizabeth. *Lion In The Valley.* 1986 Atheneum.
1986.18   15646157
   Ferrars, E X. *The Other Devil's Name.* 1986 Doubleday.
   Dobyns, Stephen. *Saratoga Snapper.* 1986 Viking.
   Lovell, Marc. *Good Spies Don't Grow On Trees.* 1986 Doubleday.

1986

1986.19   15068770
  Hammond, Gerald. *Pursuit Of Arms.* 1985 St Martins.
  Wood, Ted. *Fool's Gold.* 1986 Scribner.
  King, Pauline. *Snares Of The Enemy.* 1985 Scribner.
1986.20   16827773
  Yorke, Margaret. *Safely to the Grave.* 1986 St Martins.
  DeGrave, Philip. *Keep the Baby, Faith.* 1986 Doubleday.
  Hamilton, Nan. *Shape of Fear.* 1986 Dodd, Mead.
1986.21   15645783
  Babson, Marian. *Unfair Exchange.* 1986 Walker.
  Langton, Jane. *Good and Dead.* 1986 St Martins.
  Keating, H R F. *Under a Monsoon Cloud.* 1986 Viking.

1987

1987.01   18718863
  Holme, Timothy. *At the Lake of Sudden Death.* 1987 Walker.
  Biggle Jr., Lloyd. *Interface for Murder.* 1987 Doubleday.
  Barnao, Jack. *Lockestep.* 1987 Scribner.
1987.02   17572014
  Francis, Dick. *Bolt.* 1986 Putnam.
  Ashford, Jeffrey. *A Question Of Principle.* 1986 St Martin.
  Weeks, Dolores. *The Cape Murders.* 1987 Dodd, Mead.
1987.03   19788657
  Davey, Jocelyn. *A Dangerous Liaison.* 1987.
  Stewart, Michael. *Blindsight.* 1987 St Martins.
  Linscott, Gillian. *Whiff of Sulphur.* 1987 St Martins.
1987.04   17699794
  Page, Emma. *Final Moments.* 1987 Doubleday.
  Breen, Jon and Ball, John. *Murder California Style.* 1987 St Martins.
  Fraser, Anthea. *Pretty Maids all in a Row.* 1987 Doubleday.
1987.05   17672662
  Grimes, Martha. *The Five Bells And Bladebone.* 1987 Little, Brown.
  Dunlap, Susan. *A Dinner To Die For.* 1987 St Martins.
  Underwood, Michael. *The Uninvited Corpse.* 1987 St Martins.
1987.06   16971970
  Webster, Noah. *A Flight from Paris.* 1987 Doubleday.
  Paul, Barbara. *A Chorus of Detectives.* 1987 St Martins.
  Hebden, Mark. *Pel and the Pirates.* 1987 Walker.
1987.07   17165577
  Bagley, Desmond. *Juggernaut.* 1985 St Martins.
  Greenwood, John. *The Mind of Mr. Mosley.* 1987 Walker.
  Goodrum, Charles. *The Best Cellar.* 1987 St Martins.

1987

1987.08	18718904

McClintick, Malcolm. *The Key.* 1987 Doubleday.
Hilton, John Buxton. *Slickensides: A Derbyshire Mystery.* 1987 St Martins.
Berry, Carole. *The Letter of The Law.* 1987 St Martins.

1987.09	16532794

Pentecost, Hugh. *Kill and Kill Again.* 1987 Dodd, Mead.
Babson, Marian. *Reel Murder.* 1986 St Martins.
Elkins, Aaron J. *A Deceptive Clarity.* 1987 Walker.

1987.10	17278112

Kittredge, Mary. *Murder in Mendocino.* 1987 Walker.
McClintick, Malcolm. *Mary's Grave.* 1987 Doubleday.
Simpson, Dorothy. *Dead on Arrival.* 1986 Scribner.

1987.11	17700081

Waugh, Hillary. *Murder on Safari.* 1987 Dodd, Mead.
McBriarty, Douglas. *Whitewater VJ.* 1987 Walker.
Serafin, David. *Port of Light.* 1987 St Martins.

1987.12	16188483

Woods, Sara. *Naked Villainy.* 1987 St Martins.
Dunlap, Susan. *Too Close to the Edge.* 1987 St Martins.
Bagley, Desmond. *Night or Error.* 1987 St Martins.

1987.13	18765953

Jeffries, Roderic. *Relatively Dangerous.* 1987 St Martins.
Hess, Joan. *Dear Miss Demeanor.* 1987 St Martins.
McInerny, Ralph. *Cause and Effect.* 1987 Atheneum.

1987.14	17165657

Hillerman, Tony. *Skinwalkers.* 1986 Harper.
Mitchell, Gladys. *St Peter's Finger.* 1986 St Martins.
DeAndrea, William L. *Azrael.* 1987 Mysterious Press.

1987.15	17672578

MacDonald, John D. *Slam the Big Door.* 1987 Mysterious Press.
Yorke, Margaret. *Evidence to Destroy.* 1987 Viking.
Keating, H R F. *The Body in the Billiard Room.* 198t Viking.

1987.16	16827360

Borthwick, J S. *Student Body.* 1986 St Martins.
Engel, Howard. *City Called July.* 1986 Viking.
Craig, M S. *Flash Point.* 1987 Dodd, Mead.

1987.17	17571932

Babson, Marian. *There Must Be Some Mistake.* 1987 St Martins.
Singer, Shelley. *Spit In The Ocean.* 1987 St Martins.
Ballard, Mignon F. *Cry At Dusk.* 1987 Dodd, Mead.

1987

1987.18   16972030
Peters, Elizabeth. *Trojan Gold.* 1987 Atheneum.
Resnicow, Herbert. *The Dead Room.* 1987 Dodd, Mead.
Babson, Marian. *Murder on a Mystery Tour.* 1987 Walker.

1988

1988.01   18544524
Knox, Bill. *Dead Man's Mooring.* 1988 Doubleday.
Beck, K K. *Young Mrs. Cavendish And The Kaiser's Men.* 1987 Walker.
Dewhurst, Eileen. *A Nice Little Business.* 1987 Doubleday.
1988.02   19743850
Dentinger, Jane. *Death Mask.* 1988 Scribner.
Karl, M S. *Killer's Ink.* 1988 Dodd, Mead.
Doherty, P C. *The Crown in Darkness.* 1988 St Martins.
1988.03   19788619
Smith, Bridget A. *Death of an Alaskan Princess.* 1988 St Martins.
Meek, M R D. *Worm of Doubt.* 1987 Scribner.
Livingston, Nancy. *Incident at Parga.* 1987 St Martins.
1988.04   18718796
Hilton, John Buxton. *Displaced Person.* 1987 St Martins.
Wolzien, Valerie. *Murder at the PTA Luncheon.* 1988 St Martins.
Williams, David. *Divided Treasure.* 1987 St Martins.
1988.05   18544491
Cleary, Jon. *Dragons At The Party.* 1987 Morrow.
Elkins, Aaron. *Old Bones.* 1987 Grand Central.
MacKenzie, Donald. *A Savage State Of Grace.* 1988 Doubleday.
1988.06   19365113
Underwood, Michael. *Dual Enigma.* 1988 St Martins.
Resnicow, Herbert. *The Gold Gamble.* 1988 St Martins.
Weeks, Dolores. *The Friday Harbor Murders.* 1988 Dodd, Mead.
1988.07   18545181
Peters, Ellis. *The Hermit Of Eyton Forest.* 1988 Mysterious Press.
Taylor, L A. *Poetic Justice.* 1988 Walker.
Babson, Marian. *So Soon Done For.* 1988 Walker.
1988.08   15200045
Innes, Hammond. *High Stand.* 1988 Atheneum.
MacKenzie, Donald. *Nobody Here By That Name.* 1986 Doubleday.
Melville, James. *Go Gently, Gaijin.* 1986 St Martins.
1988.09   24251639
Ashford, Jeffrey. *The Honourable Detective.* 1988 St Martins.
Livingston, Nancy. *Death in a Distant Land.* 1988 St Martins.
Hammond, Gerald. *Adverse Report.* 1987 St Martins.

1988

1988.10   18859768
  Symons, Julian. *The Kentish Manor Murders.* 1988 Viking.
  Melville, James. *The Reluctant Ronin.* 1988 Scribner.
  Wilcox, Collin. *Bernhardt's Edge.* 1988 Tor.
1988.11   18859694
  DeAndrea, William L. *Killed in Paradise.* 1988 Mysterious Press.
  Greenwood, L B. *Sherlock Holmes and the Case of Sabina Hall.* 1988 Simon & Schuster.
  Noguchi, Thomas T and Lyons, Arthur. *Unnatural Causes.* 1988 Putnam.
1988.12   18544644
  Melville, James. *Kimono for a Corpse.* 1987 St Martins.
  Morice, Anne. *Treble Exposure.* 1987 St Martins.
  Gillespie, Robert B. *The Last of the Honeywells.* 1988 Dodd, Mead.
1988.13   20060814
  Innes, Hammond. *Medusa.* 1988 Scribner.
  Martin, Lee. *Death Warmed Over.* 1988 St Martins.
  Barnard, Robert. *At Death's Door.* 1988 Scribner.
1988.14   19364942
  Pentecost, Hugh. *Murder Goes Round and Round.* 1988 Dodd, Mead.
  Babson, Marian. *Cover-Up Stories.* 1988 St Martins.
  Ashford, Jeffrey. *A Crime Remembered.* 1988 St Martins.
1988.15   19743829
  Tourney, Leonard. *Old Saxon Blood.* 1988 St Martins.
  Roberts, Les. *Pepper Pike.* 1988 St Martins.
  Llewellyn, Caroline. *Masks of Rome.* 1988 Scribner.
1988.16   19743745
  Hart, Roy. *A Pretty Place for Murder.* 1987 St Martins.
  Hall, Robert Lee. *Murder at San Simeon.* 1988 St Martins.
  Drummond, John Keith. *'Tis the Season to Be Dying.* 1988 St Martins.
1988.17   18544962
  Westlake, Donald E. *Trust Me On This.* 1988 Mysterious Press.
  Morice, Anne. *Design for Dying.* 1988 St Martins.
  Greenwood, John. *What, Me, Mr. Mosley?.* 1988 Walker.
1988.18   19743808
  Berry, Carole. *The Year of the Monkey.* 1988 St Martins.
  Hall, Robert Lee. *Benjamin Franklin Takes the Case.* 1988 St Martins.
  Huxley, Elspeth. *African Poison Murders.* 1988 Viking.

1989

1989.01   21055319
  Underwood, Michael. *A Compelling Case.* 1989 St Martins.
  Elkins, Aaron J. *Curses!.* 1989 Mysterious Press.
  Cook, Thomas H. *Flesh And Blood.* 1989 Putnam.

1989

1989.02   20922256
   Peters, Ellis. *The Confession Of Brother Haluin.* 1988 Mysterious Press.
   Clark, Dick and Francis, Paul. *Murder On Tour.* 1989 Mysterious Press.
   Elkins, Charlotte and Aaron. *A Wicked Slice.* 1989 St Martins.
1989.03   24251673
   Jeffries, Roderic. *Dead Clever.* 1989 St Martins.
   Boylan, Eleanor. *Working Murder.* 1989 Holt.
   Ballinger, John. *Williamsburg Forgeries.* 1989 St Martins.
1989.04   25567016
   Llewellyn, Sam. *Death Roll.* 1989 Summitt.
   Meek, M R D. *Loose connection.* 1989 Scribner.
   Gerson, Jack. *Death squad London.* 1989 St Martins.
1989.05   24251759
   Waugh, Hillary. *A Death in Town.* 1989 Carroll & Graf.
   Borgenicht, Miriam. *Undue Influence.* 1989 St Martins.
   Butler, Gwendoline. *Coffin Underground.* 1989 St Martins.
1989.06   21282953
   Ball, John. *The Kiwi Target.* 1989 Carroll & Graf.
   Ballard, Mignon F. *Deadly Promise.* 1989 Carroll & Graf.
   Greenwood, L B. *Sherlock Holmes and the Thistle of Scotland.* 1989 Simon & Schuster.
1989.07   24251715
   Wainwright, John. *The Man Who Wasn't There.* 1989 St Martins.
   Williams, David. *Holy Treasure!.* 1989 St Martins.
   Turnbull, Peter. *Condition Purple.* 1989 St Martins.
1989.08   23848365
   Meek, M R D. *A Mouthful of Sand.* 1989 Scribner.
   Jordan, Jennifer. *Murder Under The Mistletoe.* 1988 St Martins.
   Hardwick, Mollie. *The Bandersnatch.* 1989 St MArtins.
1989.09   21282908
   Gilbert, Michael. *Paint, Gold and Blood.* 1989 Harper.
   Melville, James. *A Haiku for Hanae.* 1989 Scribner.
   Forrest, Richard. *Death on the Mississippi.* 1989 St Martins.
1989.10   25027565
   Doherty, P C. *Spy in Chancery.* 1988 St Martins.
   Barth, Richard. *Blood Doesn't Tell.* 1989 St Martins.
   Shuman, M K. *The Maya Stone Murders.* 1989 St Martins.
1989.11   20901025
   Hillerman, Tony. *Talking God.* 1988 Harper.
   Cornwell, Bernard. *Killer's Wake.* 1989 Putnam.
   Cook, Thomas H. *Streets of Fire.* 1989 Putnam.

1989

1989.12	20408929

    Hillerman, Tony. *A Thief Of Time.* 1988 Harper.
    Nabb, Magdalen. *The Marshal And The Madwoman.* 1988 Scribner.
    Wood, Ted. *When The Killing Starts.* 1989 Scribner.

1989.13	18719131

    Radley, Sheila. *Who Saw Him Die?.* 1987 Scribner.
    Gault, William Campbell. *Cat & Mouse.* 1988 St Martins.
    Giroux, E X. *Death for a Dietician.* 1989 Ballantine.

1989.14	77798064

    Gardner, John. *Win, Lose or Die.* 1989 Putnam.
    Morice, Anne. *Fatal Charm.* 1988 St Martins.
    Keating, H R F. *Dead on Time.* 1989 Mysterious Press.

1990

1990.01	23279247

    Yorke, Margaret. *Admit to Murder.* 1990 Viking.
    Paul, Barbara. *In-Laws and Outlaws.* 1990 Scribner.
    Doherty, P C. *Serpent Amongst the Lilies.* 1990 St Martins.

1990.02

    Steed, Neville. *Black Eye.* 1990 St Martins.
    Alexander, Gary. *Kiet and the Golden Peacock.* 1989 St Martins.
    Page, Katherine Hall. *The Body in the Belfry.* 1990 St Martins.

1990.03	23364034

    Karl, M S. *Death Notice.* 1990 St Martins.
    McQuillan, Karin. *Deadly Safari.* 1990 St Martins.
    Holt, Hazel. *Mrs. Mallory investigates.* 1989 St Martins.

1990.04	23063810

    Westlake, Donald E. *Drowned Hope.* 1990 Mysterious Press.
    Wood, Ted. *On the Inside.* 1990 Scribner.
    Dobyns, Stephen. *Saratoga Hexameter.* 1990 Viking.

1990.05	24160101

    Babson, Marian. *Encore Murder.* 1990 St Martins.
    Melville, James. *The Bogus Buddha.* 1990 Scribner.
    Cornwell, Bernard. *Crackdown.* 1990.

1990.06	23279194

    Babson, Marian. *In the Teeth of Adversity.* 1990 St Martins.
    Borthwick, J S. *Bodies of Water.* 1990 St Martins.
    Ashford, Jeffrey. *Conflict of Interests.* 1989 St Martins.

1990.07	26486491

    Marston, Edward. *The Merry Devils.* 1989 St Martins.
    Yaffe, James. *Mom Meets Her Maker.* 1990 St Martins.
    Cook, Bob. *Paper Chase.* 1989 St Martins.

1990

1990.08	22835223

Pentecost, Hugh. *Pattern for Terror.* 1990 Carroll & Graf.
Gollin, James. *Broken Consort.* 1989 St Martins.
Doherty, P C. *Angel of Death.* 1990 St Martins.

1990.09	25566602

Hart, Roy. *Robbed Blind.* 1990 St Martins.
Roberts, Les. *Snake Oil.* 1990 St Martins.
Crider, Bill. *Evil at the Root.* 1990 St Martins.

1990.10	22835286

Underwood, Michael. *Rosa's Dilemma.* 1990 St Martins.
Gilbert, Michael. *Anything for a Quiet Life.* 1990 Carroll & Graf.
Martin, Lee. *Deficit Ending.* 1990 St Martins.

1990.11	25012510

Wright, Eric. *A Sensitive Case.* 1990 Scribner.
McInerny, Ralph. *Savings And Loam.* 1990 Atheneum.
Llewellyn, Caroline. *The Lady Of The Labyrinth.* 1990 Scribner.

1990.12	23063824

Cullen, Robert. *Soviet Sources.* 1990 Atlantic Monthly Press.
Kaminsky, Stuart M. *Poor Butterfly.* 1990 Mysterious Press.
Zollinger, Norman. *Lautrec.* 1990 Dutton.

1990.13	24159883

Deighton, Len. *Spy Sinker.* 1990 Harper.
Keating, H R F. *The Iciest Sin.* 1990 Mysterious Press.
Jeffries, Roderic. *Too Clever By Half.* 1990 St Martins.

1990.14	26486543

Francis, Dick. *Straight.* 1989 Putnam.
Jovanovich, William. *Money Trail.* 1990 Harcourt, Brace & Jovanovich.
Giroux, E X. *Death for a Double.* 1990 St Martins.

1990.15	23364022

Radley, Sheila. *This Way Out.* 1989 Scribner.
Beechcroft, William. *Pursuit of Fear.* 1990 Carroll & Graf.
Berry, Carole. *Good Night, Sweet Prince.* 1990 St Martins.

1990.16	797037818

Babson, Marian. *Tourists Are for Trapping.* 1989 St Martins.
Cleary, Jon. *Babylon South.* 1989 Morrow.
Dunlap, Susan. *Diamond in the Buff.* 1990 St Martins.

1991

1991.01	28901915

Sibley, Celestine. *Ah, Sweet Mystery.* 1991 Harper.
Zimmerman, Bruce. *Thicker Than Water.* 1991 Harper.
Wright, Jim. *Last Man Standing.* 1991 Carroll & Graf.

1991

1991.02   28901734
  Cooper, Natasha. *A Common Death.* 1990 Crown.
  Westbrook, Robert. *Lady Left.* 1990 Crown.
  D'Amato, Barbara. *Hard Tack.* 1991 Scribner.
1991.03   28901790
  Llewellyn, Sam. *Deadeye.* 1991 Summit.
  Mortimer, John. *Rumpole a La Carte.* 1990 Viking.
  Norman, Geoffrey. *Sweetwater Ranch.* 1990 Atlantic Monthly Press.
1991.04   25480818
  Peters, Ellis. *Flight of the Witch.* 1991 Mysterious Press.
  Hitt, Jack. *Perfect Murder.* 1991 Harper.
  McInerny, Ralph. *Search Committee.* 1991 Scribner.
1991.05   24676848
  Elkins, Aaron J. *A Glancing Light.* 1991 Scribner.
  Wright, Eric. *Final Cut.* 1991 Scribner.
  Chesbro, George C. *The Fear In Yesterday's Rings.* 1991 Mysterious Press.
1991.06   24676892
  Wilcox, Collin. *Hire a Hangman.* 199 Holt.
  Rendell, Ruth. *Going Wrong.* 1990 Mysterious Press.
  Henry, Sue. *Murder on the Iditarod Trail.* 1991 Atlantic Monthly Pres.
1991.07   25480742
  Gardner, Erle Stanley. *Honest Money.* 1991 Carroll & Graf.
  Gilbert, Michael. *The Queen Against Karl Mullen.* 1991 Carroll & Graf.
  Ballard, Mignon F. *The Widow's Woods.* 1991 Carroll & Graf.
1991.08   27362266
  Deighton, Len. *Mamista.* 1991 Harper.
  Warga, Wayne. *Singapore Transfer.* 1991 Vikiing.
  Kelly, Susan. *And Soon I'll Come to Kill You.* 1991 Villard.
1991.09   28901538
  Maxwell, A E. *Money Burns.* 1991 Villard.
  Brennan, Carol. *Headhunt.* 1991 Carroll & Graf.
  Rossiter, Elizabeth. *Lemon Garden.* 1991 Carroll & Graf.
1991.10   28901884
  Allen, Steve. *Murder in Vegas.* 1991 Zebra.
  Roome, Annette. *Second Shot in the Dark.* 1990 Crown.
  Wright, Laurali. *Fall From Grace.* 1991 Penguin.
1991.11   28901693
  Cooper, Natasha. *Poison Flowers.* 1990 Crown.
  Rothenberg, Rebecca. *Bulrush Murders.* 1991 Carroll & Graf.
  Bowers, Elisabeth. *No Forwarding Address.* 1991 Seal Press.

1991

1991.12	27362261

Gorman, E & Greenberg, M H. *Solved.* 1991 Carroll & Graf.
Burns, Rex. *Body Guard.* 1991 Penguin.
Kenrick, Tony. *Glitterbug.* 1991 Carroll & Graf.

1992

1992.01   28480939

Westlake, Donald E. *Humans.* 1992 Grand Central Publishing.
Pronzini, Bill. *Quarry.* 1991 Delacourte.
Ballard, Mignon F. *Final Curtain.* 1992 Carroll & Graf.

1992.02   28480944

Elkins, Aaron J. *Make No Bones.* 1991 Mysterious Press.
Rendell, Ruth. *Copper Peacock.* 1991 Grand Central Publishing.
Langton, Jane. *God in Concord.* 1992 Viking.

1992.03   29217053

Hill, Donna. *Murder Uptown.* 1992 Carroll & Graf.
Trocheck, Kathy Hogan. *Every Crooked Nanny.* 1992 Harper.
Tucker, Kerry. *Cold Feet.* 1992 Harper.

1992.04   29217033

Press, Margaret L. *Requiem For A Postman.* 1992 Carroll & Graf.
Davis, Lindsey. *Venus in Copper.* 1991 Crown.
O'Marie, Carol Anne. *Murder in Ordinary Time.* 1991 Delacorte.

1993

1993.01   30375186

Wilcox, Collin. *Dead Center.* 1992 Holt.
Giroux, E X. *A Death For A Dodo.* 1993 St Martins.
Wright, Eric. *A Fine Italian Hand.* 1992 Scribner.

1993.02   559084512

Boyle, Gerry. *Deadline.* 1993 North Country Press.
Sibley, Celestine. *Dire Happenings at Scratch Ankle.* 1993 Harper.
Pronzini, Bill. *Carmody's Run.* 1992 Dark Harvest.

1993.03   31948830

Tucker, Kerry. *Death Echo.* 1993 Harper.
Naslund, Sena Jeter. *Sherlock in Love.* 1993 David R. Godine.
Gieson, Judith Van. *The Lies That Bind.* 1993 Harper.

1993.04   30530657

Allen, Steve. *The Murder Game.* 1993 Kensington.
Beaton, M C. *Death of a Prankster.* 1992 St Martins.
Hall, Robert Lee. *Murder At Drury Lane.* 1992 St Martins.

1993

1993.05   31153570
  Boylan, Eleanor. *Pushing Murder.* 1993 Holt.
  Wilcox, Collin. *Switchback.* 1993 Holt.
  Trocheck, Kathy Hogan. *To Live and Die in Dixie.* 1993 Harper.
1993.06   30530570
  Lewis, Roy. *A Secret Dying.* 1993 St Martins.
  Bowen, Michael. *Act of Faith.* 1992 St Martins.
  Chesbro, George C. *An Incident at Bloodtide.* 1993 Mysterious Press.
1993.07   30375141
  Babson, Marian. *Shadows In Their Blood.* 1993 St Martins.
  Doherty, P C. *The Prince Of Darkness.* 1993 St Martins.
  Meek, M R D. *Touch And Go.* 1992 Scribner.
1993.08   31698949
  Ferrars, E X. *Thy Brother Death.* 1993 Doubleday.
  Babson, Marian. *Nine Lives To Murder.* 1992 St Martins.
  Cleary, Jon. *Bleak Spring.* 1993 Morrow.
1993.09   38155236
  Moyes, Patricia. *Twice in a Blue Moon.* 1993 Holt.
  Jones, D J H. *Murder at the MLA.* 1993 University of George Press.
  Ruell, Patrick. *The Only Game.* 1993 Foul Play.

1994

1994.01   34057621
  Thomas, Ross. *Ah, Treachery!.* 1994 Mysterious Press.
  Hill, Reginald. *Blood Sympathy.* 1994 St Martins.
  Martin, Lee. *Inherited Murder.* 1994 St Martins.
1994.02   32209756
  Keating, H R F. *Cheating Death.* 1992 Mysterious Press.
  Westlake, Donald E. *Baby, Would I Lie?.* 1994 Mysterious Press.
  Doherty, P C. *The Assassin in the Greenwood.* 1993 St Martins.
1994.03   40549594
  McQuillan, Karin. *The Cheetah Chase.* 1994 Ballantine.
  Shaffer, Louise. *All My Suspects.* 1994 Putnam.
  Caverly, Carol. *All the Old Lions.* 1994 Write Way.
1994.04   34057623
  Butler, Gwendoline. *A Coffin For Charley.* 1993 St Martins.
  Hensley, Joe L. *Grim City.* 1994 St Martins.
  Tucker, Kerry. *Drift Away.* 1994 Harper.
1994.05   37248109
  Hart, Roy. *A Deadly Schedule.* 1993 St Martins.
  Beaton, M C. *Agatha Raisin and the Potted Gardener.* 1994 Minotaur.
  Page, Katherine Hall. *The Body in the Basement.* 1994 St Martins.

1994

| 1994.06 | 31698925 |

Peters, Ellis. *Fallen Into the Pit.* 1994 Mysterious Press.
Dobyns, Stephen. *Saratoga Backtalk.* 1994 Norton.
Freeling, Nicolas. *You Who Know.* 1994 Mysterious Press.

| 1994.07 | 40549701 |

Gosling, Paula. *A Few Dying Words.* 1993 Mysterious Press.
Holt, Hazel. *The Shortest Journey.* 1994 St Martins.
Hall, Robert Lee. *Benjamin Franklin and a Case of Artful Murder.* 1994 St Martins.

| 1994.08 | 32909767 |

McDonald, Gregory. *Fletch Reflected.* 1994 Putnam.
Dibdin, Michael. *Dead Lagoon.* 1994 Pantheon.
Lovesey, Peter. *Bertie And The Crime Of Passion.* 1993 Mysterious Press.

| 1994.09 | 34954119 |

Tourney, Leonard. *Frobisher's Savage.* 1994 St Martins.
Friedman, Kinky. *Armadillos and Old Lace.* 1994 Simon & Schuster.
Ramsey, Diana. *Killing Words.* 1994 St Martins.

| 1994.10 | 38587261 |

Underwood, Michael. *Guilty Conscience.* 1993 St Martins.
Burley, W J. *Wycliffe and the Dunes Mystery.* 1994 St Martins.
Melville, Jennie. *Whoever Has the Heart.* 1994 St Martins.

| 1994.11 | 31789607 |

Ashford, Jeffrey. *Judgement Deferred.* 1994 St Martins.
Biggle Jr., Lloyd. *Where Dead Soldiers Walk.* 1994 St Martins.
Nabb, Magdalen. *The Marshal at Villa Torrini.* 1993 Harper.

| 1994.12 | 32209529 |

Van de Wetering, Janwillem. *Just a Corpse at Twilight.* 1994 Soho.
Harrington, William. *Columbo: The Helter Skelter Murders.* 1994 Tom Doherty Assoc..
Aird, Catherine. *A Going Concern.* 1994 St Martins.

| 1994.13 | 32871662 |

Roberts, Les. *The Lake Effect.* 1994 Minotaur.
Hammond, Gerald. *Thin Air.* 1994 St Martins.
Frommer, Sara Hoskinson. *Buried In Quilts.* 1994 St Martins.

| 1994.14 | 32871514 |

Block, Lawrence. *A Long Line Of Dead Men.* 1994 Morrow.
Jeffries, Roderic. *Death Takes Time.* 1994 St Martins.
Law, Janice. *Backfire.* 1994 St Martins.

| 1994.15 | 32871704 |

Crider, Bill. *Murder Most Fowl.* 1994 St Martins.
Dawson, Janet. *Don't Turn Your Back on the Ocean.* 1994 Ballantine.
Bannister, Jo. *Charisma.* 1994 St Martins.

1994

1994.16   32871573
>   Davis, Lindsey. *Poseidon's Gold.* 1992 Crown.
>   Berlinski, David. *Less Than Meets the Eye.* 1994 St Martins.
>   Pearce, Michael. *The Mamur Zapt and the Girl in the Nile.* 1992 Mysterious Press.

1995

1995.01   33391724
>   Cleary, Jon. *Autumn Maze.* 1994 Morrow.
>   Yorke, Margaret. *Almost The Truth.* 1994 Little, Brown.
>   Beaton, M C. *Agatha Raisin And The Walkers Of Dembley.* 1994 St Martins.

1995.02   35190785
>   Barnard, Robert. *The Bad Samaritan.* 1995 Scribner.
>   Chesbro, George C. *Bleeding In The Eye Of A Brainstorm.* 1995 Simon & Schuster.
>   Granger, Ann. *Flowers For His Funeral.* 1995 St Martins.

1995.03   33267088
>   Boyle, Gerry. *Bloodline.* 1995 Putnam.
>   Sibley, Celestine. *Plague of Kinfolks.* 1995 Harper.
>   Landrum, Graham. *Sensational Music Club Mystery.* 1994 St Martins.

1995.04   32909927
>   Eyre, Elizabeth. *Bravo for the Bride.* 1995 St Martins.
>   Van Gieson, Judith. *Parrot Blues.* 1995 Harper.
>   Yeager, Dorian. *Murder Will Out.* 1994 St Martins.

1995.05   34497144
>   Beck, K K. *Cold Smoked.* 1995 Mysterious Press.
>   Lee, Barbara. *Death in Still Waters.* 1995 St Martins.
>   Comfort, B. *Elusive Quarry.* 1995 Countryman Press.

1995.06   33391735
>   Lewis, Roy. *The Cross Bearer.* 1995 St Martins.
>   Berry, Carole. *The Death Of A Difficult Woman.* 1994 Berkley.
>   Fraser, Anthea. *Three, Three, The Rivals.* 1995 St Martins.

1995.07   35190714
>   Casley, Dennis. *Death Undertow.* 1994 St Martins.
>   Doss, Jame D. *The Shaman Laughs.* 1994 St Martins.
>   Myers, Tamar. *Parsley, Sage, Rosemary And Crime.* 1995 Doubleday.

1995.08   33808279
>   Melville, Jennie. *A Death in the Family.* 1993 St Martins.
>   Palmer, Leonard. *The Sherman Letter.* 1994 Write Way.
>   Bannister, Jo. *A Taste for Burning.* 1995 St Martins.

1995.09   34497053
>   Lewin, Michael Z. *Family Business.* 1995 Foul Play.
>   Robb, Candice. *The Nun's Tale.* 1995 St Martins.
>   Smith, Barbara Burnett. *Dust Devils of the Purple Sage.* 1995 St Martins.

1995

1995.10	32909695

Shoemaker, Bill. *Fire Horse.* 1995 Ballantine.
Robitaille, Julie. *Iced.* 1994 St Martins.
Irvine, Robert. *Hosanna Shout.* 1994 St Martins.

1995.11	32909867

Wilcox, Collin. *Full Circle.* 1994 Forge.
Doherty, P C. *A Time For The Death Of A King.* 1994 St Martins.
Kaminsky, Stuart M. *Tomorrow Is Another Day.* 1995 Mysterious Press.

1995.12	35227423

Keating, H R F. *The Good Detective.* 1995 Scribner.
Burley, W J. *Wycliffe And The House Of Fear.* 1995 St Martins.
Kruger, Mary. *No Honeymoon For Death.* 1995 Kensington.

1995.13	34497099

Ferrars, E X. *A Hobby Of Murder.* 1995 Doubleday.
Roberts, Les. *The Duke Of Cleveland.* 1995 St Martins.
Hall, Robert L. *Murder By The Waters.* 1995 Minotaur.

1995.14	33808303

Kittredge, Mary. *Kill or Cure.* 1995 St Martins.
Cooper, Natasha. *Rotten Apples.* 1995 St Martins.
Dunn, Carola. *Winter Garden Mystery.* 1995 Kensington.

1995.15	35227501

Nolan, William F. *The Marble Orchard.* 1994 St Martins.
Hammond, Gerald. *Carriage of Justice.* 1995 St Martins.
O'Marie, Carol Anne. *Death Goes on Retreat.* 1995 Random House.

1995.16	34884433

Allen, Steve. *Murder on the Atlantic.* 1995 Kensington.
Rubino, Jane. *Death of a DJ.* 1994 Write Way.
Pearce, Michael. *Mamur Zapt and the Spoils of Egypt.* 1992 Mysterious Press.

1995.17	33391731

James, P D. *Original Sin.* 1994 Knopf.
Gilman, Dorothy. *Mrs. Pollifax Pursued.* 1995 Fawcett.
Barnard, Robert. *Dead Mr. Mozart.* 1995 St Martins.

1995.18	35190457

Dukthas, Ann. *The Prince Lost To Time.* 1995 St Martins.
Irvine, Robert. *Pillar Of Fire.* 1995 St Martins.
Linscott, Gillian. *Crown Witness.* 1995 St Martins.

1995.19	33808289

O'Donnell, Lillian. *The Raggedy Man.* 1995 Putnam.
Doherty, P C. *An Ancient Evil.* 1995 St Martins.
Trocheck, Kathy Hogan. *Happy Never After.* 1995 Harper.

1995

1995.20   34497397
  Marston, Edward. *The Roaring Boy.* 1995 St Martins.
  Borthwick, J S. *Dolly Is Dead.* 1995 St Martins.
  Hammond, Gerald. *Sting In The Tail.* 1995 St Martins.
1995.21   34497201
  Dobyns, Stephen. *Saratoga Fleshpot.* 1995 Norton.
  Satterthwait, Walter. *Escapade.* 1995 St Martins.
  Babson, Marian. *Diamond Cat.* 1994 St Martins.
1995.22   34884498
  Doherty, P C. *The Song of a Dark Angel.* 1995 St Martins.
  Martin, Lee. *Bird In A Cage.* 1995 St Martins.
  Holtzer, Susan. *Curly Smoke.* 1995 St Martins.
1995.23   33808296
  Michaels, Barbara. *Stitches in Time.* 1995 Harper.
  Hill, Reginald. *Born Guilty.* 1995 Harper.
  Linscott, Gillian. *An Easy Day for a Lady.* 1995 St Martins.
1995.24   34497326
  Black, Veronica. *A Vow of Devotion.* 1995 St Martins.
  Shone, Anna. *Mr. Donaghue Investigates.* 1994 St Martins.
  Brown, Lizbie. *Turkey Tracks.* 1995 St Martins.

1996

1996.01   35720645
  Jeffries, Roderic. *An Arcadian Death.* 1995 Harper.
  Gosling, Paula. *The Dead of Winter.* 1995 Little Brown.
  Kaminsky, Stuart M. *Dancing in the Dark.* 1996 Grand Central.
1996.02   36370395
  Shoemaker, Bill. *Dark Horse.* 1996 Ballantine.
  Martin, Lee. *Genealogy of Murder.* 1996 St Martins.
  Shone, Anna. *Secrets in Stone.* 1996 Minotaur.
1996.03   35981955
  DeAndrea, William L. *Killed In Fringe Time.* 1995 Simon & Schuster.
  Boylan, Eleanor. *Murder Crossed.* 1996 Holt.
  Fraser, Anthea. *The Gospel Makers.* 1996 St Martins.
1996.04   38155568
  Kaminsky, Stuart. *Lieberman's Law.* 1996 Holt.
  Trocheck, Kathy Hogan. *Heart Trouble.* 1996 Harper.
  Bell, Nancy. *Biggie And The Poisoned Politician.* 1996 St Martins.
1996.05   36876333
  Wilhelm, Kate. *Malice Prepense.* 1996 St Martins.
  Hunt, Richard. *Murder Benign.* 1996 St Martins.
  Black, Veronica. *Vow of Poverty.* 1996 St Martins.

1996

1996.06   37505844

    Kruger, Mary. *Masterpiece of Murder.* 1996 Kensington.
    Baxt, George. *The Fred Astaire and Ginger Rogers Murder Case.* 1996 St Martins.
    Curzon, Clare. *Close Quarters.* 1996 St Martins.

1996.07   35981956

    Gilman, Dorothy. *Mrs. Pollifax and the Lion Killer.* 1996 Fawcett.
    Doherty, P C. *A Tapestry of Murders.* 1996 Gardner.
    Ferrars, E X. *Seeing is Believing.* 1996 Doubleday.

1996.08   37307278

    Koch, Ed. *Murder On Broadway.* 1996 Kensington.
    Holtzer, Susan. *Bleeding Maize and Blue.* 1996 St Martins.
    Caverly, Carol. *Frogskin and Muttonfat.* 1996 Write Way.

1996.09   37307276

    Eddenden, A E. *Murder at the Movies.* 1996 Chicago Review Press.
    McGown, Jill. *Shred of Evidence.* 1995 Fawcett.
    Melville, Jennie. *Morbid Kitchen.* 1995 St Martins.

1996.10   36370398

    Yorke, Margaret. *Serious Intent.* 1995 Mysterious Press.
    Crider, Bill. *Winning Can Be Murder.* 1996 St Martins.
    Berlinski, David. *The Body Shop.* 1996 St Martins.

1996.11   36642881

    Rothenberg, Rebecca. *The Shy Tulip Murders.* 1996 Mysterious Press.
    Palmer, Frank. *Nightwatch.* 1994 St Martins.
    Lipinski, Thomas. *A Picture of Her Tombstone.* 1996 St Martins.

1996.12   38159298

    Edwards, Ruth Dudle. *Ten Lords A Leaping.* 1995 St Martins.
    Page, Katherine Hall. *The Body In The Bog.* 1996 Morrow.
    Sullivan, Winona. *Dead South.* 1996 St Martins.

1996.13   35981953

    Eyre, Elizabeth. *Axe for an Abbot.* 1996 St Martins.
    Ashford, Jeffrey. *The Bitter Bite.* 1996 St Martins.
    Black, Veronica. *A Vow of Fidelity.* 1995 St Martins.

1996.14   36370394

    Wright, Eric. *Buried In Stone.* 1995 Scribner.
    Harrington, Jonathan. *The Death Of Cousin Rose.* 1995 Write Way Publishing.
    Gleiter, Jan. *Lie Down With Dogs.* 1996 St Martins.

1996.15   38155374

    Granger, Ann. *Candle For A Corpse.* 1996 St Martins.
    Winslow, Don. *While Drowning In The Desert.* 1996 St Martins.
    Curzon, Clare. *Past Mischief.* 1994 Little, Brown.

1996

1996.16   37307269

   Dawson, Janet. *A Credible Threat.* 1996 Ballantine.
   Harrington, William. *Columbo: The Game Show Killer.* 1996 Forge.
   Hammond, Gerald. *Mad Dogs and Scotsmen.* 1996 St Martins.

1996.17   36642871

   King, Peter. *The Gourmet Detective.* 1994 St Martins.
   Sipherd, Ray. *Dance Of The Scarecrows.* 1996 St Martins.
   Templeton, Aline. *The Last Act Of All.* 1996 St Martins.

1996.18   45209359

   Landrum, Graham. *The Historical Society Murder Mystery.* 1996 St Martins.
   Ripley, Ann. *Death Of A Garden Pest.* 1996 St Martins.
   Grace, C L. *The Book Of Shadows.* 1996 Minotaur.

1996.19   36370397

   D'Amato, Barbara. *Killer.app.* 1996 Doherty Associates.
   Morson, Ian. *Falconer's Judgement.* 1995 St Martins.
   Yeager, Dorian. *Ovation by Death.* 1996 St Martins.

1996.20   35227556

   Cleary, Jon. *Winter Chill.* 1995 Morrow.
   Babson, Marian. *Even Yuppies Die.* 1996 St Martins.
   Butler, Gwendoline. *The Coffin Tree.* 1996 St Martins.

1996.21   36876327

   Roberts, Les. *Collision Bend.* 1995 St Martins.
   Beaton, M C. *Agatha Raisin And The Murderous Marriage.* 1996 St Martins.
   Chesbro, George C. *Dream Of A Falling Eagle.* 1996 Simon & Schuster.

1996.22   37307270

   Butler, Gwendoline. *A Dark Coffin.* 1996 St Martins.
   Dukthas, Ann. *The Time of Murder at Mayerling.* 1996 St Martins.
   Yeager, Dorian. *Summer Will End.* 1996 St Martins.

1996.23   36642876

   Gieson, Judith Van. *Hotshots.* 1996 Harper.
   Bannister, Jo. *No Birds Sing.* 1996 Minotaur.
   Crespi, Camilla. *The Trouble With A Bad Fit.* 1996 Harper.

1996.24   38158454

   Marston, Edward. *The Laughing Hangman.* 1996 St Martins.
   Eccles, Marjorie. *The Company She Kept.* 1996 St Martins.
   St. Edmunds, Anne. *Red Right Returning.* 1996 St Martins.

1996.25   37307289

   Kaminsky, Stuart M. *The Rockford Files: The Green Bottle.* 1996 Forge.
   Aird, Catherine. *After Effects.* 1996 Minotaur.
   Wright, Eric. *Death of a Sunday Writer.* 1996 Foul Play Press.

1996

1996.26   37307293
    Doherty, P C. *Satan's Fire.* 1996 Minotaur.
    Satterthwait, Walter. *Accustomed To The Dark.* 1996 St Martins.
    Fraser, Anthea. *I'll Sing You Two-O.* 1996 St Martins.

1997

1997.01   39366642
    Fawcett, Quinn. *Against the Brotherhood.* 1997 Tom Doherty Assoc.
    Boyle, Alistair. *Unlucky Seven.* 1997 Allan A Knoll.
    Heber, R W. *Murder at Wittenham Park.* 1997 St Martins.
1997.02   38841622
    Jeffries, Roderic. *An Artistic Way To Go.* 1997 St Martins.
    Crossman, David. *A Show Of Hands.* 1997 Down East Books.
    Hammond, Gerald. *Sink Or Swim.* 1996 St Martins.
1997.03   37505822
    Keating, H R F. *Asking Questions.* 1996 St Martins.
    Dunn, Carola. *Murder on the Flying Scotsman.* 1996 St Martins.
    Shaber, Sarah R. *Simon Said.* 1997 St Martins.
1997.04   37505826
    Babson, Marian. *Break a Leg, Darling.* 1997 St Martins.
    O'Marie, Carol Anne. *Death of an Angel.* 1996 Minotaur.
    Linscott, Gillian. *Dead Man's Sweetheart.* 1996 St Martins.
1997.05   46986746
    Babson, Marian. *Canapes For The Kitties.* 1996 St Martins.
    Baxt, George. *The Clark Gable And Carole Lombard Murder Case.* 1997 St Martins.
    Holtzer, Susan. *Black Diamond.* 1997 St Martins.
1997.06   37927808
    Eyre, Elizabeth. *Dirge for a Doge.* 1996 Headline.
    MacPherson, Rett. *Family Skeletons.* 1997 St Martins.
    Peel, Colin D. *Blood of Your Sisters.* 1997 St Martins.
1997.07   38841623
    Marston, Edward. *The Fair Maid Of Bohemia.* 1997 St Martins.
    Bell, Nancy. *Biggie And The Mangled Mortician.* 1997 St Martins.
    Boyle, Alistair. *The Missing Link.* 1995 Allen A Knoll.
1997.08   37927809
    Morson, Ian. *Falconer and the Face of God.* 1996 Sy Martins.
    Shelton, Connie. *Partnerships Can Kill.* 1997 Intrigue Press.
    Carlon, Patricia. *The Whispering Wall.* 1996 Soho.
1997.09   38841624
    Lee, Barbara. *Final Closing.* 1997 St Martins.
    Quill, Monica. *Half Past Nun.* 1997 St Martins.
    Fraser, Anthea. *Motive For Murder.* 1997 Severn House.

1997

1997.10   37927812
   Borthwick, J S. *The Garden Plot.* 1997 St Martins.
   Jones, D J H. *The Buchan Papers.* 1996 St Martins.
   Emerson, Kathy Lynn. *Face Down In The Marrow-Bone Pie.* 1997 Minotaur.
1997.11   38841625
   Hill, Reginald. *Killing the Lawyers.* 1997 St Martins.
   Harrington, William. *Columbo: the Glitter Murder.* 1997 Forge.
   Ruth Dudley. *Murder in a Cathedral.* 1997 St Martins.
1997.12   38841626
   Peters, Ray. *The Lafitte Case.* 1997 Write Way.
   Chinchinian, Harry. *Murder in the Mountains.* 1997 Plum Tree Press.
   Law, Janice. *Cross-check.* 1997 St Martins.
1997.13   38841627
   Bannister, Jo. *The Lazarus Hotel.* 1997 St Martins.
   Healy, R Austin. *Sweetfeed.* 1996 Marshall Jones.
   Robb, Candace M. *Riddle of St. Leonard's.* 1997 St Martins.
1997.14   39741959
   Hall, Robert Lee. *London Blood.* 1997 St Martins.
   Roberts, Les. *Cleveland Local.* 1997 St Martins.
   Beaton, M C. *Agatha Raisin and the Terrible Tourist.* 1997 St Martins.
1997.15   40275872
   Burton, David. *Manmade For Murder.* 1997 Write Way.
   Kemprecos, Paul. *Bluefin Blues.* 1997 St Martins.
   Boyle, Alistair. *The Con.* 1996 Allan A Knoll.
1997.16   38841628
   Frommer, Sara Hoskinson. *Murder & Sullivan.* 1997 St Martins.
   Champion, David. *Mountain Massacres.* 1995 Allan A Knoll.
   Meek, M R D. *Postscript to Murder.* 1997 St Martins.
1997.17   39742408
   Connor, Beverly. *Questionable Remains.* 1997 Sourcebooks.
   Dunn, Carola. *Damsel in Distress.* 1997 St Martins.
   Champion, David. *Celebrity Trouble.* 1997 Allen A Knoll.
1997.18   37927813
   Granger, Ann. *A Touch of Mortality.* 1997 St Martins.
   Laurence, Janet. *Death at the Table.* 1997 St Martins.
   Piccirilli, Tom. *The Dead Past.* 1997 Write Way Pub.
1997.19   39724849
   Doherty, P C. *A Tournament Of Murders.* 1996 Headline.
   Hensley, Joe L. *Robak's Witch.* 1997 St Martins.
   Chittenden, Margaret. *Dead Men Don't Dance.* 1997 Kensington.

1997

1997.20   37505855
  Allen, Steve. *Wake Up To Murder.* 1996 Kensington.
  Eccles, Marjorie. *An Accidental Shroud.* 1997 St Martins.
  Cooper, Natasha. *Drowning Pool.* 1997 St Martins.

1998

1998.01   40704238
  Yorke, Margaret. *Act of Violence.* 1997 Little, Brown.
  Koch, Edward I. *The Senator Must Die.* 1998 Kensington.
  Cohn, R J. *Baker's Gold.* 1998 Four Seasons.
1998.02   39670962
  Weber, Ronald. *The Aluminum Hatch.* 1998 Harlequin.
  Dukthas, Ann. *In The Time Of The Poisoned Queen.* 1998 St Martins.
  Crider, Bill. *Death By Accident.* 1998 St Martins.
1998.03   39670963
  Hammond, Gerald. *Bloodlines.* 1998 St Martins.
  Smith, Barbara Burnett. *Mistletoe from Purple Sage.* 1997 St Martins.
  Sprague, Gretchen. *Death in Good Company.* 1997 St Martins.
1998.04   41686025
  Block, Lawrence. *The Burglar Who Painted Like Mondrian.* 1998 Dutton.
  Scott, Willard with Crider, Bill. *Murder In The Mist.* 1998 Dutton.
  Zimler, Richard. *The Last Kabbalist Of Lisbon.* 1998 Overlook.
1998.05   40704240
  Linscott, Gillian. *Dance on Blood.* 1998 St Martins.
  Thrasher, L L. *Charlie's Bones.* 1998 Write Way.
  Emerson, Kathy Lynn. *Face Down Upon a Herbal.* 1997 St Martins.
1998.06   39670965
  Doherty, P C. *The Devil's Hunt.* 1998 St Martins.
  Yeager, Dorian. *Libation By Death.* 1998 St Martins.
  Bannister, Jo. *Primrose Convention.* 1998 St Martins.
1998.07   40978931
  Butler, Gwendoline. *A Double Coffin.* 1998 St Martins.
  Sipherd, Ray. *The Audubon Quartet.* 1998 Thomas Dunne.
  Granger, Ann. *A Word After Dying.* 1996 Headline.
1998.08   39670966
  King, Peter. *Dying on the Vine.* 1998 St Martins.
  Eslick, Tom. *Tracked in the Whites.* 1997 Write Way.
  Smith, Frank. *Stone Dead.* 1998 St Martins.
1998.09   40652520
  Graham, Caroline. *Faithful Unto Death.* 1998 St Martins.
  Boyle, Alistair. *Bluebeard's Last Stand.* 1998 Allan A Knoll.
  Evans, Penelope. *Freezing.* 1997 Soho Crime.

1998

1998.10	40275869

D'Amato, Barbara. *Good Cop, Bad Cop.* 1998 Tom Doherty Assoc.
Briody, Thomas. *Rogue's Wager.* 1997 St Martins.
Abresch, Peter E. *Bloody Bonsai.* 1998 Write Way.

1998.11	39670967

Elkjer, Thom. *Hook, Line And Murder.* 1997 Write Way Pub.
Curzon, Clare. *All Unwary.* 1998 St Martins.
Allen, Irene. *Quaker Indictment.* 1998 St Martins.

1998.12	40978930

Satterthwait, Walter. *Masquerade.* 1998 St. Martins.
Gleiter, Jan. *A House by the side of the road.* 1998 St. Martins.
Berry, Linda. *Death and the Easter Bunny.* 1998 Write Way.

1998.13	39670968

Jeffries, Roderic. *A Maze Of Murders.* 1998 St Martins.
Allen, Steve. *Die Laughing.* 1998 Kensington.
Meier, Leslie. *Back To School Murder.* 1997 Kensington.

1998.14	41830681

Trocheck, Kathy Hogan. *Midnight Clear.* 1998 Harper.
Staub, Wendy Corsi. *Fade to Black.* 1998 Kensington.
Branham, Mary. *Little Green Man in Ireland.* 1997 Sunstone.

1998.15	40978928

Scott, Williard and Crider, Bill. *Murder Under Blue Skies.* 1998 Dutton.
Jaffe, Jody. *In Colt Blood.* 1998 Fawcett.
Comfort, Barbara. *A Pair for the Queen.* 1998 Norton.

1998.16	40275873

Champion, David. *Nobody Roots For Goliath.* 1996 Allen A Knoll.
Shelton, Connie. *Small Towns Can Be Murder.* 1998 Intrigue Press.
Matthews, Alex. *Vendetta's Victim.* 1998 Intrigue Press.

1998.17	41830680

Healy, Jeremiah. *The Only Good Lawyer.* 1998 Atria Books.
Adamson, Lydia. *A Cat Of One's Own.* 1998 Dutton.
Seranella, Barbara. *No Offense Intended.* 1998 HarperCollins.

1998.18	40978929

Kelly, Lelia. *Presumption of Guilt.* 1997 Kensington.
Edwards, Martin. *Eve of Destruction.* 1998 Norton.
Skinner, Robert. *Cat-Eyed Trouble.* 1998 Kensington.

1998.19	39670969

Ashford, Jeffrey. *The Price of Failure.* 1998 St Martins.
Kelner, Toni L P. *Tight as a Tick.* 1997 Kensington.
Black, Veronica. *Vow of Adoration.* 1998 St Martins.

1998

1998.20 40704239

 Mitchell, Kay. *A Rage of Innocents.* 1997 St Martins.
 MacPherson, Rett. *Veiled Antiquity.* 1998 St Martins.
 Trow, M J. *The Adventures of Inspector Lestrade.* 1998 Regnery.

1998.21 40275877

 Kaminsky, Stuart M. *The Rockford Files: Devils On My Doorstep.* 1998 Forge.
 Hathaway, Robin. *The Doctor Digs A Grave.* 1998 Thomas Dunne.
 Eccles, Marjorie. *A Death Of Distinction.* 1998 St Martins.

1998.22 40704236

 Roberts, Les. *A Shoot in Cleveland.* 1998 Thomas Dunne.
 Beaton, M C. *Agatha Raisin and the Wellspring of Death.* 1998 St Martins.
 Westfall, Patricia Tichenor. *Mother of the Bride.* 1998 Minotaur.

1998.23 40704241

 Champion, David. *The Snatch.* 1994 Allan A Knoll.
 Bruno, Anthony. *Double Espresso.* 1998 Forge.
 King-Wente, Sami. *Baby Girl.* 1998 Pen & Ivy Press.

1998.24 40704242

 Cooper, Natasha. *Sour Grapes.* 1997 Simon & Schuster.
 Maness, Larry. *Strangler.* 1998 Presidio.
 Landrum, Graham G & Landrum, R G. *The Garden Club Mystery.* 1998 Thomas Dunne.

1998.25 40978927

 Block, Lawrence. *Tanner on Ice.* 1997 Dutton.
 Holt, Hazel. *Mrs. Malory and the Only Good Lawyer.* 1997 Dutton.
 Van Gieson, Judith. *Ditch Rider.* 1998 HarperCollins.

1999

1999.01 43920500

 Block, Lawrence. *The Burglar In The Rye.* 1997 Dutton.
 Harris, Charlaine. *A Fool And His Honey.* 1999 Minotaur.
 Cobb, James H. *West On 66.* 1999 Minotaur.

1999.02 43920503

 Shubin, Seymour. *The Captain.* 1982 Stein & Day.
 Trow, M J. *Lestrade and the Deadly Game.* 1999 Regnery.
 Menkes, John. *Angry Puppet Syndrome.* 1999 Demos.

1999.03 45062001

 Hunter, David. *The Dancing Savior.* 1999 Cumberland House.
 Shubin, Seymour. *Anyone's My Name.* 1998 Creative Arts.
 Hammond, Gerald. *Twice Bitten.* 1999 Minotaur.

1999.04 43395919

 Lee, Barbara. *Dead Man's Fingers:A Chesapeake Bay mystery.* 1999 St Martins.
 Harrington, Jonathan. *The Second Sorrowful Mystery.* 1999 Write Way Publishing.
 Trow, M J. *Lestrade and the Leviathan.* 1999 Gateway.

1999

1999.05   43395917
   Conant, Susan. *Evil Breeding: A dog lover's mystery.* 1999 Doubleday.
   Morson, Ian. *Falconer and the Great Beast.* 1998 St Martins.
   Neri, Kris. *Revenge of the Gypsy Queen.* 1999 Rainbow Books.
1999.06   43920502
   Emerson, Kathy Lynn. *Face Down Among The Winchester Geese.* 1999 Minotaur.
   Cameron, Kate. *Under The Wolf's Head.* 1999 St Kitts Press.
   Sloan, Bob. *Bliss Jumps The Gun.* 1999 Norton.
1999.07   41830678
   Foglia, Leonard & Richards, David Richards. *Face Down in the Park.* 1999 Pocket Books.
   Murphy, Shirley Rousseau. *Cat in the Dark.* 1998 Harper.
   Branham, Mary. *Big Black Dog in Vallarta.* 1998 Sunstone.
1999.08   45062000
   Shubin, Seymour. *Fury's Children.* 1997 Write Way.
   Goldberg, Marshall. *Deadly Operation.* 1996 Dufour.
   Shelton, Connie. *Memories Can Be Murder.* 1999 Intrigue.
1999.09   42388101
   Ferrigno, Robert. *Heartbreaker.* 1999 Pantheon.
   Trow, M J. *Brigade: the further adventures of Lestrade.* 1998 Gateway.
   Matthews, Alex. *Wanton's web.* 1999 Intrigue Press.
1999.10   41830677
   McKinney, Meagan. *In the dark.* 1998 Kensington.
   Shubin, Seymour. *My face among strangers.* 1999 Write Way.
   Meier, Leslie. *Valentine murder.* 1999 Kensington.
1999.11   43920504
   James, Bill. *The Lolita Man.* 1986 Foul Play Press.
   Martin, Valerie. *Italian Fever.* 1999 Knopf.
   Collins, Max Allan. *Majic Man.* 1999 Dutton.
1999.12   41830683
   Dibdin, Michael. *A Long Finish.* 1998 Pantheon.
   Henry, April. *Circles Of Confusion.* 1998 HarperCollins.
   Pye, Michael. *Taking Lives.* 1999 Knopf.
1999.13   42872304
   Marshall, Evan. *Missing Marlene.* 1999 Kensington.
   Struthers, Betsy. *Found: A Body.* 1992 Simon & Pierre.
   Schunk, Laurel. *Black and Secret Midnight.* 1998 St Kitts.
1999.14   41830682
   Allen, Steve. *Murder In Hawaii.* 1999 Kensington.
   Hanson, Rick. *Extreme Odds.* 1998 Kensington.
   Piccirilli, Tom. *Sorrow's Crown.* 1999 Write Way Publishing.

1999

1999.15	43484453

Engel, Howard. *Murder in Montparnasse.* 1999 Abrams.
Wright, Eric. *Death on the rocks.* 1999 Minotaur.
Bowen, Michael. *Collateral damage.* 1999 St Martins.

1999.16	42872302

Horrock, Henry. *Potomac Fever.* 1999 Little, Brown.
Chittenden, Margaret. *Don't Forget To Die.* 1999 Kensington.
Trow, M J. *Lestrade And The Hallowed House.* 1999 Gateway.

1999.17	44078981

Slater, Susan. *The Pumpkin Seed Massacre.* 1999 Intrigue.
Abresch, Peter E. *Killing Thyme.* 1999 Write Way.
Trow, M J. *Lestrade and the Brother of Death.* 1999 Regnery.

1999.18	42388103

James, Bill. *Roses, Roses.* 1998 Norton.
Dibdin, Michael. *Cosi Fan Tutti.* 1996 Pantheon.
Thrasher, L L. *Dogsbody, Inc..* 1999 Write Way

1999.19	42872305

MacGregor, T J. *The Seventh Sense.* 1999 Kensington.
Skinner, Robert. *Daddy's Gone A-Hunting.* 1999 Poisoned Pen Press.
Bowen, Gail. *Verdict in Blood.* 1998 McClelland & Stewart.

1999.20	43395920

Smith, Rosamond. *Starr Bright Will Be With You Soon.* 1999 Dutton.
Katz, Jon. *Death Row.* 1998 Doubleday.
Gordon, Alan. *Thirteenth Night.* 1998 St Martins.

1999.21	42872303

James, Bill. *Top Banana.* 1998 W. W. Norton.
Wishnia, K J A. *Soft Money.* 1999 Dutton.
Sultan, Faye and Kennedy, Teresa. *Helpline.* 1999 Random House.

1999.22	45061999

McKinney, Mel. *Where There's Smoke.* 1999 St Martins.
Bartholomew, Nancy. *Drag Strip.* 1999 St Martins.
McInerny, Ralph M. *Irish Tenure.* 1999 Minotaur.

1999.23	45132027

Bannister, Jo. *The hireling's tale.* 1999 St. Martins.
Cosin, Elizabeth M. *Zen and the city of angels.* 1999 Minotaur.
Eccles, Marjorie. *Killing me softly.* 1999 Minotaur.

1999.24	44078979

Keating, H R F. *The Bad Detective.* 1999 Minotaur Books.
Frommer, Sara Hoskinson. *The Vanishing Violinist.* 1999 Minotaur Books.
Ballard, Mignon F. *Angel At Troublesome Creek.* 1999 Minotaur Books.

1999

1999.25	44078977

Allen, Conrad. *Murder On The Lusitania.* 1999 Minotaur Books.
James, Bill. *Gospel.* 1997 Foul Play Press.
Boyle, Alistair. *Ship Shapely.* 1999 Allen A Knoll.

2000

2000.01	45625861

Dibdin, Michael. *Blood Rain.* 1999 Pantheon.
Keating, H R F. *Hard Detective.* 2000 St Martins.
Stansberry, Domenic. *Manifesto For the Dead.* 2000 Permanent Press.

2000.02	45625860

Wishnia, K J A. *The Glass Factory.* 2000 Dutton.
Morton, C W. *Sea Trials.* 1999 St Martins.
Roberts, John Maddox. *Saturnalia: SPQR V.* 1999 Minotaur.

2000.03 *May*	45179431

Seranella, Barbara. *Unwanted Company.* 1999 Harper.
Franscell, Ron. *The Deadline.* 1999 Write Way.
Goldberg, Marshall. *Intelligence.* 1996 Dufour.

The Detective Book Club 1942-2000 Author Index

Abbey, Kieran
  Beyond the Dark 1944.07
Abbot, Anthony
  The Shudders 1943.02
Abresch, Peter E
  Bloody Bonsai 1998.10
  Killing Thyme 1999.17
Adamson, Lydia
  A Cat Of One's Own 1998.17
Aird, Catherine
  After Effects 1996.25
  A Going Concern 1994.12
  Harm's Way 1984.06
  Last Respects 1983.03
  Passing Strange 1981.10
  Some Die Eloquent 1980.10
Alan, Marjorie
  Dark Prophecy 1945.12
Albrand, Martha
  The Door Fell Shut 1966.09
  The Mask Of Alexander 1955.08
  Zurich/AZ900 1974.18
Alding, Peter
  Murder Is Suspected 1979.09
Alexander, David
  Death Of Humpty Dumpty 1958.02
  Die, Little Goose 1956.05
  Hush-A-Bye Murder 1957.09
  The Murder Of Whistler's Brother 1957.04
  Pennies From Hell 1960.12
  Shoot A Sitting Duck 1956.03
Alexander, Gary
  Kiet and the Golden Peacock 1990.02
Allbeury, Ted
  The Man With The President's Mind 1978.16
  The Man With the President's Mind 1978.24
  Omega-Minus 1975.10
Allen, Conrad
  Murder On The Lusitania 1999.25
Allen, Irene
  Quaker Indictment 1998.11
Allen, Steve
  Die Laughing 1998.13
  The Murder Game 1993.04
  Murder In Hawaii 1999.14
  Murder in Vegas 1991.10
  Murder on the Atlantic 1995.16
  Wake Up To Murder 1997.20
Allingham, Margery
  Cargo Of Eagles 1968.08
  The China Governess 1963.04
  Deadly Duo 1949.10
  The Estate Of The Beckoning Lady 1955.06
  The Mind Readers 1965.12
  More Work for the Undertaker 1949.04
  Pearls Before Swine 1945.07
Ambler, Eric
  Judgement On Deltchev 1951.08
Ames, Delano
  Coffin For Christopher 1954.11
Amos, Alan
  Borderline Murder 1948.03
  Fatal Harvest 1958.03
  Panic In Paradise 1952.02
  They're Going To Kill Me 1956.02
Anderson, J R L
  Death In The Channel 1977.02
  Death In The City 1983.02
  Death in the Greenhouse 1983.10
  Festival 1980.07
  A Sprig Of Sea Lavender 1979.02
Angus, Sylvia
  Arson And Old Lace 1973.05
  Dead To Rites 1979.05
  Death Of A Hittite 1969.11
Anthony, Evelyn
  The Company Of Saints 1984.03
Archer, Frank
  The Malabang Pearl 1965.03
Armstrong, Anthony
  A Room At The Hotel Ambre 1956.03
Armstrong, Charlotte
  The Better To Eat You 1954.10
  Dream Of Fair Woman 1966.06
  The Protege 1970.05
  The Unsuspected 1946.05
Arrighi, Mel
  Turkish White 1977.19
Ashe, Gordon
  The Big Call 1975.14
  The Big Call 1975.20
  A Blast of Trumpets 1976.07
  A Clutch Of Coppers 1969.12
  The Croaker 1973.11
  Elope To Death 1977.20
  A Herald Of Doom 1975.03
  The Kidnaped Child 1971.15
  The Kidnaped Child 1972.17
  The Kidnapped Child 1971.08
  A Life For A Death 1973.15

Murder With Mushrooms — 1974.09
A Plague Of Demons — 1977.07
A Rabble Of Rebels — 1972.15
A Shadow of Death — 1976.11
A Shadow of Death — 1976.22
Wait For Death — 1972.10
Ashford, Jeffrey
The Anger Of Fear — 1979.15
The Bitter Bite — 1996.13
Conflict of Interests — 1990.06
A Crime Remembered — 1988.14
The Honourable Detective — 1988.09
Hostage To Death — 1978.09
An Ideal Crime — 1986.10
Judgement Deferred — 1994.11
The Loss Of The Culion — 1982.03
The Price of Failure — 1998.19
A Question Of Principle — 1987.02
A Recipe For Murder — 1980.22
A Sense Of Loyalty — 1985.15
Slow Down The World — 1977.05
Asimov, Isaac
Banquets of the Black Widowers — 1984.01
More Tales Of The Black Widowers — 1977.01
Audemars, Pierre
And One For The Dead — 1981.22
Babson, Marian
Bejewelled Death — 1982.13
Break a Leg, Darling — 1997.04
Canapes For The Kitties — 1997.05
Cover-Up Stories — 1988.14
The Cruise of a Deathtime — 1985.12
Dangerous To Know — 1981.22
Death Beside The Sea — 1983.09
Death Swap — 1985.13
Death Warmed Up — 1983.04
Diamond Cat — 1995.21
Encore Murder — 1990.05
Even Yuppies Die — 1996.20
A Fool for Murder — 1984.08
In the Teeth of Adversity — 1990.06
Line Up For Murder — 1982.08
The Lord Mayor of Death — 1980.03
Murder on a Mystery Tour — 1987.18
Murder, Murder, Little Star — 1980.14
Nine Lives To Murder — 1993.08
Reel Murder — 1987.09
Shadows In Their Blood — 1993.07
So Soon Done For — 1988.07
There Must Be Some Mistake — 1987.17

Tourists Are for Trapping — 1990.16
A Trail Of Ashes — 1985.17
Twelve Deaths of Christmas — 1980.23
Unfair Exchange — 1986.21
Bagby, George
A Big Hand for the Corpse — 1953.10
The Body In The Basket — 1954.12
Corpse Candle — 1968.02
Country and Fatal — 1980.21
Dead Drunk — 1954.01
Dirty Pool — 1967.02
The Golden Creep — 1982.21
Guaranteed To Fade — 1979.03
Honest Reliable Corpse — 1969.05
Mysteriouser an Mysteriouser — 1965.09
A Question Of Quarry — 1981.16
Shadow on the Window — 1955.12
The Sitting Duck — 1982.08
The Three-Time Losers — 1958.04
Bagley, Desmond
Bahama Crisis — 1983.18
The Enemy — 1978.12
Flyaway — 1979.17
Juggernaut — 1987.07
Night or Error — 1987.12
The Spoilers — 1970.07
Windfall — 1982.24
Baker, Ivon
Grave Doubt — 1973.08
Ball, John
Five Pieces Of Jade — 1972.13
A Killing In The Market — 1978.10
The Kiwi Target — 1989.06
Mark One: The Dummy — 1974.17
Police Chief — 1977.18
Police Chief — 1977.21
Police Chief — 1977.24
Singapore — 1986.03
Then Came Violence — 1980.11
Trouble For Tallon — 1981.12
Ball, John [editor]
Cop Cade — 1979.05
Ballard, Helen Mabry
To the Tune of Murder — 1952.07
Ballard, Mignon F
Angel At Troublesome Creek — 1999.24
Cry At Dusk — 1987.17
Deadly Promise — 1989.06
Final Curtain — 1992.01
Raven Rock — 1986.01

The Widow's Woods   1991.07
Ballinger, Bill S
  The Heir Hunters   1966.08
  The Tooth And The Nail   1955.09
Ballinger, John
  Williamsburg Forgeries   1989.03
Banks, Oliver
  The Rembrandt Panel   1980.23
Bannister, Jo
  Charisma   1994.15
  The Lazarus Hotel   1997.13
  No Birds Sing   1996.23
  Primrose Convention   1998.06
  A Taste for Burning   1995.08
  The hireling's tale   1999.23
Barnao, Jack
  Lockestep   1987.01
Barnard, Robert
  At Death's Door   1988.13
  The Bad Samaritan   1995.02
  The Case Of The Missing Bronte   1983.09
  Dead Mr. Mozart   1995.17
  Death And The Princess   1983.04
  Death By Sheer Torture   1982.08
  Death In A Cold Climate   1981.10
  Death Of A Mystery Writer   1979.20
  Death of A Literary Widow   1980.22
Barroll, Clare
  A Strange Place For A Murder   1979.15
Barry, Nora
  Sherbourne's Folly   1979.06
Barth, Richard
  Blood Doesn't Tell   1989.10
Bartholomew, Nancy
  Drag Strip   1999.22
Baxt, George
  The Clark Gable And Carole
    Lombard Murder Case   1997.05
  The Fred Astaire and Ginger Rogers
    Murder Case   1996.06
  I, Said the Demon!   1969.07
Bayer, Oliver Weld
  An Eye For An Eye   1945.08
Beaton, M C
  Agatha Raisin And The Murderous
    Marriage   1996.21
  Agatha Raisin And The Walkers Of
    Dembley   1995.01
  Agatha Raisin and the Potted
    Gardener   1994.05
  Agatha Raisin and the Terrible
    Tourist   1997.14
  Agatha Raisin and the Wellspring of
    Death   1998.22
  Death of a Prankster   1993.04
Beck, K K
  Cold Smoked   1995.05
  Murder in a Mummy Case   1986.16
  Young Mrs. Cavendish And The
    Kaiser's Men   1988.01
Beechcroft, William
  Pursuit of Fear   1990.15
Bell, Josephine
  A Question Of Inheritance   1981.18
Bell, Nancy
  Biggie And The Mangled Mortician   1997.07
  Biggie And The Poisoned Politician   1996.04
Bellairs, George
  All Roads To Sospel   1982.10
  Devious Murder   1981.06
Bennett, Ken
  Passport For A Renegade   1955.11
Benson, Ben
  Stamped for Murder   1952.05
Berckman, Evelyn
  The Strange Bedfellow   1956.07
Berlinski, David
  The Body Shop   1996.10
  Less Than Meets the Eye   1994.16
Berry, Carole
  The Death Of A Difficult Woman   1995.06
  Good Night, Sweet Prince   1990.15
  The Letter of The Law   1987.08
  The Year of the Monkey   1988.18
Berry, Linda
  Death and the Easter Bunny   1998.12
Biggle Jr., Lloyd
  Interface for Murder   1987.01
  The Quallsford Inheritance   1986.13
  Where Dead Soldiers Walk   1994.11
Bingham, John
  Murder Off The Record   1958.01
Bird, Brandon
  Downbeat For A Dirge   1952.12
  Hawk Watch   1954.09
Black, Gavin
  A Big Wind For Summer   1976.12
Black, Veronica
  Vow of Adoration   1998.19
  A Vow of Devotion   1995.24

A Vow of Fidelity	1996.13		*The Missing Link*	1997.07
Vow of Poverty	1996.05		*Ship Shapely*	1999.25
Blanc, Suzanne			*Unlucky Seven*	1997.01
The Green Stone	1962.02		Boyle, Gerry	
The Rose Window	1967.05		*Bloodline*	1995.03
The Yellow Villa	1964.06		*Deadline*	1993.02
Blankenship, William D			Braddon, Russell	
The Leavenworth Irregulars	1974.05		*The Thirteenth Trick*	1974.06
Blazer, J S			Bradley, Mary Hastings	
Deal Me Out	1973.17		*Murder In The Family*	1951.10
Blizard, Marie			Bramhall, Marion	
Conspiracy of Silence	1954.09		*Button Button*	1944.09
The Dark Corner	1950.05		Brand, Christianna	
The Watch Sinister	1951.09		*Cat And Mouse*	1951.01
Block, Lawrence			Branham, Mary	
The Burglar In The Rye	1999.01		*Big Black Dog in Vallarta*	1999.07
The Burglar Who Painted Like			*Little Green Man in Ireland*	1998.14
Mondrian	1998.04		Braun, Lilian Jackson	
A Long Line Of Dead Men	1994.14		*The Cat Who Could Read Backwards*	1966.10
Tanner on Ice	1998.25		Brean, Herbert	
Block, Libbie			*The Darker the Night*	1949.05
Bedeviled	1947.06		Breen, Jon L	
Bohle, Edgar			*Triple Crown*	1986.07
The Wife That Died Twice	1962.06		Breen, Jon and Ball, John	
Bonett, John and Emery			*Murder California Style*	1987.04
Dead Lion	1949.07		Bremner, Marjorie	
Booton, Kage			*Murder Most Familiar*	1954.04
The Toy	1976.02		Brennan, Carol	
Borgenicht, Miriam			*Headhunt*	1991.09
Don't Look Back	1956.05		Brett, John	
Undue Influence	1989.05		*Who'd Hire Brett*	1981.19
Borthwick, J S			Brett, Simon	
Bodies of Water	1990.06		*An Amateur Corpse*	1978.16
Dolly Is Dead	1995.20		*Dead Giveaway*	1986.04
The Garden Plot	1997.10		*The Dead Side Of The Mike*	1981.02
Student Body	1987.16		*Murder In The Title*	1983.17
Bowen, Gail			*Situation Tragedy*	1981.23
Verdict in Blood	1999.19		Briody, Thomas	
Bowen, Michael			*Rogue's Wager*	1998.10
Act of Faith	1993.06		Broun, Daniel	
Collateral damage	1999.15		*Egypt's Choice*	1964.02
Bowers, Elisabeth			Brown, Fredric	
No Forwarding Address	1991.11		*The Five-Day Nightmare*	1962.10
Boylan, Eleanor			Brown, J E	
Murder Crossed	1996.03		*Incident at 125th Street*	1970.06
Pushing Murder	1993.05		Brown, Lizbie	
Working Murder	1989.03		*Turkey Tracks*	1995.24
Boyle, Alistair			Bruce, Leo	
Bluebeard's Last Stand	1998.09		*Death In Albert Park*	1979.20
The Con	1997.15		Bruno, Anthony	
			Double Espresso	1998.23

Bunce, Frank
So Young a Body — 1950.02
Burley, W J
Wycliffe And The House Of Fear — 1995.12
Wycliffe And The Scapegoat — 1979.16
Wycliffe In Paul's Court — 1981.03
Wycliffe and the Beales — 1984.15
Wycliffe and the Dunes Mystery — 1994.10
Wycliffe and the Quiet Virgin — 1986.11
Wycliffe's Wild Goose Chase — 1983.03
Burns, Rex
Body Guard — 1991.12
Burton, David
Manmade For Murder — 1997.15
Butler, Gwendoline
A Coffin For Charley — 1994.04
The Coffin Tree — 1996.20
Coffin Underground — 1989.05
A Dark Coffin — 1996.22
A Double Coffin — 1998.07
Byrne, Robert
The Tunnel — 1977.19
Caldwell, Taylor
The Late Clara Beame — 1963.09
Cameron, Kate
Under The Wolf's Head — 1999.06
Campbell, Alice
Ringed With Fire — 1942.08
Veiled Murder — 1950.01
Candy, Edward
Which Doctor? — 1954.07
Canning, Victor
Birdcage — 1979.17
Birds Of A Feather — 1985.17
Burden of Proof — 1956.08
The Doomsday Carrier — 1977.14
Fall From Grace — 1981.12
The Kingsford Mark — 1976.13
Memory Boy — 1982.09
The Painted Tent — 1974.14
The Satan Sampler — 1980.09
Twist Of The Knife — 1955.05
Vanishing Point — 1983.05
Carey, Bernice
The Missing Heiress — 1952.09
Carleton, Marjorie
Vanished — 1955.05
Carlon, Patricia
The Whispering Wall — 1997.08
Carmichael, Harry
The Motive — 1977.15

Carnac, Carol
It's Her Own Funeral — 1952.10
The Late Miss Trimming — 1957.07
Carr, John Dickson
He Who Whispers — 1946.05
Scandal At High Chimneys — 1959.10
The Sleeping Sphinx — 1947.03
The Third Bullet and Other Stories — 1954.08
Till Death Do Us Part — 1944.10
Carson, Robert
The Golden Years Caper — 1971.04
Carter, Diana
The Ghost Writer — 1975.13
Carvic, Heron
Miss Seeton Draws The Line — 1970.08
Odds On Miss Seeton — 1976.10
Picture Miss Seeton — 1969.01
Witch Miss Seaton — 1971.11
Casley, Dennis
Death Undertow — 1995.07
Caspary, Vera
The Murder In The Stork Club — 1946.07
Cavanaugh, Arthur
The Children Are Gone — 1966.07
Caverly, Carol
All the Old Lions — 1994.03
Frogskin and Muttonfat — 1996.08
Chaber, M E
The Bonded Dead — 1971.07
Born to be Hanged — 1973.16
Jade for a Lady — 1962.07
A Man In The Middle — 1968.01
Six Who Ran — 1964.12
Wild Midnight Falls — 1968.10
Champion, David
Celebrity Trouble — 1997.17
Mountain Massacres — 1997.16
Nobody Roots For Goliath — 1998.16
The Snatch — 1998.23
Charteris, Leslie
Catch the Saint — 1976.01
Count on the Saint — 1981.01
The Fantastic Saint — 1983.05
The Saint And The People Importers — 1972.07
The Saint And The Templar Treasure — 1979.21
The Saint In Trouble — 1979.08
The Saint In Trouble — 1979.23
The Saint in Pursuit — 1971.03
Salvage for the Saint — 1983.18
Send for the Saint — 1978.13

Chesbro, George C
 Bleeding In The Eye Of A
 Brainstorm   1995.02
 Dream Of A Falling Eagle   1996.21
 The Fear In Yesterday's Rings   1991.05
 An Incident at Bloodtide   1993.06
Cheyney, Peter
 Dance Without Music   1948.05
 Dark Bahama   1951.06
 Dark Duet   1943.09
 Dark Interlude   1947.08
 Dark Wanton   1949.03
 Ladies Won't Wait   1951.10
 Lady, Beware   1950.12
 The Man Nobody Saw   1949.11
 One of Those Things   1950.03
 Sinister Errand   1945.11
 The Stars are Dark   1944.01
 They Never Say When   1945.02
 The Urgent Hangman   1952.06
Chinchinian, Harry
 Murder in the Mountains   1997.12
Chittenden, Margaret
 Dead Men Don't Dance   1997.19
 Don't Forget To Die   1999.16
Christie, Agatha
 At Bertram's Hotel   1967.01
 Blood Will Tell   1952.01
 The Body in the Library   1942.03
 The Clocks   1964.11
 Dead Man's Folly   1956.12
 Death Comes as the End   1944.12
 Double Sin and Other Stories   1961.12
 Endless Night   1968.05
 Evil Under The Sun   1942.01
 Funerals Are Fatal   1953.03
 Hallowe'en Party   1970.03
 The Hollow   1946.10
 A Murder Is Announced   1950.09
 Nemesis   1972.01
 Nemesis   1973.19
 Ordeal by Innocence   1959.05
 The Pale Horse   1962.11
 So Many Steps to Death   1955.04
 There is a Tide   1948.03
 The Under Dog And Other Stories   1952.03
 The Witness for the Prosecution   1949.01
Clark, Dick and Francis, Paul
 Murder On Tour   1989.02
Clark, Douglas
 Roast Eggs   1982.06

Clark, Mary Higgins
 Where Are The Children?   1975.09
Clark, Philip
 The Dark River   1949.07
Clarke, Anna
 Desire To Kill   1982.19
 The Last Judgement   1985.12
 Letter From The Dead   1981.19
 The Mystery Lady   1986.05
 One Of Us Must Die   1981.06
 We The Bereaved   1983.07
Cleary, Jon
 Autumn Maze   1995.01
 Babylon South   1990.16
 Bleak Spring   1993.08
 City of Fading Light   1985.16
 Dragons At The Party   1988.05
 The Faraway Drums   1982.16
 The Golden Sabre   1982.04
 Peter's Pence   1974.05
 Ransom   1973.10
 The Safe House   1975.12
 A Sound of Lightning   1976.14
 Vortex   1978.14
 Winter Chill   1996.20
Clemeau, Carol
 The Ariadne Clue   1983.03
Cobb, James H
 West On 66   1999.01
Cody, Liza
 Dupe   1982.03
Cohen, Anthea
 Angel of Death   1985.01
 Angel of Vengeance   1984.07
Cohn, R J
 Baker's Gold   1998.01
Coles, Manning
 Among Those Absent   1948.10
 Concrete Crime   1960.03
 Dangerous by Nature   1950.11
 Death Of An Ambassador   1957.09
 The Fifth Man   1946.01
 A Knife For The Juggler   1965.04
 Let the Tiger Die   1947.10
 The Man In The Green Hat   1955.03
 Night Train To Paris   1952.03
 Search For A Sultan   1961.09
Collins, Max Allan
 Majic Man   1999.11
Collins, Michael
 Act Of Fear   1968.02

The Detective Book Club 1942-2000 Author Index

The Brass Rainbow	*1969.06*
Colter, Eli	
Cheer For The Dead	*1947.05*
Comfort, B	
Elusive Quarry	*1995.05*
Comfort, Barbara	
A Pair for the Queen	*1998.15*
Conant, Susan	
Evil Breeding: A dog lover's mystery	*1999.05*
Connor, Beverly	
Questionable Remains	*1997.17*
Constantine, K C	
A Fix Life This	*1976.07*
The Rocksburg Railroad Murders	*1973.11*
Cook, Bob	
Paper Chase	*1990.07*
Cook, Thomas H	
Flesh And Blood	*1989.01*
Streets of Fire	*1989.11*
Cooper, Natasha	
A Common Death	*1991.02*
Drowning Pool	*1997.20*
Poison Flowers	*1991.11*
Rotten Apples	*1995.14*
Sour Grapes	*1998.24*
Cores, Lucy	
The Misty Curtain	*1964.10*
Painted for the Kill	*1943.08*
Cornish, Constance	
Dead Of Winter	*1959.07*
Cornwell, Bernard	
Crackdown	*1990.05*
Killer's Wake	*1989.11*
Cosin, Elizabeth M	
Zen and the city of angels	*1999.23*
Coxe, George Harmon	
Double Identity	*1970.04*
An Easy Way To Go	*1969.01*
The Frightened Fiancee	*1951.02*
The Hollow Needle	*1949.02*
The Inside Man	*1974.12*
Lady Killer	*1949.06*
No Place for Murder	*1976.01*
The Silent Witness	*1973.06*
Woman With a Gun	*1972.09*
Craig, Alisa	
The Grub-And-Stakers Quilt A Bee	*1985.08*
The Grub-and-Stakers Move A	
Mountain	*1981.10*
A Pint of Murder	*1980.23*

The Terrible Tide	*1983.14*
Craig, John	
If You Want To See Your Wife	
Again...	*1972.05*
Craig, M S	
Flash Point	*1987.16*
Crane, Caroline	
Circus Day	*1986.15*
The Foretelling	*1982.22*
Someone At The Door	*1985.08*
Crane, Frances	
The Amethyst Spectacles	*1944.11*
The Applegreen Cat	*1944.02*
Black Cypress	*1949.02*
The Buttercup Case	*1959.11*
The Cinnamon Murder	*1946.09*
The Coral Princess Murders	*1954.14*
Death in Lilac Time	*1955.04*
Death-Wish Green	*1960.12*
The Flying Red horse	*1949.11*
Horror on the Ruby X	*1956.10*
The Indigo Necklace	*1945.03*
The Man in Gray	*1958.08*
Murder In Bright Red	*1954.02*
Murder On The Purple Water	*1947.09*
The Pink Umbrella	*1943.10*
The Yellow Violet	*1943.01*
Creasey, John	
The Beauty Queen Killer	*1956.06*
Death of a Racehorse	*1962.08*
Figure in the Dusk	*1953.12*
Hang the Little Man	*1965.02*
Hit and Run	*1959.12*
Inspector West Takes Charge	*1973.06*
Inspector West at Home	*1974.03*
The Killing Strike	*1961.05*
Lame Dog Murder	*1973.02*
Look Three Ways At Murder	*1965.08*
Murder, London - New York	*1962.03*
Murder, London-Australia	*1966.03*
Murder: One Two Three	*1960.12*
Policeman's Dread	*1964.07*
The Scene Of The Crime	*1963.12*
A Sharp Rise in Crime	*1979.11*
A Splinter Of Glass	*1972.14*
Take A Body	*1972.12*
The Theft of the Magna Carta	*1973.12*
Crespi, Camilla	
The Trouble With A Bad Fit	*1996.23*
Crider, Bill	
Death By Accident	*1998.02*

Evil at the Root 1990.09
Murder Most Fowl 1994.15
Winning Can Be Murder 1996.10
Crisp, N J
The London Deal 1979.05
Crispin, Edmund
Dead and Dumb 1947.11
Frequent Hearses 1982.11
The Long Divorce 1951.12
Sudden Vengeance 1950.06
Crofts, Freemont Wills
Fear Comes To Chalfont 1942.07
Cromie, Alice
Lucky To Be Alive? 1979.09
Crossman, David
A Show Of Hands 1997.02
Cullen, Robert
Soviet Sources 1990.12
Cumberland, Marten
The House In The Forest 1951.04
Cunningham, A B
The Great Yant Mystery 1943.12
Cunningham, E V
The Case Of The One-Penny Orange 1978.04
The Case Of The Russian Diplomat 1978.13
The Case Of The Russian Diplomat 1978.21
Curtiss, Ursula
Danger: Hospital Zone 1967.02
Dog In The Manger 1982.24
Don't Open That Door 1968.12
*The House on Plymouth Street and
Other Stories* 1985.14
The Iron Cobweb 1953.04
Letter Of Intent 1971.09
The Menace Within 1979.09
Out Of The Dark 1964.09
The Poisoned Orchard 1980.15
The Second Sickle 1950.04
The Stairway 1957.12
Voice Out of Darkness 1948.09
The Wasp 1963.07
Curzon, Clare
All Unwary 1998.11
Close Quarters 1996.06
Past Mischief 1996.15
D'Alton, Martina
Fatal Finish 1983.02
D'Amato, Barbara
Good Cop, Bad Cop 1998.10
Hard Tack 1991.02

Killer.app 1996.19
Dale, Celia
The Deception 1980.15
Daly, Elizabeth
And Dangerous To Know 1949.11
Arrow Pointing Nowhere 1944.05
The Book Of The Crime 1951.06
The Book Of The Dead 1944.09
The Book of the Lion 1948.07
Death And Letters 1950.09
Evidence of Things Seen 1943.09
Night Walk 1948.02
Nothing Can Rescue Me 1943.04
Somewhere In The House 1946.03
The Wrong Way Down 1946.09
Davey, Jocelyn
A Dangerous Liaison 1987.03
Murder In Paradise 1982.19
Davis, Dorothy Salisbury
A Death In The Life 1976.17
Death Of An Old Sinner 1957.07
The Little Brothers 1974.02
Scarlet Night 1980.16
Davis, Frederick C
Another Morgue Heard From 1955.01
Drag The Dark 1953.08
Night Drop 1955.14
Davis, Lindsey
Poseidon's Gold 1994.16
Venus in Copper 1992.04
Davis, Mildred
Tell Them What's-Her-Name Called 1975.04
Three Minutes To Midnight 1972.07
Dawson, Janet
A Credible Threat 1996.16
Don't Turn Your Back on the Ocean 1994.15
DeAndrea, William L
Azrael 1987.14
Killed In Fringe Time 1996.03
Killed In The Act 1982.07
Killed On The Ice 1984.03
Killed With A Passion 1983.11
Killed in Paradise 1988.11
The Lunatic Fringe 1981.07
DeGrave, Philip
Keep the Baby, Faith 1986.20
Dean, Amber
Be Home By Eleven 1973.17
Bullet Proof 1960.06
Collectors Item 1953.05

Deadly Contact 1963.05

Encounter with Evil 1961.05

Dean, S F X

Such Pretty Toys 1982.23

Dean, Spencer

Dishonor Among Thieves 1958.09

The Merchant Of Murder 1959.01

Murder After A Fashion 1961.02

Deighton, Len

Catch A Falling Spy 1977.01

Mamista 1991.08

SS-GB 1979.14

Spy Sinker 1990.13

Spy Story 1974.18

Delving, Michael

Die Like a Man 1970.12

A Shadow Of Himself 1972.06

Smiling the Boy Fell Dead 1967.05

Denham, Bertie

The Man Who Lost His Shadow 1980.07

Dent, Lester

Dead at the Take-Off 1946.06

Lady To Kill 1947.01

Dentinger, Jane

Death Mask 1988.02

First Hit of the Season 1984.15

Derby, Mark

The Big Water 1953.11

Devine, Dominic

Sunk Without a Trace 1980.02

Dewey, Thomas B

As Good As Dead 1946.09

Deadline 1966.11

Death and Taxes 1967.10

Draw The Curtain Close 1948.02

The Girl Who Wasn't There 1960.06

The Love-Death Thing 1970.01

A Sad Song Singing 1964.02

The Taurus Trip 1971.02

Dewhurst, Eileen

Curtain Fall 1982.22

Drink This 1981.18

The House that Jack Built 1984.07

A Nice Little Business 1988.01

Whoever I Am 1983.11

Dibdin, Michael

Blood Rain 2000.01

Cosi Fan Tutti 1999.18

Dead Lagoon 1994.08

The Last Sherlock Holmes Story 1978.20

The Last Sherlock Holmes Story 1978.23

A Long Finish 1999.12

Dickson, Carter

The Curse of the Bronze Lamp 1945.09

He Wouldn't Kill Patience 1944.04

My Late Wives 1946.08

She Died A Lady 1943.03

Disney, Doris Miles

The Chandler Policy 1972.02

Cry For Help 1975.06

The Day Miss Bessie Lewis

Disappeared 1972.16

The Departure Of Mr. Gaudette 1964.12

Did She Fall Or Was She Pushed 1959.10

Do Not Fold, Spindle Or Mutilate 1971.06

Don't Go Into The Woods Today 1974.12

Find the Woman 1963.02

Here Lies... 1963.12

The Hospitality Of The House 1964.05

The Last Straw 1955.02

Method In Madness 1957.06

Money For The Taking 1968.03

My Neighbor's Wife 1958.01

Night of Clear Choice 1967.08

No Next Of Kin 1960.03

Only Couples Need Apply 1973.10

Should Auld Acquaintance 1962.03

Three's A Crowd 1971.10

Trick Or Treat 1955.13

Unappointed Rounds 1957.01

Winifred 1976.08

Disney, Dorothy Cameron

Explosion 1948.05

The Hangman's Tree 1949.08

Dobyns, Stephen

Saratoga Backtalk 1994.06

Saratoga Fleshpot 1995.21

Saratoga Hexameter 1990.04

Saratoga Snapper 1986.18

Saratoga Swimmer 1982.03

Doherty, P C

An Ancient Evil 1995.19

Angel of Death 1990.08

The Assassin in the Greenwood 1994.02

The Crown in Darkness 1988.02

The Devil's Hunt 1998.06

The Prince Of Darkness 1993.07

Satan's Fire 1996.26

Serpent Amongst the Lilies 1990.01

The Song of a Dark Angel 1995.22

Spy in Chancery	1989.10	Durrenmatt, Friedrich	
A Tapestry of Murders	1996.07	*The Judge And His Hangman*	1955.10
A Time For The Death Of A King	1995.11	Eberhart, Mignon G	
A Tournament Of Murders	1997.19	*Another Man's Murder*	1958.02
Dolson, Hildegarde		*Another Woman's House*	1947.05
Beauty Sleep	1977.18	*The Bayou Road*	1979.04
Doss, Jame D		*Call After Midnight*	1965.02
The Shaman Laughs	1995.07	*Casa Madrone*	1980.12
Drachman, Theodore S, M.D.		*The Cup, The Blade Or The Gun*	1961.09
Something For The Birds	1958.07	*Danger Money*	1975.02
Driscoll, Peter		*Danger Money*	1975.18
The Barboza Credentials	1976.19	*Danger Money*	1975.19
In Connection With Kilshaw	1974.08	*Danger Money*	1976.20
Pangolin	1979.08	*Dead Men's Plans*	1952.10
The White Lie Assignment	1975.15	*Deadly is the Diamond*	1958.09
The Wilby Conspiracy	1973.05	*El Rancho Rio*	1971.01
Drummond, Ivor		*Enemy in the House*	1962.12
The Diamonds Of Loreta	1980.10	*Family Affair*	1981.16
A Stench Of Poppies	1979.02	*Family Fortune*	1976.17
Drummond, John Keith		*Family Fortune*	1977.23
'Tis the Season to Be Dying	1988.16	*Family Fortune*	1977.25
Du Bois, Theodora		*Five Passengers From Lisbon*	1946.07
It's Raining Violence	1950.03	*House of Storm*	1949.09
DuBois, Theodora		*Hunt With the Hounds*	1950.10
The Face Of Hate	1949.03	*Jury Of One*	1960.08
Fowl Play	1951.12	*Man Missing*	1954.04
Shannon Terror	1964.08	*Melora*	1959.08
Dukthas, Ann		*Message from Hong Kong*	1969.03
In The Time Of The Poisoned Queen	1998.02	*Murder In Waiting*	1973.13
The Prince Lost To Time	1995.18	*Next of Kin*	1982.20
The Time of Murder at Mayerling	1996.22	*Nine O'Clock Tide*	1978.04
Duncan, Robert L		*Nine O'Clock Tide*	1978.24
Brimstone	1980.20	*Postmark Murder*	1956.04
Dragons At The Gate	1976.02	*R.S.V.P. Murder*	1965.11
Fire Storm	1979.03	*Run Scared*	1963.11
In The Enemy Camp	1985.23	*Two Little Rich Girls*	1972.03
Temple Dogs	1977.16	*Two Little Rich Girls*	1972.18
Dunlap, Susan		*Two Little Rich Girls*	1973.20
As a Favor	1984.07	*The Unknown Quantity*	1953.08
The Bohemian Connection	1985.07	*The White Dress*	1946.10
Diamond in the Buff	1990.16	*With This Ring*	1942.02
A Dinner To Die For	1987.05	*Witness At Large*	1967.03
Not Exactly A Brahmin	1985.23	*Wolf In Man's Clothing*	1943.02
Too Close to the Edge	1987.12	*The Woman On The Roof*	1968.01
Dunn, Carola		Eby, Lois and Fleming, John	
Damsel In Distress	1997.17	*Death Begs The Question*	1952.10
Murder on the Flying Scotsman	1997.03	Eccles, Marjorie	
Winter Garden Mystery	1995.14	*An Accidental Shroud*	1997.20
Dunn, Dorothy		*The Company She Kept*	1996.24
Murder's Web	1950.06	*A Death Of Distinction*	1998.21

The Detective Book Club 1942-2000 Author Index

Killing me softly 1999.23

Eddenden, A E
Murder at the Movies 1996.09

Eden, Matthew
Conquest Before Autumn 1973.16

Edwards, Martin
Eve of Destruction 1998.18

Edwards, Ruth Dudle
Ten Lords A Leaping 1996.12

Egan, Lesley
Against the Evidence 1963.02
The Borrowed Alibi 1962.08
Run To Evil 1963.11

Ehrlich, Max
Reincarnation in Venice 1979.11
Reincarnation in Venice 1979.23

Einstein, Charles
The Blackjack Hijack 1976.12

Elkins, Aaron
Old Bones 1988.05

Elkins, Aaron J
Curses! 1989.01
The Dark Place 1983.16
A Deceptive Clarity 1987.09
Fellowship Of Fear 1983.07
A Glancing Light 1991.05
Make No Bones 1992.02
Murder In The Queen's Armes 1985.18

Elkins, Charlotte and Aaron
A Wicked Slice 1989.02

Elkjer, Thom
Hook, Line And Murder 1998.11

Emerson, Kathy Lynn
Face Down Among The Winchester Geese 1999.06
Face Down In The Marrow-Bone Pie 1997.10
Face Down Upon a Herbal 1998.05

Engel, Howard
City Called July 1987.16
Murder in Montparnasse 1999.15

Erskine, Margaret
The Dead Don't Speak 1955.02
Dead by Now 1954.06
Look Behind You, Lady 1952.12

Eslick, Tom
Tracked in the Whites 1998.08

Estes, Carroll Cox
The Moon Gate 1954.10

Ethan, John B
The Black Gold Murders 1959.08

Evans, Penelope
Freezing 1998.09

Eyre, Elizabeth
Axe for an Abbot 1996.13
Bravo for the Bride 1995.04
Dirge for a Doge 1997.06

Fair, A A
All Grass Isn't Green 1970.05
Bachelors Get Lonely 1961.07
Bats Fly At Dusk 1942.09
Bedrooms Have Windows 1949.02
Beware The Curves 1957.02
Cats Prowl At Night 1943.10
The Count Of Nine 1958.07
Crows Can't Count 1946.05
Cut Thin to Win 1965.05
Double or Quits 1942.03
Fish or Cut Bait 1963.05
Fools Die on Friday 1947.08
Give 'Em The Ax 1944.10
Kept Women Can't Quit 1960.11
Pass The Gravy 1959.03
Shills Can't Cash Chips 1962.03
Some Slips Don't Show 1957.10
Some Women Won't Wait 1953.10
Top Of The Heap 1952.03
Traps Need Fresh Bait 1967.05
Try Anything Once 1962.09
Up For Grabs 1964.05
Widows Wear Weeds 1966.05
You Can Die Laughing 1957.05

Farrell, Henry
Death On The Sixth Day 1961.07
Whatever Happened To Baby Jane? 1960.10

Fawcett, Quinn
Against the Brotherhood 1997.01

Fenisong, Ruth
Dead Yesterday 1952.05
The Lost Caesar 1945.10

Fenwick, Elizabeth
A Long Way Down 1959.03
Poor Harriet 1957.09

Ferguson, Austin
Jet Stream 1974.06

Ferrars, E X
Alive And Dead 1975.12
Alive And Dead 1975.20
Blood Flies Upwards 1977.11
Count The Cost 1957.11
The Crime and the Crystal 1985.14

The Detective Book Club 1942-2000 Author Index

Depart This Life	1958.10
Drowned Rat	1976.04
Enough To Kill A Horse	1956.01
Experiment with Death	1981.20
Frog In The Throat	1981.04
Hanged Man's House	1974.18
A Hobby Of Murder	1995.13
I Met Murder	1986.10
In At The Kill	1979.13
Kill Or Cure	1957.03
Last Will And Testament	1979.03
Last Will And Testament	1979.22
Murders Anonymous	1978.17
No Peace For The Wicked	1966.10
The Other Devil's Name	1986.18
The Pretty Pink Shroud	1978.01
Root Of All Evil	1984.09
Seeing is Believing	1996.07
Skeleton In Search Of A Closet	1983.01
Something Wicked	1984.05
Thinner Than Water	1982.17
Thy Brother Death	1993.08
We Haven't Seen Her Lately	1956.10
Witness Before the Fact	1980.13

Ferrigno, Robert
| *Heartbreaker* | 1999.09 |

Finer, Alex
| *Deepwater* | 1985.10 |

Fischer, Bruno
| *The Hornet's Nest* | 1944.05 |

Fish, Robert L
Always Kill A Stranger	1967.03
Brazilian Sleigh Ride	1966.03
The Bridge That Went Nowhere	1968.05
The Diamond Bubble	1965.05
The Green Hell Treasure	1971.06
A Gross Carriage Of Justice	1979.13
The Hochman Miniatures	1967.10
Isle of Snakes	1963.06
Pursuit	1979.07
Rub-A-Dub-Dub	1971.13
The Shrunken Head	1964.03
Trouble In Paradise	1975.09
The Wager	1974.13
The Xavier Affair	1969.07

Fisher, Steve
| *Saxon's Ghost* | 1969.12 |

Fitzsimmons, Cortland
| *Death Rings a Bell* | 1942.08 |

Fleming, Ian
| *Thunderball* | 1961.08 |

Fleming, Joan
Alas Poor Father	1973.07
Be a Good Boy	1972.08
Every Inch A Lady	1978.10
How To Live Dangerously	1975.08
The Man Who Looked Back	1952.09
You Won't Let Me Finnish	1974.05

Fletcher, Lucille
| *80 Dollars To Stamford* | 1976.06 |

Foglia, Leonard & Richards, David Richards
| *Face Down in the Park* | 1999.07 |

Foley, Rae
An Ape In Velvet	1951.11
Back Door to Death	1963.06
The Barclay Place	1976.03
Bones of Contention	1950.02
The Brownstone House	1974.15
A Calculated Risk	1971.03
Call It Accident	1966.02
Dangerous To Me	1960.01
The Dark Hill	1975.05
Death And Mr. Potter	1955.03
Escape To Fear	1958.04
Fatal Lady	1964.04
Fear of a Stranger	1967.07
The First Mrs. Winston	1973.01
Girl From Nowhere	1949.06
Girl on a High Wire	1970.01
The Hundreth Door	1951.03
It's Murder, Mr Potter	1961.04
The Last Gamble	1957.02
Malice Domestic	1968.07
The Man In The Shadow	1953.02
No Hiding Place	1969.08
No Tears for the Dead	1948.07
Ominous Star	1971.13
One O'Clock At The Gotham	1974.12
Put Out The Light	1976.19
Reckless Lady	1973.16
Repent at Leisure	1962.12
Run For Your Life	1957.04
Scared To Death	1967.03
The Shelton Conspiracy	1967.11
Sleep Without Morning	1972.10
The Slippery Step	1977.13
Suffer A Witch	1965.04
This Woman Wanted	1971.08
Wake The Sleeping Wolf	1952.06
Where Helen Lies	1976.13
Wild Night	1966.08

The Detective Book Club 1942-2000 Author Index

Foote-Smith, Elizabeth
  Gentle Albatross — 1976.18
  Never Say Die — 1977.09
Footner, Hulbert
  Orchids To Murder — 1945.03
Forbes, Stanton
  A Business Of Bodies — 1967.01
  But I Wouldn't Want To Die There — 1972.13
  If Two of Them are Dead — 1968.09
  The Name's Death, Remember Me? — 1970.03
  Relative To Death — 1965.10
  The Sad, Sudden Death Of My Fair Lady — 1971.07
  She Was Only the Sheriff's Daughter — 1970.07
Ford, Leslie
  The Bahamas Murder Case — 1952.04
  The Devil's Stronghold — 1948.08
  The Girl From The Mimosa Club — 1957.06
  Honolulu Story — 1946.08
  Invitation To Murder — 1954.12
  Murder Comes To Eden — 1955.10
  Murder Is The Pay-Off — 1951.04
  The Woman In Black — 1947.07
Forrest, Richard
  The Death At Yew Corner — 1981.02
  Death Through The Looking Glass — 1978.09
  Death Under the Lilacs — 1985.06
  Death in the Willows — 1980.02
  Death on the Mississippi — 1989.09
Foxx, Jack
  Dead Run — 1975.17
Francis, Dick
  Banker — 1983.14
  Bolt — 1987.02
  High Stakes — 1976.08
  High Stakes — 1976.22
  High Stakes — 1976.24
  In The Frame — 1977.11
  In The Frame — 1977.24
  Knockdown — 1975.11
  Knockdown — 1975.18
  Proof — 1985.17
  Reflex — 1981.13
  Reflex — 1981.25
  Slay-Ride — 1974.07
  Smokescreen — 1973.09
  Smokescreen — 1973.20
  Straight — 1990.14
  Twice Shy — 1982.13
Franklin, Max
  Justice Has No Sword — 1953.12

Franklin, Steve
  The Chickens In The Airshaft — 1972.15
Franscell, Ron
  The Deadline — 2000.03
Fraser, Anthea
  The Gospel Makers — 1996.03
  I'll Sing You Two-O — 1996.26
  Motive For Murder — 1997.09
  Pretty Maids all in a Row — 1987.04
  A Shroud for Delilah — 1986.06
  Three, Three, The Rivals — 1995.06
Freeling, Nicolas
  You Who Know — 1994.06
Freeman, R Austin
  The Unconscious Witness — 1942.04
Freemantle, Brian
  Charlie Muffin, USA — 1980.18
Fremlin, Celia
  Appointment With Yesterday — 1973.03
  A Lovely Day To Die — 1984.09
  The Spider-Orchid — 1978.12
Friedman, Kinky
  Armadillos and Old Lace — 1994.09
Frimmer, Steven
  Dead Matter — 1982.06
Frome, David
  Homicide House — 1950.07
Frommer, Sara Hoskinson
  Buried In Quilts — 1994.13
  Murder & Sullivan — 1997.16
  Murder in C Major — 1986.04
  The Vanishing Violinist — 1999.24
Frost, Barbara
  Innocent Bystander — 1955.13
Gage, Edwin
  Phoenix No More — 1979.06
Gallagher, Gale
  I Found Him Dead — 1947.11
Gardiner, Dorothy
  Lion In Wait — 1963.08
  What Crime Is It? — 1956.12
Gardner, Erle Stanley
  The Case Of The Amorous Aunt — 1964.01
  The Case Of The Angry Mourner — 1951.12
  The Case Of The Backward Mule — 1946.08
  The Case Of The Beautiful Beggar — 1965.09
  The Case Of The Bigamous Spouse — 1961.11
  The Case Of The Black-Eyed Blonde — 1944.12
  The Case Of The Black-Eyed Blonde — 1947.12
  The Case Of The Blonde Bonanza — 1962.07

The Detective Book Club 1942-2000 Author Index

The Case Of The Borrowed Brunette	*1947.01*
The Case Of The Borrowed Brunette	*1947.12*
The Case Of The Buried Clock	*1943.06*
The Case Of The Calendar Girl	*1958.11*
The Case Of The Careless Cupid	*1968.09*
The Case Of The Crimson Kiss	*1971.05*
The Case Of The Crooked Candle	*1944.07*
The Case Of The Crying Swallow	*1972.01*
The Case Of The Daring Decoy	*1957.11*
The Case Of The Daring Divorce	*1964.03*
The Case Of The Deadly Toy	*1959.01*
The Case Of The Demure Defendant	*1956.06*
The Case Of The Drowning Duck	*1942.07*
The Case Of The Drowsy Mosquito	*1943.11*
The Case Of The Dubious Bridegroom	*1949.03*
The Case Of The Duplicate Daughter	*1960.07*
The Case Of The Empty Tin	*1942.01*
The Case Of The Fabulous Fake	*1970.01*
The Case Of The Fabulous Fake	*1972.17*
The Case Of The Fan-Dancer's Horse	*1947.06*
The Case Of The Fenced-In Woman	*1973.01*
The Case Of The Fiery Fingers	*1951.07*
The Case Of The Foot-Loose Doll	*1958.05*
The Case Of The Fugitive Nurse	*1954.03*
The Case Of The Gilded Lady	*1956.11*
The Case Of The Glamorous Ghost	*1955.03*
The Case Of The Golddigger's Purse	*1945.07*
The Case Of The Green-Eyed Sister	*1954.01*
The Case Of The Grinning Gorilla	*1953.01*
The Case Of The Half-Wakened Wife	*1945.12*
The Case Of The Half-Wakened Wife	*1947.12*
The Case Of The Hesitant Hostess	*1953.07*
The Case Of The Horrified Heir	*1965.01*
The Case Of The Ice-Cold Hands	*1963.01*
The Case Of The Irate Witness	*1972.06*
The Case Of The Irate Witness	*1972.18*
The Case Of The Lazy Lover	*1947.10*
The Case Of The Lonely Heiress	*1948.05*
The Case Of The Long-Legged Models	*1958.01*
The Case Of The Lucky Loser	*1957.01*
The Case Of The Mischievous Doll	*1963.03*
The Case Of The Moth-Eaten Mink	*1952.08*
The Case Of The Mythical Monkeys	*1959.07*
The Case Of The Negligent Nymph	*1950.01*
The Case Of The Nervous Accomplice	*1955.13*
The Case Of The One-Eyed Witness	*1951.01*
The Case Of The Phantom Fortune	*1964.09*
The Case Of The Postponed Murder	*1973.07*
The Case Of The Postponed Murder	*1973.19*
The Case Of The Queenly Contestant	*1967.07*
The Case Of The Reluctant Model	*1962.01*
The Case Of The Restless Redhead	*1955.01*
The Case Of The Runaway Corpse	*1954.08*
The Case Of The Screaming Woman	*1957.07*
The Case Of The Shapely Shadow	*1961.01*
The Case Of The Singing Skirt	*1959.11*
The Case Of The Smoking Chimney	*1943.03*
The Case Of The Spurious Spinster	*1961.05*
The Case Of The Step-Daughter's Secret	*1963.09*
The Case Of The Sun Bather's Diary	*1955.07*
The Case Of The Terrified Typist	*1956.02*
The Case Of The Troubled Trustee	*1965.03*
The Case Of The Vagabond Virgin	*1948.08*
The Case Of The Waylaid Wolf	*1960.01*
The Case Of The Worried Waitress	*1966.09*
The Case of the Careless Cupid	*1971.15*
The D.A. Breaks A Seal	*1946.02*
The D.A. Breaks An Egg	*1949.12*
The D.A. Calls A Turn	*1944.02*
The D.A. Cooks A Goose	*1942.02*
The D.A. Takes a Chance	*1948.09*
Honest Money	*1991.07*
Two Clues	*1947.04*

Gardner, John

Win, Lose or Die	*1989.14*

Garfield, Brian

Death Sentence	*1976.03*
Death Sentence	*1976.20*
Death Wish	*1973.03*
Hopscotch	*1975.06*
Necessity	*1984.09*
Recoil	*1977.13*
Recoil	*1977.24*
Relentless	*1972.12*
The Romanov Succession	*1975.02*
The Threepersons Hunt	*1974.10*

Garve, Andrew

Boomerang	*1970.11*
By-Line For Murder	*1952.02*
The Case Of Robert Quarry	*1972.11*
Counterstroke	*1978.18*
The End Of The Track	*1956.09*
The Golden Deed	*1960.07*
Home to Roost	*1977.03*
The Late Bill Smith	*1971.12*

The Detective Book Club 1942-2000 Author Index

The Lester Affair	1974.07
Murder Through the Looking Glass	1952.07
Prisoner's Friend	1962.10
A Very Quiet Place	1968.04

Gash, Jonathan

Pearlhanger	1985.13
The Sleepers Of Erin	1983.12
Spend Game	1981.17
The Vatican Rip	1982.09

Gatenby, Rosemary

Hanged For A Sheep	1973.08
The Third Identity	1980.09

Gault, William Campbell

Cat & Mouse	1989.13

George, Theodore

The Deadly Homecoming	1973.04

Gerson, Jack

Death squad London	1989.04

Gieson, Judith Van

Hotshots	1996.23
The Lies That Bind	1993.03

Gilbert, Anthony

After The Verdict	1962.02
And Death Came Too	1956.07
Black Death	1954.02
By Hook or Crook	1947.02
A Case for Mr. Crook	1952.11
Death Against The Clock	1958.04
Death At The Door	1945.03
Death Casts A Long Shadow	1960.01
Death Knocks Three Times	1950.05
Death Lifts The Latch	1946.03
Death Won't Wait	1954.09
Death in the Wrong Room	1948.01
The Fingerprint	1965.06
The Innocent Bottle	1949.04
The Looking Glass Murder	1967.08
Missing From Her Home	1969.08
The Missing Widow	1948.06
Mr. Crook Lifts The Mask	1971.01
Murder Anonymous	1969.02
Murder Comes Home	1951.07
Murder's A Waiting Game	1972.13
Mystery In The Woodshed	1942.07
A Nice Little Killing	1974.09
No Dust In The Attic	1963.09
Out For The Kill	1961.01
Passenger To Nowhere	1966.11
Prelude To Murder	1959.08
A Question Of Murder	1955.10

Riddle of a Lady	1956.11
Ring for a Noose	1964.04
Tenant For The Tomb	1971.10
Uncertain Death	1963.02
The Visitor	1967.12
The Voice	1966.04
The Woman In Red	1943.10
The Wrong Body	1951.11

Gilbert, Michael

After The Fine Weather	1963.08
Anything for a Quiet Life	1990.10
The Black Seraphim	1984.02
The Empty House	1979.14
End-Game	1982.21
He Didn't Mind Danger	1949.09
The Long Journey Home	1985.08
Paint, Gold and Blood	1989.09
The Queen Against Karl Mullen	1991.07

Gill, Bartholomew

Death Drop	1980.10
McGarr At The Dublin Horse Show	1980.07
McGarr On The Cliffs Of Moher	1978.16
McGarr and the Politician's Wife	1977.19

Gill, Josephine Eckert

The House That Died	1955.07

Gillespie, Robert B

The Empress of Coney Island	1986.07
The Last of the Honeywells	1988.12
Print-Out	1983.07

Gilman, Dorothy

The Amazing Mrs. Pollifax	1970.08
The Elusive Mrs. Pollifax	1972.04
Mrs. Pollifax And The Hong Kong Buddha	1985.11
Mrs. Pollifax On Safari	1977.07
Mrs. Pollifax On The China Station	1983.17
Mrs. Pollifax Pursued	1995.17
Mrs. Pollifax and the Lion Killer	1996.07
A Nun In The Closet	1975.11
A Palm For Mrs. Pollifax	1973.15
The Unexpected Mrs. Pollifax	1966.05

Giroux, E X

A Death For A Dodo	1993.01
Death for a Dietician	1989.13
Death for a Double	1990.14

Gleiter, Jan

A House by the side of the road	1998.12
Lie Down With Dogs	1996.14

Godden, Jon

In Her Garden	1981.11

Goldberg, Marshall
Deadly Operation — 1999.08
Intelligence — 2000.03
Goldman, Lawrence
Fall Guy For Murder — 1943.08
Goldstein, Arthur D
Nobody's Sorry He Got Killed — 1976.05
A Person Shouldn't Die Like That — 1972.11
You're Never Too Old To Die — 1974.17
Goldthwaite, Eaton K
Root Of Evil — 1948.04
Goller, Nicholas
Tomorrow's Silence — 1980.18
Gollin, James
Broken Consort — 1990.08
The Philomel Foundation — 1980.06
The Verona Passamezzo — 1985.04
Goodis, David
Nightfall — 1948.04
Of Missing Persons — 1950.09
Goodrum, Charles
The Best Cellar — 1987.07
Carnage of the Realm — 1979.12
Gordon, Alan
Thirteenth Night — 1999.20
Gordons, The
The Big Frame — 1957.08
Captive — 1957.12
Catnapped — 1975.04
Night Before the Wedding — 1969.05
Race for the Golden Tide — 1983.18
Tiger On My Back — 1960.05
Undercover Cat — 1963.10
Gorman, E & Greenberg, M H
Solved — 1991.12
Gosling, Paula
The Dead of Winter — 1996.01
A Few Dying Words — 1994.07
Woman in Red — 1984.10
Wychford Murders — 1986.16
Grace, C L
The Book Of Shadows — 1996.18
Grafton, C W
The Rat Began To Gnaw The Rope — 1943.07
Graham, Caroline
Faithful Unto Death — 1998.09
Granger, Ann
Candle For A Corpse — 1996.15
Flowers For His Funeral — 1995.02
A Touch of Mortality — 1997.18

A Word After Dying — 1998.07
Gray, Malcolm
Look Back on Murder — 1986.13
Green, William M
Avery's Fortune — 1973.02
See How They Run — 1976.10
Greenan, Russell H
The Bric-A-Brac Man — 1977.06
Greenwood, John
The Mind of Mr. Mosley — 1987.07
The Missing Mr. Mosley — 1985.09
What, Me, Mr. Mosley? — 1988.17
Greenwood, L B
Sherlock Holmes and the Case Of The Raleigh Legacy — 1986.14
Sherlock Holmes and the Case of Sabina Hall — 1988.11
Sherlock Holmes and the Thistle of Scotland — 1989.06
Grew, William
Doubles In Death — 1953.09
Grimes, Martha
The Five Bells And Bladebone — 1987.05
The Man With A Load Of Mischief — 1981.22
The Old Fox Deceiv'd — 1982.23
Griswold, George
A Checkmate for the Colonel — 1953.06
The Pinned Man — 1955.07
Gruber, Frank
Beagle Scented Murder — 1947.03
Bridge Of Sand — 1963.10
Brothers of Silence — 1962.04
The Etruscan Bull — 1969.06
The Gift Horse — 1943.01
The Gold Gap — 1968.04
The Greek Affair — 1964.10
The Leather Duke — 1949.08
The Limping Goose — 1954.14
Little Hercules — 1966.02
The Lock and the Key — 1948.10
The Lonesome Badger — 1954.05
The Mighty Blockhead — 1942.02
Run, Fool, Run — 1966.12
The Scarlet Feather — 1948.06
The Spanish Prisoner — 1970.05
The Twilight Man — 1967.06
The Whispering Master — 1947.09
Guthrie Jr., A B
The Genuine Article — 1977.20
Haddad, C A
The Academic Factor — 1980.18

Operation Apricot — 1978.06

Hagen, Miriam-Ann
Dig Me Later — 1949.08

Haggard, William
The Antagonists — 1964.10
The Conspirators — 1968.06
A Cool Day for Killing — 1969.04
The High Wire — 1964.02
The Kinsmen — 1975.05
The Median Line — 1981.20
The Mischief Makers — 1982.21
The Money Men — 1982.05
The Notch On The Knife — 1973.18
The Powder Barrel — 1966.01
The Power House — 1967.06
The Protectors — 1973.04
The Unquiet Sleep — 1963.03
Venetian Blind — 1960.06
Visa To Limbo — 1980.08
Yesterday's Enemy — 1977.10

Hall, Robert L
Murder By The Waters — 1995.13

Hall, Robert Lee
Benjamin Franklin Takes the Case — 1988.18
Benjamin Franklin and a Case of Artful Murder — 1994.07
London Blood — 1997.14
Murder At Drury Lane — 1993.04
Murder at San Simeon — 1988.16

Hallahan, William H
Catch Me, Kill Me — 1977.16
Catch Me, Kill Me — 1978.23
Keeper Of The Children — 1979.04

Halliday, Brett
The Blonde Cried Murder — 1956.07
Blood on the Black Market — 1943.12
Murder Is My Business — 1945.05
Murder Wears A Mummer's Mask — 1943.04

Hamilton, Donald
Murder Twice Told — 1950.12

Hamilton, Nan
Shape of Fear — 1986.20

Hammond, Gerald
Adverse Report — 1988.09
Bloodlines — 1998.03
Carriage of Justice — 1995.15
Fair Game — 1982.19
Mad Dogs and Scotsmen — 1996.16
Pursuit Of Arms — 1986.19
Sink Or Swim — 1997.02

Sting In The Tail — 1995.20
Thin Air — 1994.13
Twice Bitten — 1999.03

Hansen, Robert P
Back To The Wall — 1958.02
Deadly Purpose — 1958.12
Mark Three For Murder — 1957.02
Murder is Where You Find It — 1956.06
There's Always A Payoff — 1960.02
Walk A Wicked Mile — 1955.08

Hanson, Rick
Extreme Odds — 1999.14

Hardwick, Mollie
The Bandersnatch — 1989.08

Hardy, William
A Little Sin — 1958.10
Malice Domestic — 1957.03

Harper, David
Hijacked — 1971.01

Harrington, Jonathan
The Death Of Cousin Rose — 1996.14
The Second Sorrowful Mystery — 1999.04

Harrington, William
Columbo: The Game Show Killer — 1996.16
Columbo: The Helter Skelter Murders — 1994.12
Columbo: the Glitter Murder — 1997.11

Harris, Charlaine
A Fool And His Honey — 1999.01

Harris, John Norman
The Weird World Of Wes Beattie — 1963.10

Harrison, Harry
Montezuma's Revenge — 1973.02

Harriss, Will
The Bay Psalm Book Murder — 1983.15

Hart, Roy
A Deadly Schedule — 1994.05
A Pretty Place for Murder — 1988.16
Robbed Blind — 1990.09

Hathaway, Robin
The Doctor Digs A Grave — 1998.21

Hawkins, John and Ward
Death Watch — 1958.09

Hays, Sue Brown
Go Down, Death — 1946.06

Heal, Anthony
Man In The Middle — 1980.22

Healey, Ben
Midnight Ferry to Venice — 1982.15

Healy, Jeremiah
The Only Good Lawyer — 1998.17

The Detective Book Club 1942-2000 Author Index

Healy, R Austin
  Sweetfeed — 1997.13
Hebden, Mark
  The Dark Side of the Island — 1974.04
  Death Set to Music — 1983.13
  The Eyewitness — 1967.11
  Pel And The Faceless Corpse — 1982.23
  Pel and the Pirates — 1987.06
  A Pride Of Dolphins — 1975.06
Heber, R W
  Murder at Wittenham Park — 1997.01
Henderson, M R
  By Reason Of — 1986.08
Henissart, Paul
  The Winter Spy — 1977.12
Henry, April
  Circles Of Confusion — 1999.12
Henry, Sue
  Murder on the Iditarod Trail — 1991.06
Hensley, Joe L
  Grim City — 1994.04
  Outcasts — 1981.11
  Robak's Witch — 1997.19
Herber, William
  Death Paints a Portrait — 1958.08
Hervey, Evelyn
  The Man of Gold — 1985.20
Hess, Joan
  Dear Miss Demeanor — 1987.13
Hewens, Frank E
  The Murder Of The Dainty-Footed Model — 1968.03
Heyes, Douglas
  The 12th Of Never — 1963.11
Highsmith, Patricia
  The Boy Who Followed Ripley — 1980.20
  Ripley's Game — 1974.08
Hill, Donna
  Murder Uptown — 1992.03
Hill, Peter
  The Enthusiast — 1979.12
Hill, Reginald
  Blood Sympathy — 1994.01
  Born Guilty — 1995.23
  A Killing Kindness — 1981.15
  Killing the Lawyers — 1997.11
Hillerman, Tony
  The Blessing Way — 1970.10
  The Dark Wind — 1982.05
  The Fly On The Wall — 1972.03

  The Ghostway — 1985.05
  People Of Darkness — 1981.02
  Skinwalkers — 1987.14
  Talking God — 1989.11
  A Thief Of Time — 1989.12
Hilton, John Buxton
  Displaced Person — 1988.04
  Green Frontier — 1982.15
  Moondrop to Murder — 1986.08
  Slickensides: A Derbyshire Mystery — 1987.08
  Some Run Crooked — 1978.19
Hinxman, Margaret
  The Night They Murdered Chelsea — 1985.19
Hitchens, Bert and Dolores
  The Man Who Followed Women — 1960.05
Hitchens, Dolores
  The Bank With The Bamboo Door — 1965.06
  The Baxter Letters — 1971.12
  Beat Back The Tide — 1954.06
  The Man Who Cried All The Way Home — 1967.04
Hitt, Jack
  Perfect Murder — 1991.04
Holbrook, Marion
  Crime Wind — 1945.05
Holden, Genevieve
  Deadlier Than The Male — 1961.08
  Killer Loose! — 1953.06
  Sound An Alarm — 1954.05
Holding, Elisabeth Sanxay
  The Blank Wall — 1948.01
  The Innocent Mrs. Duff — 1946.04
  Lady Killer — 1942.04
  Widow's Mite — 1953.04
Holme, Timothy
  At the Lake of Sudden Death — 1987.01
  A Funeral Of Gondolas — 1983.11
  The Neapolitan Streak — 1981.03
Holt, Hazel
  Mrs. Mallory investigates — 1990.03
  Mrs. Malory and the Only Good Lawyer — 1998.25
  The Shortest Journey — 1994.07
Holton, Leonard
  A Corner Of Paradise — 1977.07
  Deliver Us From Wolves — 1963.04
  The Devil to Play — 1974.03
  Flowers by Request — 1964.04
  The Mirror of Hell — 1972.09
  Out Of The Depths — 1966.12

The Detective Book Club 1942-2000 Author Index

A Pact With Satan — 1960.09
A Problem in Angels — 1970.03
The Secret Of The Doubting Saint — 1961.12
A Touch Of Jonah — 1968.12

Holtzer, Susan
  Black Diamond — 1997.05
  Bleeding Maize and Blue — 1996.08
  Curly Smoke — 1995.22
Homes, Geoffrey
  Six Silver Handles — 1944.06
Horrock, Henry
  Potomac Fever — 1999.16
Hough Jr., John
  The Guardian — 1975.11
Hubbard, P M
  High Tide — 1970.12
  The Holm Oaks — 1966.06
  The Tower — 1967.10
Huff, T E
  Meet A Dark Stranger — 1974.11
Huggins, Roy
  The Double Take — 1946.01
  Too Late For Tears — 1947.09
Hughes, Dorothy B
  The Blackbirder — 1943.12
  The Delicate Ape — 1944.06
  Dread Journey — 1945.09
Hunt, Kyle
  Kill Once, Kill Twice — 1957.01
Hunt, Richard
  Murder Benign — 1996.05
Hunter, Alan
  Gently Between The Tides — 1983.10
Hunter, David
  The Dancing Savior — 1999.03
Huntsberry, William E
  Oscar Mooney's Head — 1961.06
Huston, H C
  With Murder For Some — 1953.08
Huxley, Elspeth
  African Poison Murders — 1988.18
Hymers, John
  Utter Death — 1954.03
Iams, Jack
  Do Not Murder Before Christmas — 1950.03
  What Rhymes With Murder? — 1950.07
Inchbald, Peter
  Short Break in Venice — 1984.10
Innes, Hammond
  The Big Footprints — 1977.17

The Black Tide — 1983.08
The Golden Soak — 1973.14
High Stand — 1988.08
Medusa — 1988.13
North Star — 1975.08
Solomons Seal — 1981.08
Innes, Michael
  Dead Man's Shoes — 1954.12
Irish, William
  Deadline at Dawn — 1944.03
  Eyes That Watch You — 1952.12
  Phantom Lady — 1942.06
  Strangler's Serenade — 1951.06
Irvine, Robert
  Hosanna Shout — 1995.10
  Pillar Of Fire — 1995.18
Jackson, Giles
  Court Of Shadows — 1943.07
Jaffe, Jody
  In Colt Blood — 1998.15
James, Bill
  Gospel — 1999.25
  The Lolita Man — 1999.11
  Roses, Roses — 1999.18
  Top Banana — 1999.21
James, Breni
  Night Of The Kill — 1961.09
James, P D
  Death of an Expert Witness — 1978.07
  Death of an Expert Witness — 1978.21
  Death of an Expert Witness — 1978.24
  Innocent Blood — 1980.17
  Original Sin — 1995.17
  The Skull Beneath The Skin — 1983.05
Jeffers, H Paul
  Murder on Mike — 1985.21
Jeffries, Roderic
  Almost Murder — 1986.01
  An Arcadian Death — 1996.01
  An Artistic Way To Go — 1997.02
  Dead Clever — 1989.03
  Death Takes Time — 1994.14
  A Maze Of Murders — 1998.13
  Murder Begets Murder — 1980.03
  Relatively Dangerous — 1987.13
  Too Clever By Half — 1990.13
  Unseemly End — 1982.14
Jobson, Hamilton
  To Die A Little — 1979.16
John, Owen
  Sabotage — 1973.17

The Detective Book Club 1942-2000 Author Index

Johns, Veronica Parker
Murder by the Day — 1953.07

Johnston, Velda
Along a Dark Path — 1967.09
Deveron Hall — 1977.08
The Etruscan Smile — 1977.13
The Etruscan Smile — 1977.23
The Face In The Shadows — 1971.14
The Frenchman — 1976.11
The Frenchman — 1976.22
The Hour Before Midnight — 1978.11
The Hour Before Midnight — 1979.22
The House On The Left Bank — 1975.03
A Howling In The Woods — 1969.01
I Came to a Castle — 1970.02
I Came to the Highlands — 1974.10
The Light in the Swamp — 1971.04
The Mourning Tree — 1972.05
The People From The Sea — 1980.01
The People on the Hill — 1971.05
The Phantom Cottage — 1970.06
A Presence In An Empty Room — 1980.09
The Silver Dolphin — 1979.07
The Silver Dolphin — 1979.23
The White Pavilion — 1974.01

Jones, D J H
The Buchan Papers — 1997.10
Murder at the MLA — 1993.09

Jordan, Jennifer
Murder Under The Mistletoe — 1989.08

Jovanovich, William
Money Trail — 1990.14

Kaminsky, Stuart
Lieberman's Law — 1996.04

Kaminsky, Stuart M
Dancing in the Dark — 1996.01
Down For The Count — 1985.03
Poor Butterfly — 1990.12
The Rockford Files: Devils On My Doorstep — 1998.21
The Rockford Files: The Green Bottle — 1996.25
Tomorrow Is Another Day — 1995.11

Kane, Henry
Conceal And Disguise — 1967.01
Laughter In The Alehouse — 1968.08
The Midnight Man — 1966.09

Karl, M S
Death Notice — 1990.03
Killer's Ink — 1988.02

Katz, Jon
Death Row — 1999.20

Keating, H R F
Asking Questions — 1997.03
The Bad Detective — 1999.24
Bats Fly Up for Inspector Ghote — 1974.16
The Body in the Billiard Room — 1987.15
Cheating Death — 1994.02
Dead on Time — 1989.14
Filmi, Filmi, Inspector Ghote — 1977.17
Go West, Inspector Ghote — 1981.13
The Good Detective — 1995.12
Hard Detective — 2000.01
The Iciest Sin — 1990.13
Inspector Ghote Breaks An Egg — 1971.14
Inspector Ghote Draws The Line — 1979.14
Inspector Ghote Goes By Train — 1972.15
Inspector Ghote Trusts The Heart — 1973.13
Mrs. Craggs: Crimes Cleaned Up — 1986.02
A Remarkable Case Of Burglary — 1976.15
A Rush For The Ultimate — 1983.01
The Sheriff Of Bombay — 1984.13
Under a Monsoon Cloud — 1986.21

Keech, Scott
Ciphered — 1980.11

Keith, Carlton
The Hiding Place — 1965.07
Missing, Presumed Dead — 1961.11
A Taste Of Sangria — 1968.10

Kelland, Clarence Budington
The Artless Heiress — 1962.05
Death Keeps A Secret — 1956.05
The Great Mail Robbery — 1951.10
The Key Man — 1952.09
Murder Makes An Entrance — 1955.09
The Nameless Corpse — 1957.08
The Sinister Strangers — 1961.12
Stolen Goods — 1950.11
Where There's Smoke — 1959.05

Kelly, Lelia
Presumption of Guilt — 1998.18

Kelly, Susan
And Soon I'll Come to Kill You — 1991.08

Kelner, Toni L P
Tight as a Tick — 1998.19

Kelsey, Vera
Whisper Murder! — 1946.03

Kemprecos, Paul
Bluefin Blues — 1997.15

Kendrick, Baynard
The Aluminum Turtle — 1960.08

Hot Red Money 1959.11
Out Of Control 1945.08
Reservations For Death 1957.05
Kenrick, Tony
Glitterbug 1991.12
A Tough One to Lose 1972.16
King, Pauline
Snares Of The Enemy 1986.19
King, Peter
Dying on the Vine 1998.08
The Gourmet Detective 1996.17
King, Rufus
Lethal Lady 1948.04
King-Wente, Sami
Baby Girl 1998.23
Kirk, Michael
All Other Perils 1975.10
Cargo Risk 1981.06
A Cut In Diamonds 1986.09
Dragonship 1977.12
Mayday From Malaga 1983.16
Salvage Job 1979.04
Kirk, Russell
The Old House Of Fear 1961.10
Kittredge, Mary
Kill or Cure 1995.14
Murder in Mendocino 1987.10
Knight, Clifford
The Affair Of The Dead Stranger 1944.11
The Affair Of The Fainting Butler 1943.11
Affair Of The Jade Monkey 1943.05
The Affair of the Splintered Heart 1942.08
Dark Abyss 1949.01
Death And The Little Brother 1952.08
Knight, Kathleen Moore
Akin To Murder 1953.04
The Bass Derby Murder 1950.04
Beauty Is A Beast 1959.06
Death Goes to a Reunion 1952.07
Dying Echo 1949.05
High Rendezvous 1954.07
Intrigue For Empire 1944.10
Invitation To Vengeance 1961.01
Port Of Seven Strangers 1945.11
The Robineau Look 1955.05
The Silent Partner 1951.05
Stream Sinister 1945.04
Three Of Diamonds 1953.11
The Trouble At Turkey Hill 1946.04
Valse Macabre 1952.11

Knotts, Raymond
And the Deep Blue Sea 1944.06
Knox, Bill
Blacklight 1968.02
Bloodtide 1983.12
Blueback 1970.06
Bombship 1980.21
The Crossfire Killings 1986.02
Dead Man's Mooring 1988.01
Devilweed 1966.08
Figurehead 1969.03
The Hanging Tree 1984.05
Hellspout 1977.04
A Killing In Antiques 1981.24
Live Bait 1979.18
Rally to Kill 1975.17
Seafire 1972.03
Stormtide 1973.11
Wavecrest 1985.23
Whitewater 1974.17
Witchrock 1978.10
Koch, Ed
Murder On Broadway 1996.08
Koch, Edward I
The Senator Must Die 1998.01
Kruger, Mary
Masterpiece of Murder 1996.06
No Honeymoon For Death 1995.12
Kruger, Paul
Weave a Wicked Web 1967.09
Kyle, Duncan
Flight Into Fear 1972.14
Terror's Cradle 1975.04
LaRosa, Linda J and Tannenbaum, Barry
The Random Factor 1978.19
Land, Myrick
Last Flight 1975.13
Landrum, Graham
*The Historical Society Murder
  Mystery* 1996.18
Sensational Music Club Mystery 1995.03
Landrum, Graham G & Landrum, R G
The Garden Club Mystery 1998.24
Langton, Jane
Emily Dickinson Is Dead 1984.11
God in Concord 1992.02
Good and Dead 1986.21
Natural Enemy 1982.10
Lanham, Edwin
Passage to Danger 1962.06

Lariar, Lawrence
  The Girl With the Frightened Eyes — 1945.12
  The Man With the Lumpy Nose — 1944.07
Laurence, Janet
  Death at the Table — 1997.18
Law, Janice
  Backfire — 1994.14
  The Big Payoff — 1976.05
  Cross-check — 1997.12
  Death Under Par — 1981.05
  Gemini Trip — 1978.02
  The Shadow Of The Palms — 1980.12
  Under Orion — 1978.19
Lawrence, Hilda
  Blood Upon The Snow — 1945.02
  Death of a Doll — 1947.03
  Duet of Death — 1949.05
  The Pavilion — 1946.02
Layne, Marion Margery
  The Balloon Affair — 1982.02
Leather, Edwin
  The Mozart Score — 1979.20
  The Vienna Elephant — 1978.05
Leather, Sir Edward
  The Duveen Letter — 1980.19
Lee, Barbara
  Dead Man's Fingers:A Chesapeake
    Bay mystery — 1999.04
  Death in Still Waters — 1995.05
  Final Closing — 1997.09
Lemarchand, Elizabeth
  The Affacombe Affair — 1985.04
  Change For The Worse — 1981.15
  Light Through Glass — 1986.11
  Troubled Waters — 1983.02
Leonard, Charles
  Search for a Scientist — 1948.01
Leonard, Constance
  The Other Maritha — 1972.09
Letton, Jennette
  Allegra's Child — 1969.07
  Incident at Hendon — 1968.04
Lewin, Michael Z
  Family Business — 1995.09
  Missing Woman — 1981.23
  Night Cover — 1976.15
Lewis, Roy
  A Blurred Reality — 1985.02
  The Cross Bearer — 1995.06
  The Manuscript Murders — 1982.18

  Most Cunning Workmen — 1985.10
  A Secret Dying — 1993.06
  Where Agents Fear to Tread — 1984.14
  A Wolf by the Ears — 1973.09
Linklater, J Lane
  Black Opal — 1947.11
  Shadow For A Lady — 1947.05
Linscott, Gillian
  Crown Witness — 1995.18
  Dance on Blood — 1998.05
  Dead Man's Sweetheart — 1997.04
  An Easy Day for a Lady — 1995.23
  Whiff of Sulphur — 1987.03
Lipinski, Thomas
  A Picture of Her Tombstone — 1996.11
Little, Constance and Gwyneth
  The Black Iris — 1953.03
Livingston, Nancy
  Death in a Distant Land — 1988.09
  Incident at Parga — 1988.03
Llewellyn, Caroline
  The Lady Of The Labyrinth — 1990.11
  Masks of Rome — 1988.15
Llewellyn, Sam
  Deadeye — 1991.03
  Death Roll — 1989.04
Lockridge, Frances and Richard
  Death On The Aisle — 1942.04
  Death Takes a Bow — 1943.08
  Hanged For A Sheep — 1942.09
  Killing the Goose — 1944.03
  Murder Within Murder — 1946.02
  Murder is Served — 1949.01
  Payoff For The Banker — 1945.04
  A Pinch Of Poison — 1942.01
  Quest of the Bogeyman — 1964.03
  Untidy Murder — 1947.10
Lockridge, Richard
  Death In A Sunny Place — 1972.10
  The Tenth Life — 1977.22
  The Tenth Life — 1978.03
  Troubled Journey — 1970.04
Lockridge, Richard and Frances
  I Want to Go Home — 1948.06
  Spin Your Web Lady — 1949.04
Lorac, E C R
  Accident by Design — 1951.09
  I Could Murder Her — 1952.04
  Place For A Poisoner — 1949.06
Lord, Garland
  Murder with Love — 1944.01

The Detective Book Club 1942-2000 Author Index

Lovell, Marc
  Apple Spy In The Sky — 1983.10
  Good Spies Don't Grow On Trees — 1986.18
  Spy On The Run — 1982.22
  The Spy Who Barked In The Night — 1986.15
  The Spy Who Got His Feet Wet — 1985.22
Lovesey, Peter
  Bertie And The Crime Of Passion — 1994.08
Lowe, Kenneth
  No Tears For Shirley Minton — 1956.03
Luard, Nicholas
  The Orion Line — 1977.02
Lyall, Gavin
  The Secret Servant — 1981.03
MacDonald, John D
  A Deadly Shade of Gold — 1975.01
  A Deadly Shade of Gold — 1975.19
  The Deep Blue Good-By — 1975.12
  The Deep Blue Good-By — 1976.21
  The Dreadful Lemon Sky — 1975.03
  The Dreadful Lemon Sky — 1976.21
  The Dreadful Lemon Sky — 1976.23
  The Empty Copper Sea — 1978.14
  The Empty Copper Sea — 1978.23
  Free Fall in Crimson — 1981.09
  The Green Ripper — 1979.21
  Nightmare In Pink — 1976.04
  Nightmare In Pink — 1976.21
  One Fearful Yellow Eye — 1977.23
  One Fearful Yellow Eye — 1978.01
  Purple Place for Dying — 1977.03
  Slam the Big Door — 1987.15
  The Turquoise Lament — 1974.01
  The Turquoise Lament — 1974.19
MacDonald, Philip
  Something To Hide — 1953.02
MacGregor, T J
  The Seventh Sense — 1999.19
MacKenzie, Donald
  Nobody Here By That Name — 1988.08
  Raven And The Ratcatcher — 1977.09
  Raven Settles a Score — 1979.01
  Raven and the Paperhangers — 1981.08
  Raven's Shadow — 1985.05
  A Savage State Of Grace — 1988.05
MacLeod, Charlotte
  The Curse Of The Giant Hogweed — 1985.15
  The Luck Runs Out — 1980.03
  Rest You Merry — 1979.06
MacLeod, Robert
  The Iron Sanctuary — 1968.06

MacPherson, Rett
  Family Skeletons — 1997.06
  Veiled Antiquity — 1998.20
Macdonald, Ross
  The Ferguson Affair — 1961.02
  Lew Archer Private Investigator — 1977.21
  The Underground Man — 1971.07
Mace, Merlda
  Headlong For Murder — 1943.06
  Motto For Murder — 1943.11
Mackay, Amanda
  Death Is Academic — 1977.05
  Death On The Eno — 1982.02
Mackenzie, Donald
  Raven After Dark — 1980.04
  Raven And The Kamikaze — 1978.02
  Raven's Longest Night — 1984.02
  Raven's Revenge — 1982.12
  The Spreewald Collection — 1975.10
Madden, E S
  Craig's Spur — 1963.07
Magee, Bill and Schenck, Craig
  Columbo and the Samurai Sword — 1980.02
Malcolm-Smith, George
  Come Out, Come Out — 1965.11
  The Lady Finger — 1962.11
Maling, Arthur
  Bent Man — 1975.16
  Decoy — 1970.02
  Go-Between — 1971.03
  The Koberg Link — 1980.05
  Loophole — 1971.13
  Lucky Devil — 1978.11
  The Rheingold Route — 1979.10
  Ripoff — 1976.11
  Schroeder's Game — 1977.15
  A Taste Of Treason — 1983.17
Maness, Larry
  Strangler — 1998.24
Mantell, Laurie
  Murder and Chips — 1982.14
Maron, Margaret
  Bloody Kin — 1985.02
  Death in Blue Folders — 1985.22
  Death of a Butterfly — 1984.06
Marric, J J
  Gideon's Art — 1972.05
  Gideon's Art — 1972.18
  Gideon's Drive — 1977.04
  Gideon's Fog — 1975.05

The Detective Book Club 1942-2000 Author Index

Gideon's Fog	*1975.20*
Gideon's Force	*1985.06*
Gideon's Law	*1986.03*
Gideon's Men	*1973.01*
Gideon's Press	*1974.01*
Gideon's Way	*1986.17*
Marsh, Ngaio	
Black As He's Painted	*1974.13*
Died in the Wool	*1945.07*
False Scent	*1960.05*
Singing In The Shrouds	*1958.06*
Marshall, Evan	
Missing Marlene	*1999.13*
Marshall, William	
The Hatchet Man	*1977.09*
Manila Bay	*1986.12*
Marston, Edward	
The Fair Maid Of Bohemia	*1997.07*
The Laughing Hangman	*1996.24*
The Merry Devils	*1990.07*
The Roaring Boy	*1995.20*
Martin, A E	
Death In The Limelight	*1946.04*
The Outsiders	*1945.06*
Martin, Lee	
Bird In A Cage	*1995.22*
A Conspiracy of Strangers	*1986.11*
Death Warmed Over	*1988.13*
Deficit Ending	*1990.10*
Genealogy of Murder	*1996.02*
Inherited Murder	*1994.01*
Too Sane a Murder	*1984.06*
Martin, Robert	
A Key To The Morgue	*1959.09*
Killer Among Us	*1959.02*
Martin, Valerie	
Italian Fever	*1999.11*
Mason, Michael	
71 Hours	*1972.12*
Mason, Sara Elizabeth	
The Whip	*1948.07*
Mason, Van Wyck	
Maracaibo Mission	*1966.01*
The Rio Casino Intrigue	*1942.03*
Trouble in Burma	*1962.09*
Zanzibar Intrigue	*1963.12*
Masterson, Whit	
711 - Officer Needs Help	*1966.01*
All Through The Night	*1955.11*
The Dark Fantastic	*1959.07*
Dead, She Was Beautiful	*1955.06*
The Death of Me Yet	*1970.12*
The Gravy Train	*1971.11*
A Hammer In His Hand	*1960.04*
Hunter Of The Blood	*1977.08*
The Last One Kills	*1969.10*
The Man With Two Clocks	*1974.11*
The Man on a Nylon String	*1963.06*
Play Like You're Dead	*1967.11*
A Shadow In The Wild	*1957.06*
The Slow Gallows	*1979.13*
The Undertaker Wind	*1973.15*
Why She Cries, I Do Not Know	*1973.04*
Matheson, Richard	
A Stir Of Echoes	*1958.06*
Mathews, D L	
The Fatal Amateur	*1959.05*
Reach Of Fear	*1958.10*
A Very Welcome Death	*1961.10*
Matthews, Alex	
Vendetta's Victim	*1998.16*
Wanton's web	*1999.09*
Maxwell, A E	
Money Burns	*1991.09*
Mayo, J K	
The Hunting Season	*1985.09*
McBain, Ed	
Ax	*1964.11*
Fuzz	*1968.10*
Hail, Hail, The Gang's All Here	*1971.08*
Jigsaw	*1970.07*
Sadie When She Died	*1972.16*
Shotgun	*1969.11*
McBriarty, Douglas	
Whitewater VJ	*1987.11*
McClintick, Malcolm	
The Key	*1987.08*
Mary's Grave	*1987.10*
McCloy, Helen	
Alias Basil Willing	*1951.09*
Burn This	*1980.24*
A Change of Heart	*1973.09*
Cue For Murder	*1942.09*
Do Not Disturb	*1943.07*
The Goblin Market	*1944.03*
He Never Came Back	*1954.13*
Long Body	*1956.01*
The One That Got Away	*1946.01*
She Walks Alone	*1948.09*
Two-Thirds Of A Ghost	*1957.03*

The Detective Book Club 1942-2000 Author Index

McCollum, Robert
And Then They Die — 1985.10

McConnaughey, James
Three For The Money — 1954.07

McCormick, Claire
Murder in Cowboy Bronze — 1985.02

McDonald, Gregory
Fletch Reflected — 1994.08

McDougald, Roman
The Deaths Of Lora Karen — 1944.05

McGerr, Pat
Fatal In My Fashion — 1954.14

McGerr, Patricia
Is There a Traitor in the House? — 1965.01

McGovern, James
The Berlin Couriers — 1960.09

McGown, Jill
Shred of Evidence — 1996.09

McGurk, Slater
The Big Dig — 1968.07

McInerny, Ralph
Cause and Effect — 1987.13
Let Us Prey — 1982.14
Savings And Loam — 1990.11
Search Committee — 1991.04

McInerny, Ralph M
Irish Tenure — 1999.22

McKinney, Meagan
In the dark — 1999.10

McKinney, Mel
Where There's Smoke — 1999.22

McLarty, Nancy
Chain of Death — 1962.05

McMahon, Thomas Patrick
Jink — 1971.12

McMullen, Mary
The Bad-News Man — 1986.02
Better Off Dead — 1982.09
A Country Kind Of Death — 1975.16
A Dangerous Funeral — 1977.16
Death By Bequest — 1978.04
Funny, Jonas, You Don't Look Dead — 1977.02
The Man With Fifty Complaints — 1979.01
Something Of The Night — 1981.04
Until Death Do Us Part — 1983.04
Welcome To The Grave — 1979.08

McQuillan, Karin
The Cheetah Chase — 1994.03
Deadly Safari — 1990.03

Mccloy, Helen
Through A Glass, Darkly — 1950.08

Meek, M R D
Hang The Consequences — 1985.09
Loose connection — 1989.04
A Mouthful of Sand — 1989.08
Postscript to Murder — 1997.16
Touch And Go — 1993.07
Worm of Doubt — 1988.03

Meier, Leslie
Back To School Murder — 1998.13
Valentine murder — 1999.10

Melville, James
The Bogus Buddha — 1990.05
The Death Ceremony — 1985.18
Death of a Daimyo — 1985.01
Go Gently, Gaijin — 1988.08
A Haiku for Hanae — 1989.09
Kimono for a Corpse — 1988.12
The Reluctant Ronin — 1988.10
Sayonara, Sweet Amaryllis — 1985.19
A Sort of Samurai — 1982.15

Melville, Jennie
A Death in the Family — 1995.08
Morbid Kitchen — 1996.09
Whoever Has the Heart — 1994.10

Menkes, John
Angry Puppet Syndrome — 1999.02

Meynell, Lawrence
The Thirteen Trumpeters — 1979.02

Michaels, Barbara
Be Buried In The Rain — 1986.03
The Grey Beginning — 1984.12
The Sea Kings' Daughter — 1976.09
Someone in the House — 1982.01
Stitches in Time — 1995.23
Wait for What Will Come — 1978.20
Wait for What Will Come — 1978.22
The Walker In Shadows — 1980.05
The Wizard's Daughter — 1981.08

Miles, Graham
Evil Mark — 1986.07

Miles, John
The Night Hunters — 1973.13

Millar, Margaret
Ask For Me Tomorrow — 1977.04
Beyond This Point Are Monsters — 1970.11
Fire Will Freeze — 1944.04
How Like An Angel — 1962.10
The Listening Walls — 1959.09
The Murder Of Miranda — 1979.10
A Stranger In My Grave — 1961.03

The Detective Book Club 1942-2000 Author Index

<table>
<tbody>
<tr><td>Vanish In An Instant</td><td>1953.02</td><td>Naslund, Sena Jeter</td><td></td></tr>
<tr><td>Millhauser, Bertram</td><td></td><td>Sherlock in Love</td><td>1993.03</td></tr>
<tr><td>Whatever Goes Up</td><td>1945.05</td><td>Nelson, Hugh Lawrence</td><td></td></tr>
<tr><td>Mitchell, Gladys</td><td></td><td>The Fence</td><td>1953.07</td></tr>
<tr><td>The Death-Cap Dancers</td><td>1982.06</td><td>Gold In Every Grave</td><td>1951.11</td></tr>
<tr><td>St Peter's Finger</td><td>1987.14</td><td>Kill With Care</td><td>1954.02</td></tr>
<tr><td>Mitchell, Kay</td><td></td><td>The Sleep Is Deep</td><td>1953.01</td></tr>
<tr><td>A Rage of Innocents</td><td>1998.20</td><td>Neri, Kris</td><td></td></tr>
<tr><td>Morice, Anne</td><td></td><td>Revenge of the Gypsy Queen</td><td>1999.05</td></tr>
<tr><td>Dead On Cue</td><td>1985.11</td><td>Neville, Margot</td><td></td></tr>
<tr><td>Death of a Heavenly Twin</td><td>1975.01</td><td>Murder of a Nymph</td><td>1950.10</td></tr>
<tr><td>Death of a Wedding Guest</td><td>1976.14</td><td>Murder of the Well-Beloved</td><td>1954.01</td></tr>
<tr><td>Design for Dying</td><td>1988.17</td><td>Nevins, Francis M</td><td></td></tr>
<tr><td>Fatal Charm</td><td>1989.14</td><td>120-Hour Clock</td><td>1986.16</td></tr>
<tr><td>Getting Away With Murder?</td><td>1984.04</td><td>Nielsen, Helen</td><td></td></tr>
<tr><td>Hollow Vengeance</td><td>1982.20</td><td>After Midnight</td><td>1966.07</td></tr>
<tr><td>The Men in Her Death</td><td>1981.20</td><td>Borrow The Night</td><td>1956.08</td></tr>
<tr><td>Murder By Proxy</td><td>1978.18</td><td>The Crime is Murder</td><td>1956.11</td></tr>
<tr><td>Murder In Mimicry</td><td>1977.11</td><td>The Fifth Caller</td><td>1959.04</td></tr>
<tr><td>Nursery Tea and Poison</td><td>1976.06</td><td>A Killer in the Street</td><td>1967.06</td></tr>
<tr><td>Nursery Tea and Poison</td><td>1976.20</td><td>Sing Me A Murder</td><td>1961.02</td></tr>
<tr><td>Publish and Be Killed</td><td>1986.12</td><td>Verdict Suspended</td><td>1964.07</td></tr>
<tr><td>Scared To Death</td><td>1978.08</td><td>Nisot, E H</td><td></td></tr>
<tr><td>Treble Exposure</td><td>1988.12</td><td>The Sleepless Men</td><td>1959.06</td></tr>
<tr><td>Morson, Ian</td><td></td><td>Noguchi, Thomas T and Lyons, Arthur</td><td></td></tr>
<tr><td>Falconer and the Face of God</td><td>1997.08</td><td>Unnatural Causes</td><td>1988.11</td></tr>
<tr><td>Falconer and the Great Beast</td><td>1999.05</td><td>Nolan, Jeannette Covert</td><td></td></tr>
<tr><td>Falconer's Judgement</td><td>1996.19</td><td>Final Appearance</td><td>1943.04</td></tr>
<tr><td>Mortimer, John</td><td></td><td>Sudden Squall</td><td>1955.06</td></tr>
<tr><td>Rumpole a La Carte</td><td>1991.03</td><td>Nolan, William F</td><td></td></tr>
<tr><td>Morton, C W</td><td></td><td>The Marble Orchard</td><td>1995.15</td></tr>
<tr><td>Sea Trials</td><td>2000.02</td><td>Norman, Geoffrey</td><td></td></tr>
<tr><td>Moyes, Patricia</td><td></td><td>Sweetwater Ranch</td><td>1991.03</td></tr>
<tr><td>The Curious Affair Of The Third Dog</td><td>1974.02</td><td>North, Jessica</td><td></td></tr>
<tr><td>Twice in a Blue Moon</td><td>1993.09</td><td>Mask Of The Jaguar</td><td>1981.07</td></tr>
<tr><td>Muller, Marcia and Pronzini, Bill</td><td></td><td>O'Donnell, Lillian</td><td></td></tr>
<tr><td>Beyond the Grave</td><td>1986.05</td><td>Aftershock</td><td>1977.17</td></tr>
<tr><td>Murphy, Shirley Rousseau</td><td></td><td>Aftershock</td><td>1977.21</td></tr>
<tr><td>Cat in the Dark</td><td>1999.07</td><td>The Baby Merchants</td><td>1975.14</td></tr>
<tr><td>Murray, Max</td><td></td><td>The Baby Merchants</td><td>1976.24</td></tr>
<tr><td>The Doctor and the Corpse</td><td>1952.11</td><td>Leisure Dying</td><td>1976.16</td></tr>
<tr><td>Good Luck To The Corpse</td><td>1952.04</td><td>Leisure Dying</td><td>1976.23</td></tr>
<tr><td>The Neat Little Corpse</td><td>1950.06</td><td>The Phone Calls</td><td>1972.06</td></tr>
<tr><td>Myers, Tamar</td><td></td><td>The Raggedy Man</td><td>1995.19</td></tr>
<tr><td>Parsley, Sage, Rosemary And Crime</td><td>1995.07</td><td>Wicked Designs</td><td>1980.24</td></tr>
<tr><td>Nabb, Magdalen</td><td></td><td>O'Farrell, William</td><td></td></tr>
<tr><td>Death Of An Englishman</td><td>1983.06</td><td>Grow Young And Die</td><td>1952.08</td></tr>
<tr><td>Death of a Dutchman</td><td>1983.15</td><td>O'Finn, Thaddeus</td><td></td></tr>
<tr><td>The Marshal And The Madwoman</td><td>1989.12</td><td>Happy Holiday</td><td>1951.04</td></tr>
<tr><td>The Marshal at Villa Torrini</td><td>1994.11</td><td>O'Marie, Carol Anne</td><td></td></tr>
<tr><td></td><td></td><td>Death Goes on Retreat</td><td>1995.15</td></tr>
</tbody>
</table>

The Detective Book Club 1942-2000 Author Index

Death of an Angel — 1997.04

Murder in Ordinary Time — 1992.04

O'Neil, Kerry

Death Strikes At Heron House — 1944.08

O'Sullivan, J B

Don't Hang Me Too High — 1954.11

Offord, Lenore Glen

Walking Shadow — 1960.02

Olsen, D B

The Cat And The Capricorn — 1952.01

Death Walks On Cat Feet — 1956.09

Something About Midnight — 1950.05

Orum, Poul

The Scapegoat — 1976.06

Osborne, Helena

The Yellow Gold of Tiryns — 1970.04

Oursler, Will

Folio On Florence White — 1942.06

Page, Emma

Final Moments — 1987.04

Last Walk Home — 1983.13

Page, Katherine Hall

The Body In The Bog — 1996.12

The Body in the Basement — 1994.05

The Body in the Belfry — 1990.02

Page, Marco

The Shadowy Third — 1947.02

Palmer, Frank

Nightwatch — 1996.11

Palmer, Leonard

The Sherman Letter — 1995.08

Palmer, Start & Fletcher, Flora

Hildegarde Withers Makes The Scene — 1969.12

Palmer, Stuart

Cold Poison — 1954.06

Four Lost Ladies — 1950.01

The Green Ace — 1951.05

Nipped In The Bud — 1952.02

Rook Takes Knight — 1968.12

Papazoglou, Orania

Death's Savage Passion — 1986.13

Paretsky, Sara

Killing Orders — 1985.07

Parker, Robert B

Early Autumn — 1981.01

The Judas Goat — 1978.17

The Judas Goat — 1978.22

Mortal Stakes — 1976.03

Mortal Stakes — 1976.23

A Savage Place — 1981.21

Wilderness — 1980.01

Paul, Barbara

A Chorus of Detectives — 1987.06

First Gravedigger — 1981.11

In-Laws and Outlaws — 1990.01

Your Eyelids Are Growing Heavy — 1981.18

Pearce, Michael

The Mamur Zapt and the Girl in the Nile — 1994.16

Mamur Zapt and the Spoils of Egypt — 1995.16

Peel, Colin

Snowtrap — 1985.21

Peel, Colin D

Blood of Your Sisters — 1997.06

Firestorm — 1984.01

Pentecost, Hugh

Bargain With Death — 1974.08

The Beautiful Dead — 1974.06

Beware Young Lovers — 1980.17

Birthday, Deathday — 1972.08

The Cannibal Who Overate — 1962.07

The Champagne Killer — 1973.03

Choice Of Violence — 1961.11

The Copycat Killers — 1984.02

Dead Woman Of The Year — 1968.03

The Deadly Friend — 1961.04

The Deadly Joke — 1971.11

Deadly Trap — 1978.20

Death After Breakfast — 1978.08

Death Mask — 1981.05

Death by FIre — 1986.05

Die After Dark — 1976.17

The Evil That Men Do — 1966.10

The Fourteen Dilemma — 1976.08

Girl Watcher's Funeral — 1969.09

The Girl With Six Fingers — 1969.06

The Golden Trap — 1967.09

Hide Her From Every Eye — 1966.04

The Homicidal Horse — 1980.08

Honeymoon With Death — 1975.15

The Judas Freak — 1974.16

Kill and Kill Again — 1987.09

The Lonely Target — 1960.02

Murder Goes Round and Round — 1988.14

Murder In Luxury — 1981.12

Murder Out of Wedlock — 1984.08

Murder Round The Clock — 1985.13

Murder Sweet and Sour — 1985.14

Murder in High Places — 1983.14

The Detective Book Club 1942-2000 Author Index

Nightmare Time	*1986.17*	Philips, Judson	
The Obituary Club	*1958.12*	*Backlash*	*1976.13*
Only the Rich Die Young	*1964.06*	*The Black Glass City*	*1965.05*
The Party Killer	*1985.16*	*A Dead Ending*	*1962.12*
Pattern for Terror	*1990.08*	*Death is a Dirty Trick*	*1981.01*
A Plague Of Violence	*1971.06*	*Five Roads To Death*	*1978.03*
The Price Of Silence	*1984.11*	*Hot Summer Killing*	*1969.03*
Random Killer	*1979.17*	*The Laughter Trap*	*1964.12*
Remember To Kill Me	*1984.12*	*A Murder Arranged*	*1978.18*
The Shape of Fear	*1965.01*	*Murder As The Curtain Rises*	*1981.24*
The Sniper	*1965.07*	*Murder Clear, Track Fast*	*1961.08*
Sow Death, Reap Death	*1982.04*	*The Power Killers*	*1974.11*
The Substitute Victim	*1984.04*	*Target For Tragedy*	*1983.01*
The Tarnished Angel	*1963.03*	*Thursday's Folly*	*1967.12*
Time of Terror	*1975.08*	*The Twisted People*	*1965.11*
Walking Dead Man	*1973.12*	*Why Murder?*	*1979.18*
With Intent To Kill	*1982.17*	Piccirilli, Tom	
Peters, Bryan		*The Dead Past*	*1997.18*
The Big H	*1963.08*	*Sorrow's Crown*	*1999.14*
Peters, Elizabeth		Pike, Robert L	
Borrower Of The Night	*1973.18*	*Bank Job*	*1974.09*
The Camelot Caper	*1969.09*	*Deadline: 2 a.m.*	*1976.10*
The Copenhagen Connection	*1982.16*	*The Gremlin's Grampa*	*1972.07*
The Curse Of The Pharaohs	*1981.17*	*Mute Witness*	*1964.01*
The Dead Sea Cipher	*1970.10*	*Police Blotter*	*1965.12*
Die For Love	*1984.04*	*The Quarry*	*1964.09*
The Jackal's Head	*1968.11*	*Reardon*	*1970.09*
Lion In The Valley	*1986.17*	Piper, Peter	
The Love Talker	*1980.20*	*The Corpse That Came Back*	*1954.10*
The Mummy Case	*1985.12*	Potts, Jean	
Street Of The Five Moons	*1978.14*	*Dark Destination*	*1955.11*
Summer Of The Dragon	*1979.18*	*Go, Lovely Rose*	*1954.08*
Trojan Gold	*1987.18*	*The Little Lie*	*1969.04*
Peters, Ellis		*The Man With The Cane*	*1957.10*
The Confession Of Brother Haluin	*1989.02*	*My Brother's Killer*	*1976.05*
Dead Man's Ransom	*1985.03*	*The Trash Stealer*	*1968.06*
The Devil's Novice	*1984.03*	*The Troublemaker*	*1973.06*
An Excellent Mystery	*1986.09*	Powell, Richard	
Fallen Into the Pit	*1994.06*	*Shark River*	*1949.12*
Flight of the Witch	*1991.04*	*Shell Game*	*1950.08*
The Hermit Of Eyton Forest	*1988.07*	Press, Margaret L	
The Horn Of Roland	*1975.02*	*Requiem For A Postman*	*1992.04*
The Leper of Saint Giles	*1982.24*	Price, Anthony	
Monk's-Hood	*1981.16*	*Gunner Kelly*	*1984.15*
Never Pick Up Hitch-Hikers!	*1977.01*	Priestley, J B	
Rainbow's End	*1980.04*	*Salt Is Leaving*	*1975.07*
Saint Peter's Fair	*1982.12*	Proctor, Maurice	
The Virgin In The Ice	*1983.12*	*Devil's Due*	*1961.04*
Who Lies Here?	*1965.10*	Pronzini, Bill	
Peters, Ray		*Bones*	*1985.11*
The Lafitte Case	*1997.12*		

Carmody's Run	*1993.02*	*The Caper*	*1969.10*
Graveyard Plots	*1985.16*	*The Inside-Out Heist*	*1971.05*
Hoodwink	*1981.21*	Reeve, Christopher	
Labyrinth	*1980.12*	*Lady, Be Careful*	*1950.02*
Quarry	*1992.01*	*Murder Steps Out*	*1951.05*
Scattershot	*1982.12*	Reilly, Helen	
Undercurrent	*1973.14*	*The Canvas Dagger*	*1957.04*
Pronzini, Bill and Muller, Marcia		*Certain Sleep*	*1962.01*
The Lighthouse	*1986.12*	*Compartment K*	*1955.14*
Pye, Michael		*The Day She Died*	*1963.01*
Taking Lives	*1999.12*	*Ding Dong Bell*	*1958.12*
Queen, Ellery		*The Double Man*	*1952.06*
A Fine And Private Place	*1971.09*	*The Farmhouse*	*1947.08*
A Fine And Private Place	*1971.15*	*Follow Me*	*1960.09*
A Fine And Private Place	*1972.17*	*Lament For The Bride*	*1952.01*
A Fine And Private Place	*1973.19*	*Murder On Angler's Island*	*1945.04*
The Murderer is a Fox	*1945.09*	*Name Your Poison*	*1942.06*
Quentin, Patrick		*Not Me Inspector*	*1959.12*
Man In The Net	*1956.12*	*The Silver Leopard*	*1947.06*
Quest, Erica		*Staircase Four*	*1949.07*
Design For Murder	*1981.14*	*Tell Her It's Murder*	*1954.11*
The October Cabaret	*1979.19*	Rendell, Ruth	
The Silver Castle	*1978.15*	*Copper Peacock*	*1992.02*
Quill, Monica		*Going Wrong*	*1991.06*
And Then There Was Nun	*1984.05*	*A Judgement In Stone*	*1978.09*
Half Past Nun	*1997.09*	*The Lake of Darkness*	*1980.13*
Quinn, Derry		*Shake Hands Forever*	*1976.02*
The Limbo connection	*1978.02*	Resnicow, Herbert	
Radley, Sheila		*The Dead Room*	*1987.18*
The Chief Inspector's Daughter	*1981.07*	*The Gold Frame*	*1985.01*
Death In The Morning	*1979.19*	*The Gold Gamble*	*1988.06*
Fate Worse than Death	*1986.08*	Rhode, John	
A Talent For Destruction	*1983.06*	*The Mysterious Suspect*	*1953.10*
This Way Out	*1990.15*	*Too Many Suspects*	*1945.08*
Who Saw Him Die?	*1989.13*	Rice, Craig	
Ramsey, Diana		*The Fourth Postman*	*1948.10*
Killing Words	*1994.09*	Rich, Virginia	
Ransome, Stephen		*The Baked Bean Supper Murders*	*1983.13*
Alias His Wife	*1965.07*	Richards, Clay	
The Frazer Acquittal	*1955.08*	*The Gentle Assassin*	*1965.03*
The Hidden Hour	*1966.07*	Richart, Mary	
Meet In Darkness	*1964.08*	*Murder In the Town*	*1947.07*
The Men In Her Death	*1956.09*	Rinehart, Mary Roberts	
The Night, The Woman	*1963.05*	*Episode Of The Wandering Knife*	*1951.02*
One-Man Jury	*1965.02*	*The Frightened Wife*	*1953.11*
The Sin File	*1966.02*	Ripley, Ann	
Some Must Watch	*1961.03*	*Death Of A Garden Pest*	*1996.18*
Warning Bell	*1960.04*	Robb, Candace M	
Without A Trace	*1962.05*	*Riddle of St. Leonard's*	*1997.13*
Reagan, Thomas B		Robb, Candice	
Blood Money	*1971.02*	*The Nun's Tale*	*1995.09*

The Detective Book Club 1942-2000 Author Index

Roberts, John Maddox
Saturnalia: SPQR V — 2000.02

Roberts, Lee
Once A Widow — 1957.11
The Pale Door — 1955.02

Roberts, Les
Cleveland Local — 1997.14
Collision Bend — 1996.21
The Duke Of Cleveland — 1995.13
The Lake Effect — 1994.13
Pepper Pike — 1988.15
A Shoot in Cleveland — 1998.22
Snake Oil — 1990.09

Roberts, Willo Davis
The Annalise Experiment — 1985.19

Robitaille, Julie
Iced — 1995.10

Roden, H W
One Angel Less — 1945.06
Too Busy to Die — 1945.01
Wake For A Lady — 1946.07
You Only Hang Once — 1944.04

Rogers, Samuel
You'll Be Sorry! — 1945.10

Rohmer, Sax
Hangover House — 1949.12

Roome, Annette
Second Shot in the Dark — 1991.10

Roos, Kelley
Bad Trip — 1972.04
Ghost Of A Chance — 1947.07
Grave Danger — 1966.03
Murder On Martha's Vineyard — 1981.17
Necessary Evil — 1965.08
One False Move — 1966.11
Requiem For A Blonde — 1959.02
Suddenly One Night — 1971.04
To Save His Life — 1968.09
What Did Hattie See? — 1970.09
Who Saw Maggie Brown? — 1968.01

Ross, Frank
Sleeping Dogs — 1978.17

Ross, Ivan T
The Man Who Would Do Anything — 1963.07
Murder Out Of School — 1960.07
Old Students Never Die — 1962.04
Teacher's Blood — 1964.05

Ross, Z H
Overdue For Death — 1947.04

Rossiter, Elizabeth
Lemon Garden — 1991.09

Rothblatt, H B and Fish, Robert L
A Handy Death — 1973.18

Rothenberg, Rebecca
Bulrush Murders — 1991.11
The Shy Tulip Murders — 1996.11

Rowe, Anne
Fatal Purchase — 1945.06
Too Much Poison — 1945.01
Up To The Hilt — 1945.11

Roy Harley
A Cracking of Spines — 1982.07

Rubino, Jane
Death of a DJ — 1995.16

Ruell, Patrick
The Only Game — 1993.09

Russell, Charlotte M
Between Us And Evil — 1950.12

Ruth Dudley
Murder in a Cathedral — 1997.11

Rutland, Harriet
Blue Murder — 1943.01

Rutledge, Nancy
The Frightened Murderer — 1957.08
Wanted For Murder — 1956.04

Rydell, Forbes
If She Should Die — 1961.03

Sale, Richard
Benefit Performance — 1946.06

Sanders, Daphne
To Catch a Thief — 1943.06

Sanders, George
Crime on my Hands — 1945.01

Satterthwait, Walter
Accustomed To The Dark — 1996.26
Escapade — 1995.21
Masquerade — 1998.12

Scherf, Margaret
The Banker's Bones — 1968.05
The Corpse With One Shoe — 1951.08
Corpse with the Flannel Nightgown — 1965.08
The Gun in Daniel Websters Bust — 1949.10
Judicial Body — 1957.10
To Cache A Millionaire — 1972.11

Schunk, Laurel
Black and Secret Midnight — 1999.13

Scott, Virgil and Koski, Dominic
Walk-In — 1977.06

Scott, Willard with Crider, Bill
Murder In The Mist — 1998.04

Scott, Williard and Crider, Bill
Murder Under Blue Skies — 1998.15

The Detective Book Club 1942-2000 Author Index

Seaman, Donald
The Chameleon Course — 1976.12

Sela, Owen
The Bengali Inheritance — 1975.13
An Exchange Of Eagles — 1977.18
An Exchange Of Eagles — 1977.22

Serafin, David
The Body in Cadiz Bay — 1985.20
Port of Light — 1987.11
Saturday Of Glory — 1982.10

Seranella, Barbara
No Offense Intended — 1998.17
Unwanted Company — 2000.03

Shaber, Sarah R
Simon Said — 1997.03

Shaffer, Louise
All My Suspects — 1994.03

Shane, Susannah
A Lady in a Million — 1943.09

Shaw, Howard
Death Of A Don — 1982.02
Killing No Murder — 1981.14

Shelton, Connie
Memories Can Be Murder — 1999.08
Partnerships Can Kill — 1997.08
Small Towns Can Be Murder — 1998.16

Sherburne, James
Death's Clenched Fist — 1982.18
Death's Gray Angel — 1981.23
Death's Pale Horse — 1980.14

Sheridan, Juanita
The Waikiki Widow — 1954.03

Sherry, Edna
Backfire — 1956.02
Call the Witness — 1961.06
Girl Missing — 1962.09
Strictly A Loser — 1965.10

Sherwood, John
Ambush For Anatol — 1953.01

Shoemaker, Bill
Dark Horse — 1996.02
Fire Horse — 1995.10

Shone, Anna
Mr. Donaghue Investigates — 1995.24
Secrets in Stone — 1996.02

Shriber, Ione Sandberg
A Body For Bill — 1943.02
Invitation To Murder — 1944.02
Never Say Die — 1951.03
Pattern For Murder — 1945.02

Shubin, Seymour
Anyone's My Name — 1999.03
The Captain — 1999.02
Fury's Children — 1999.08
My face among strangers — 1999.10

Shuman, M K
The Maya Stone Murders — 1989.10

Sibley, Celestine
Ah, Sweet Mystery — 1991.01
Dire Happenings at Scratch Ankle — 1993.02
The Malignant Heart — 1958.06
Plague of Kinfolks — 1995.03

Siegel, Doris
How Still My Love — 1958.03

Siller, Hilda Van
The Watchers — 1969.10

Simenon, George
Maigret and the Spinster — 1977.22

Simenon, Georges
The Hatter's Phantoms — 1976.19
Inspector Maigret And The Burglar's Wife — 1956.04
Inspector Maigret And The Dead Girl — 1956.01
Maigret And The Apparition — 1976.14
Maigret And The Apparition — 1977.25
Maigret And The Loner — 1975.09
Maigret And The Loner — 1975.18
Maigret And The Nahour Case — 1983.08
Maigret And The Toy Village — 1980.04
Maigret At The Coroners — 1981.25
Maigret Has Doubts — 1982.17
Maigret In Exile — 1979.10
Maigret Loses His Temper — 1974.10
Maigret Rents a Room — 1961.06
Maigret Sets a Trap — 1972.08
Maigret and the Black Sheep — 1976.07
Maigret and the Black Sheep — 1976.24
Maigret and the Bum — 1974.04
Maigret and the Bum — 1974.19
Maigret and the Headless Corpse — 1968.07
Maigret and the Hotel Majestic — 1978.07
Maigret and the Hotel Majestic — 1978.21
Maigret and the Informer — 1973.10
Maigret and the Informer — 1973.20
Maigret and the Man on the Bench — 1976.01
Maigret and the Millionaires — 1975.01
Maigret and the Millionaires — 1975.19
Maigret and the Spinster — 1977.14
Maigret at the Coroner's — 1981.05

The Detective Book Club 1942-2000 Author Index

Maigret in New York	1955.04
Maigret in Vichy	1969.05
Maigret on the Defensive	1982.01
Maigret's Dead Man	1964.06
Maigret's Pickpocket	1968.11
Maigret's Pipe	1979.01
Maigret's Pipe	1979.22
Maigret's Rival	1980.13
No Vacation for Maigret	1953.12
None of Maigret's Business	1958.08
The Venice Train	1974.13
Simmons, Geoffrey S	
The Z-Papers	1976.15
Simon, Roger L	
Peking Duck	1979.16
Simpson, Dorothy	
Dead on Arrival	1987.10
Singer, Shelley	
Full House	1986.10
Spit In The Ocean	1987.17
Sipherd, Ray	
The Audubon Quartet	1998.07
Dance Of The Scarecrows	1996.17
Sjowall, Maj & Wahloo, Per	
The Locked Room	1974.02
The Locked Room	1974.19
The Terrorists	1977.03
The Terrorists	1977.25
Skinner, Robert	
Cat-Eyed Trouble	1998.18
Daddy's Gone A-Hunting	1999.19
Sladek, John	
Invisible Green	1979.15
Slater, Susan	
The Pumpkin Seed Massacre	1999.17
Slesar, Henry	
The Thing At The Door	1974.14
Sloan, Bob	
Bliss Jumps The Gun	1999.06
Smith, Alison	
Someone Else's Grave	1984.14
Smith, Barbara Burnett	
Dust Devils of the Purple Sage	1995.09
Mistletoe from Purple Sage	1998.03
Smith, Bridget A	
Death of an Alaskan Princess	1988.03
Smith, Frank	
Stone Dead	1998.08
Smith, Kay Nolte	
Catching Fire	1982.11

The Watcher	1980.14
Smith, Rosamond	
Starr Bright Will Be With You Soon	1999.20
Snow, C P	
A Coat Of Varnish	1980.05
Spicer, Bart	
Blues For The Prince	1950.07
Exit Running	1959.12
Sprague, Gretchen	
Death in Good Company	1998.03
St. Edmunds, Anne	
Red Right Returning	1996.24
Stadley, Pat	
Autumn Of A Hunter	1970.09
Stafford, Muriel	
X Marks the Dot	1944.01
Stang, JoAnne	
Shadows On The Sceptered Isle	1980.15
Stansberry, Domenic	
Manifesto For the Dead	2000.01
Stark, Richard	
The Blackbird	1969.11
The Dame	1969.02
The Damsel	1967.08
Lemons Never Lie	1971.10
Slayground	1972.02
Staub, Wendy Corsi	
Fade to Black	1998.14
Steed, Neville	
Black Eye	1990.02
Steiguer, Walter De	
Jewels for a Shroud	1950.10
Stein, Aaron Marc	
Alp Murder	1970.08
A Body For A Buddy	1981.21
The Bombing Run	1983.09
Deadly Delight	1967.07
The Finger	1973.07
The Garbage Collector	1984.13
Hangman's Row	1982.13
Lend Me Your Ears	1977.06
A Nose for It	1981.09
The Rolling Heads	1979.11
Stein, Benjamin	
The Croesus Conspiracy	1978.15
Stein, Marc	
Home and Murder	1962.08
Sterling, Stewart	
The Big Ear	1953.09
Stern, Richard Martin	
Death in the Snow	1973.12

The Detective Book Club 1942-2000 Author Index

Manuscript for Murder	1971.02
Merry Go Round	1969.04
Stevenson, Anne	
Coil Of Serpents	1977.15
Mask Of Treason	1980.06
Turkish Rondo	1982.01
Stewart, Michael	
Blindsight	1987.03
Stone, Hampton	
The Kid Who Came Home With A	
Corpse	1972.14
Stout, Rex	
Black Orchids	1942.05
Not Quite Dead Enough	1944.12
The Silent Speaker	1946.10
Too Many Women	1948.02
Strange, John Stephen	
Let The Dead Past	1953.05
Stratton, Ted	
Tourist Trap	1976.09
Strong, Michael	
Danger Feeds My Fear	1980.19
Struthers, Betsy	
Found: A Body	1999.13
Stuart, Ian	
The Garb of Truth	1984.01
Pictures in the Dark	1986.01
Sullivan, Winona	
Dead South	1996.12
Sultan, Faye and Kennedy, Teresa	
Helpline	1999.21
Suyker, Betty	
Death Scene	1981.19
Swiggett, Howard	
The Hidden And The Hunted	1950.11
Symons, Julian	
The Kentish Manor Murders	1988.10
A Three-Pipe Problem	1975.14
Taylor, Andrew	
Waiting for the End of the World	1984.14
Taylor, H Baldwin	
The Trouble With Tycoons	1967.12
Taylor, L A	
Footnote to Murder	1983.15
Love of Money	1986.14
Only Half a Hoax	1984.10
Poetic Justice	1988.07
Shed Light on Death	1985.20
Taylor, Matt	
The Famous McGarry Stories	1958.05
Taylor, Phoebe Atwood	
Punch With Care	1947.01
The Six Iron Spiders	1942.05
Templeton, Aline	
The Last Act Of All	1996.17
Templeton, Charles	
The Kidnapping Of The President	1975.07
Thayer, Lee	
And One Cried Murder	1962.04
Dead On Arrival	1960.11
Dead Reckoning	1954.13
Dusty Death	1966.06
Five Bullets	1944.11
Guilt Is Where You Find It	1957.05
Still No Answer	1958.05
Too Long Endured	1951.02
Two Ways To Die	1959.10
Who Benefits?	1955.12
Thielen, Bernard	
Open Season	1959.03
Thomas, Ross	
Ah, Treachery!	1994.01
Thomson, June	
Alibi In Time	1980.19
Case Closed	1977.12
A Dying Fall	1985.04
Shadow Of A Doubt	1982.18
Thrasher, L L	
Charlie's Bones	1998.05
Dogsbody, Inc.	1999.18
Togawa, Masako	
The Master Key	1985.07
Tourney, Leonard	
Frobisher's Savage	1994.09
Low Treason	1983.06
Old Saxon Blood	1988.15
Tracy, Don	
The Big Blackout	1959.06
Travis, Gretchen	
Too Old to Die	1969.02
Treat, Lawrence	
T as in Trapped	1948.03
Trial and Terror	1949.09
Trocheck, Kathy Hogan	
Every Crooked Nanny	1992.03
Happy Never After	1995.19
Heart Trouble	1996.04
Midnight Clear	1998.14
To Live and Die in Dixie	1993.05
Trow, M J	
The Adventures of Inspector	
Lestrade	1998.20

The Detective Book Club 1942-2000 Author Index

Brigade: the further adventures of
   Lestrade — 1999.09
Lestrade And The Hallowed House — 1999.16
Lestrade and the Brother of Death — 1999.17
Lestrade and the Deadly Game — 1999.02
Lestrade and the Leviathan — 1999.04

Truman, Margaret
   Murder in the White House — 1980.21

Tryon, Thomas
   The Other — 1971.14

Tucker, Kerry
   Cold Feet — 1992.03
   Death Echo — 1993.03
   Drift Away — 1994.04

Tucker, Wilson
   The Chinese Doll — 1947.04
   The Man In My Grave — 1956.08
   The Stalking Man — 1949.10

Turnbull, Peter
   Condition Purple — 1989.07

Tyre, Nedra
   Death Of An Intruder — 1953.03

Ullman, Allan and Fletcher, Lucile
   Night Man — 1951.07

Underwood, Michael
   Anything But The Truth — 1979.07
   A Compelling Case — 1989.01
   Crooked Wood — 1978.11
   Death at Deepwood Grange — 1986.04
   Double Jeopardy — 1982.05
   Dual Enigma — 1988.06
   Guilty Conscience — 1994.10
   Hand Of Fate — 1982.16
   The Hidden Man — 1985.06
   The Juror — 1975.16
   Menaces, Menaces — 1976.16
   Murder On Trial — 1957.12
   Murder With Malice — 1977.10
   A Pinch Of Snuff — 1974.14
   Rosa's Dilemma — 1990.10
   Smooth Justice — 1980.01
   The Uninvited Corpse — 1987.05
   Victim Of Circumstance — 1980.16

Unekis, Richard
   The Chase — 1963.04

Upfield, Arthur W
   Bachelors Of Broken Hill — 1951.03
   Murder Must Wait — 1953.09
   The Valley Of Smugglers — 1960.10

Van De Wetering, Janwillem
   Inspector Saito's Small Satori — 1985.03

Van Gieson, Judith
   Ditch Rider — 1998.25
   Parrot Blues — 1995.04

Van de Wetering, Janwillem
   Just a Corpse at Twilight — 1994.12

Vance, John Holbrook
   The Deadly Isles — 1969.09
   The Man In The Cage — 1960.11

Vickers, Roy
   A Date With Danger — 1944.09
   The Department Of Dead Ends — 1953.05
   Double Image — 1955.14
   Four Past Four — 1945.10
   The Girl Who Wouldn't Talk — 1959.09
   Maid To A Murder — 1950.08
   Murder Will Out — 1954.05
   Murder in Two Flats — 1952.05
   Seven Chose Murder — 1959.01
   Six Murders in the Suburbs — 1955.01
   The Sole Survivor and The Kynsard
     Affair — 1951.08
   The Whispering Death — 1947.02

Wainwright, John
   Duty Elsewhere — 1980.06
   The Man Who Wasn't There — 1989.07
   Pool Of Tears — 1978.06

Walling, R A J
   The Corpse With The Missing Watch — 1950.04
   The Corpse Without A Clue — 1944.08
   A Corpse by Any Other Name — 1943.05

Walsh, Thomas
   Dangerous Passenger — 1959.04
   The Eye of the Needle — 1962.01
   The Face Of The Enemy — 1967.04
   The Resurrection Man — 1966.05
   The Tenth Point — 1965.04
   A Thief in the Night — 1963.01
   To Hide A Rogue — 1964.07

Ward, Edmund
   The Baltic Emerald — 1982.11

Warga, Wayne
   Singapore Transfer — 1991.08

Warner, Mignon
   Devil's Knell — 1983.16
   Speak No Evil — 1985.21

Waters, T A
   The Lost Victim — 1974.04

Waugh, Hillary
   A Death in Town — 1989.05
   End Of A Party — 1965.06

Girl On The Run	*1966.04*	*Castle In The Air*	*1980.16*
The Girl Who Cried Wolf	*1959.02*	*Drowned Hope*	*1990.04*
Murder on Safari	*1987.11*	*Good Behavior*	*1986.09*
Prisoner's Plea	*1964.01*	*The Hot Rock*	*1970.11*
Pure Poison	*1967.02*	*Humans*	*1992.01*
Road Block	*1960.10*	*I Gave At The Office*	*1971.09*
Wayland, Patrick		*Jimmy The Kid*	*1974.15*
Counterstroke	*1964.11*	*Nobody's Perfect*	*1977.20*
The Waiting Game	*1965.09*	*A Travesty*	*1977.10*
Webb, Jack		*Trust Me On This*	*1988.17*
The Bad Blonde	*1956.10*	*Why Me*	*1983.08*
One For My Dame	*1961.10*	Weston, Garnett	
Webb, Martha G		*Legacy Of Fear*	*1951.01*
Even Cops' Daughters	*1986.14*	Wetering, Janwillem van de	
Weber, Ronald		*The Blond Baboon*	*1978.08*
The Aluminum Hatch	*1998.02*	*The Corpse On The Dike*	*1977.05*
Webster, Noah		*Death of a Hawker*	*1977.14*
A Flight from Paris	*1987.06*	*The Japanese Corpse*	*1978.01*
Incident In Iceland	*1979.19*	*The Japanese Corpse*	*1978.22*
A Legacy From Tenerife	*1984.11*	*Tumbleweed*	*1976.18*
A Problem In Prague	*1982.07*	Wheat, Carolyn	
Weeks, Dolores		*Where Nobody Dies*	*1986.06*
The Cape Murders	*1987.02*	White, Alan	
The Friday Harbor Murders	*1988.06*	*The Long Fuse*	*1974.16*
Wees, F S		White, Lionel	
The Country Of The Strangers	*1960.03*	*The Crimshaw Memorandum*	*1967.04*
Faceless Enemy	*1966.12*	*Flight Into Terror*	*1955.12*
Wells, Tobias		*A Grave Undertaking*	*1962.02*
Brenda's Murder	*1974.03*	*The House on K Street*	*1965.12*
A Die In The Country	*1973.05*	*Invitation to Violence*	*1958.03*
Die Quickly, Dear Mother	*1969.08*	*The Ransomed Madonna*	*1964.08*
Dinky Died	*1970.10*	White, Terence de Vere	
The Foo Dog	*1972.01*	*My Name Is Norval*	*1980.11*
Hark, Hark, The Watchdogs Bark	*1976.04*	Whitney, Alec	
Murder Most Fouled Up	*1968.11*	*Death In Darkness*	*1978.06*
The Young Can Die Protesting	*1970.02*	Wilcox, Collin	
Wentworth, Patricia		*Bernhardt's Edge*	*1988.10*
The Benevent Treasure	*1954.13*	*Dead Aim*	*1972.04*
Out of the Past	*1953.06*	*Dead Center*	*1993.01*
Poison In The Pen	*1955.09*	*Full Circle*	*1995.11*
Werry, Richard R		*Hire a Hangman*	*1991.06*
A Delicately Personal Matter	*1986.06*	*Mankiller*	*1981.04*
Westbrook, Robert		*Power Plays*	*1979.21*
Lady Left	*1991.02*	*Switchback*	*1993.05*
Westfall, Patricia Tichenor		*The Third Figure*	*1968.08*
Mother of the Bride	*1998.22*	*The Watcher*	*1978.07*
Westheimer, David		Wilde, Percival	
The Olmec Head	*1974.15*	*Tinsley's Bones*	*1942.05*
Westlake, Donald E		Wilhelm, Kate	
Baby, Would I Lie?	*1994.02*	*Malice Prepense*	*1996.05*

The Detective Book Club 1942-2000 Author Index

Williams, Alan
   Gentleman Traitor — 1976.09
Williams, Brad
   A Borderline Case — 1960.08
   The Well-Dressed Skeleton — 1962.11
Williams, Brad and Erlich, J W
   A Conflict Of Interest — 1972.02
   A Matter Of Confidence — 1973.08
Williams, David
   Divided Treasure — 1988.04
   Holy Treasure! — 1989.07
   Treasure Up In Smoke — 1978.15
   Wedding Treasure — 1985.22
Wilmer, Dale
   Dead Fall — 1954.04
Winslow, Don
   While Drowning In The Desert — 1996.15
Winslow, Pauline Glen
   The Brandenburg Hotel — 1976.18
   Copper' Gold — 1978.12
   The Counsellor Heart — 1980.24
   I, Martha Adams — 1984.13
   The Rockefeller Gift — 1981.24
   The Witch Hill Murder — 1978.05
Winter, Abigail
   Whispering Caverns — 1975.07
Wishnia, K J A
   The Glass Factory — 2000.02
   Soft Money — 1999.21
Withers, E L
   Heir Apparent — 1961.07
Wolfe, Michael
   The Panama Paradox — 1978.05
Wolffe, Katherine
   The Attic Room — 1943.03
Wolzien, Valerie
   Murder at the PTA Luncheon — 1988.04
Wood, Ted
   Fool's Gold — 1986.19
   On the Inside — 1990.04
   When The Killing Starts — 1989.12
Woodhouse, Martin
   Blue Bone — 1973.14
Woods, Sara
   The Bloody Book Of Law — 1984.12
   Cry Guilty — 1981.13
   Cry Guilty — 1981.25
   Dearest Enemy — 1982.04
   Done to Death — 1975.17
   Enter a Gentlewoman — 1982.20

   Most Deadly Hate — 1986.15
   Murder's Out Of Tune — 1985.15
   My Life Is Done — 1976.16
   Naked Villainy — 1987.12
   An Obscure Grave — 1985.05
   Proceed To Judgement — 1980.08
   Put Out the Light — 1985.18
   They Stay for Death — 1980.17
   A Thief For Two — 1978.03
Woolrich, Cornell
   The Black Path Of Fear — 1944.08
   Rendezvous In Black — 1948.08
   Violence — 1958.11
Worboys, Anne
   Run, Sara, Run — 1981.14
Wren, M K
   Curiosity Didn't Kill The Cat — 1974.07
   A Multitude Of Sins — 1975.15
   Nothing's Certain But Death — 1978.13
   Oh, Bury Me Not — 1977.08
   Seasons of Death — 1981.09
   Wake Up, Darlin' Corey — 1984.08
Wright, Eric
   Buried In Stone — 1996.14
   Death of a Sunday Writer — 1996.25
   Death on the rocks — 1999.15
   Final Cut — 1991.05
   A Fine Italian Hand — 1993.01
   A Sensitive Case — 1990.11
Wright, Jim
   Last Man Standing — 1991.01
Wright, Laurali
   Fall From Grace — 1991.10
Wylie, Philip
   Corpses At Indian Stones — 1943.05
Yaffe, James
   Mom Meets Her Maker — 1990.07
Yeager, Dorian
   Libation By Death — 1998.06
   Murder Will Out — 1995.04
   Ovation by Death — 1996.19
   Summer Will End — 1996.22
York, Jeremy
   Come Here And Die — 1960.04
   My Brother's Killer — 1959.04
   Seeds Of Murder — 1958.07
   Sight Of Death — 1958.11
   Thicker Than Water — 1962.06
Yorke, Margaret
   Act of Violence — 1998.01

Admit to Murder   1990.01
Almost The Truth   1995.01
The Come-On   1979.12
Evidence to Destroy   1987.15
Safely to the Grave   1986.20
The Scent Of Fear   1981.15
Serious Intent   1996.10
Zimler, Richard
  The Last Kabbalist Of Lisbon   1998.04
Zimmerman, Bruce
  Thicker Than Water   1991.01
Zollinger, Norman
  Lautrec   1990.12

The Detective Book Club 1942-2000 Title Index

'Tis the Season to Be Dying
(Drummond) — 1988.16
120-Hour Clock (Nevins) — 1986.16
The 12th Of Never (Heyes) — 1963.11
71 Hours (Mason) — 1972.12
711 - Officer Needs Help
(Masterson) — 1966.01
80 Dollars To Stamford (Fletcher) — 1976.06
The Academic Factor (Haddad) — 1980.18
Accident by Design (Lorac) — 1951.09
An Accidental Shroud (Eccles) — 1997.20
Accustomed To The Dark
(Satterthwait) — 1996.26
Act Of Fear (Collins) — 1968.02
Act of Faith (Bowen) — 1993.06
Act of Violence (Yorke) — 1998.01
Admit to Murder (Yorke) — 1990.01
The Adventures of Inspector
Lestrade (Trow) — 1998.20
Adverse Report (Hammond) — 1988.09
The Affacombe Affair (Lemarchand) — 1985.04
The Affair Of The Dead Stranger
(Knight) — 1944.11
The Affair Of The Fainting Butler
(Knight) — 1943.11
Affair Of The Jade Monkey (Knight) — 1943.05
The Affair of the Splintered Heart
(Knight) — 1942.08
African Poison Murders (Huxley) — 1988.18
After Effects (Aird) — 1996.25
After Midnight (Nielsen) — 1966.07
After The Fine Weather (Gilbert) — 1963.08
After The Verdict (Gilbert) — 1962.02
Aftershock (O'Donnell) — 1977.17
Aftershock (O'Donnell) — 1977.21
Against the Brotherhood (Fawcett) — 1997.01
Against the Evidence (Egan) — 1963.02
Agatha Raisin And The Murderous
Marriage (Beaton) — 1996.21
Agatha Raisin And The Walkers Of
Dembley (Beaton) — 1995.01
Agatha Raisin and the Potted
Gardener (Beaton) — 1994.05
Agatha Raisin and the Terrible
Tourist (Beaton) — 1997.14
Agatha Raisin and the Wellspring of
Death (Beaton) — 1998.22
Ah, Sweet Mystery (Sibley) — 1991.01
Ah, Treachery! (Thomas) — 1994.01
Akin To Murder (Knight) — 1953.04
Alas Poor Father (Fleming) — 1973.07

Alias Basil Willing (McCloy) — 1951.09
Alias His Wife (Ransome) — 1965.07
Alibi In Time (Thomson) — 1980.19
Alive And Dead (Ferrars) — 1975.12
Alive And Dead (Ferrars) — 1975.20
All Grass Isn't Green (Fair) — 1970.05
All My Suspects (Shaffer) — 1994.03
All Other Perils (Kirk) — 1975.10
All Roads To Sospel (Bellairs) — 1982.10
All Through The Night (Masterson) — 1955.11
All Unwary (Curzon) — 1998.11
All the Old Lions (Caverly) — 1994.03
Allegra's Child (Letton) — 1969.07
Almost Murder (Jeffries) — 1986.01
Almost The Truth (Yorke) — 1995.01
Along a Dark Path (Johnston) — 1967.09
Alp Murder (Stein) — 1970.08
The Aluminum Hatch (Weber) — 1998.02
The Aluminum Turtle (Kendrick) — 1960.08
Always Kill A Stranger (Fish) — 1967.03
An Amateur Corpse (Brett) — 1978.16
The Amazing Mrs. Pollifax (Gilman) — 1970.08
Ambush For Anatol (Sherwood) — 1953.01
The Amethyst Spectacles (Crane) — 1944.11
Among Those Absent (Coles) — 1948.10
An Ancient Evil (Doherty) — 1995.19
And Dangerous To Know (Daly) — 1949.11
And Death Came Too (Gilbert) — 1956.07
And One Cried Murder (Thayer) — 1962.04
And One For The Dead (Audemars) — 1981.22
And Soon I'll Come to Kill You
(Kelly) — 1991.08
And Then There Was Nun (Quill) — 1984.05
And Then They Die (McCollum) — 1985.10
And the Deep Blue Sea (Knotts) — 1944.06
Angel At Troublesome Creek
(Ballard) — 1999.24
Angel of Death (Cohen) — 1985.01
Angel of Death (Doherty) — 1990.08
Angel of Vengeance (Cohen) — 1984.07
The Anger Of Fear (Ashford) — 1979.15
Angry Puppet Syndrome (Menkes) — 1999.02
The Annalise Experiment (Roberts) — 1985.19
Another Man's Murder (Eberhart) — 1958.02
Another Morgue Heard From
(Davis) — 1955.01
Another Woman's House (Eberhart) — 1947.05
The Antagonists (Haggard) — 1964.10
Anyone's My Name (Shubin) — 1999.03
Anything But The Truth
(Underwood) — 1979.07

The Detective Book Club 1942-2000 Title Index

Anything for a Quiet Life (Gilbert)	*1990.10*
An Ape In Velvet (Foley)	*1951.11*
Apple Spy In The Sky (Lovell)	*1983.10*
The Applegreen Cat (Crane)	*1944.02*
Appointment With Yesterday (Fremlin)	*1973.03*
An Arcadian Death (Jeffries)	*1996.01*
The Ariadne Clue (Clemeau)	*1983.03*
Armadillos and Old Lace (Friedman)	*1994.09*
Arrow Pointing Nowhere (Daly)	*1944.05*
Arson And Old Lace (Angus)	*1973.05*
An Artistic Way To Go (Jeffries)	*1997.02*
The Artless Heiress (Kelland)	*1962.05*
As Good As Dead (Dewey)	*1946.09*
As a Favor (Dunlap)	*1984.07*
Ask For Me Tomorrow (Millar)	*1977.04*
Asking Questions (Keating)	*1997.03*
The Assassin in the Greenwood (Doherty)	*1994.02*
At Bertram's Hotel (Christie)	*1967.01*
At Death's Door (Barnard)	*1988.13*
At the Lake of Sudden Death (Holme)	*1987.01*
The Attic Room (Wolffe)	*1943.03*
The Audubon Quartet (Sipherd)	*1998.07*
Autumn Maze (Cleary)	*1995.01*
Autumn Of A Hunter (Stadley)	*1970.09*
Avery's Fortune (Green)	*1973.02*
Ax (McBain)	*1964.11*
Axe for an Abbot (Eyre)	*1996.13*
Azrael (DeAndrea)	*1987.14*
Baby Girl (King-Wente)	*1998.23*
The Baby Merchants (O'Donnell)	*1975.14*
The Baby Merchants (O'Donnell)	*1976.24*
Baby, Would I Lie? (Westlake)	*1994.02*
Babylon South (Cleary)	*1990.16*
Bachelors Get Lonely (Fair)	*1961.07*
Bachelors Of Broken Hill (Upfield)	*1951.03*
Back Door to Death (Foley)	*1963.06*
Back To School Murder (Meier)	*1998.13*
Back To The Wall (Hansen)	*1958.02*
Backfire (Law)	*1994.14*
Backfire (Sherry)	*1956.02*
Backlash (Philips)	*1976.13*
The Bad Blonde (Webb)	*1956.10*
The Bad Detective (Keating)	*1999.24*
The Bad Samaritan (Barnard)	*1995.02*
Bad Trip (Roos)	*1972.04*
The Bad-News Man (McMullen)	*1986.02*
Bahama Crisis (Bagley)	*1983.18*
The Bahamas Murder Case (Ford)	*1952.04*
The Baked Bean Supper Murders (Rich)	*1983.13*
Baker's Gold (Cohn)	*1998.01*
The Balloon Affair (Layne)	*1982.02*
The Baltic Emerald (Ward)	*1982.11*
The Bandersnatch (Hardwick)	*1989.08*
Bank Job (Pike)	*1974.09*
The Bank With The Bamboo Door (Hitchens)	*1965.06*
Banker (Francis)	*1983.14*
The Banker's Bones (Scherf)	*1968.05*
Banquets of the Black Widowers (Asimov)	*1984.01*
The Barboza Credentials (Driscoll)	*1976.19*
The Barclay Place (Foley)	*1976.03*
Bargain With Death (Pentecost)	*1974.08*
The Bass Derby Murder (Knight)	*1950.04*
Bats Fly At Dusk (Fair)	*1942.09*
Bats Fly Up for Inspector Ghote (Keating)	*1974.16*
The Baxter Letters (Hitchens)	*1971.12*
The Bay Psalm Book Murder (Harriss)	*1983.15*
The Bayou Road (Eberhart)	*1979.04*
Be Buried In The Rain (Michaels)	*1986.03*
Be Home By Eleven (Dean)	*1973.17*
Be a Good Boy (Fleming)	*1972.08*
Beagle Scented Murder (Gruber)	*1947.03*
Beat Back The Tide (Hitchens)	*1954.06*
The Beautiful Dead (Pentecost)	*1974.06*
Beauty Is A Beast (Knight)	*1959.06*
The Beauty Queen Killer (Creasey)	*1956.06*
Beauty Sleep (Dolson)	*1977.18*
Bedeviled (Block)	*1947.06*
Bedrooms Have Windows (Fair)	*1949.02*
Bejewelled Death (Babson)	*1982.13*
Benefit Performance (Sale)	*1946.06*
The Benevent Treasure (Wentworth)	*1954.13*
The Bengali Inheritance (Sela)	*1975.13*
Benjamin Franklin Takes the Case (Hall)	*1988.18*
Benjamin Franklin and a Case of Artful Murder (Hall)	*1994.07*
Bent Man (Maling)	*1975.16*
The Berlin Couriers (McGovern)	*1960.09*
Bernhardt's Edge (Wilcox)	*1988.10*
Bertie And The Crime Of Passion (Lovesey)	*1994.08*
The Best Cellar (Goodrum)	*1987.07*
Better Off Dead (McMullen)	*1982.09*
The Better To Eat You (Armstrong)	*1954.10*

The Detective Book Club 1942-2000 Title Index

Between Us And Evil (Russell)	1950.12
Beware The Curves (Fair)	1957.02
Beware Young Lovers (Pentecost)	1980.17
Beyond This Point Are Monsters (Millar)	1970.11
Beyond the Dark (Abbey)	1944.07
Beyond the Grave (Muller)	1986.05
Big Black Dog in Vallarta (Branham)	1999.07
The Big Blackout (Tracy)	1959.06
The Big Call (Ashe)	1975.14
The Big Call (Ashe)	1975.20
The Big Dig (McGurk)	1968.07
The Big Ear (Sterling)	1953.09
The Big Footprints (Innes)	1977.17
The Big Frame (Gordons)	1957.08
The Big H (Peters)	1963.08
A Big Hand for the Corpse (Bagby)	1953.10
The Big Payoff (Law)	1976.05
The Big Water (Derby)	1953.11
A Big Wind For Summer (Black)	1976.12
Biggie And The Mangled Mortician (Bell)	1997.07
Biggie And The Poisoned Politician (Bell)	1996.04
Bird In A Cage (Martin)	1995.22
Birdcage (Canning)	1979.17
Birds Of A Feather (Canning)	1985.17
Birthday, Deathday (Pentecost)	1972.08
The Bitter Bite (Ashford)	1996.13
Black As He's Painted (Marsh)	1974.13
Black Cypress (Crane)	1949.02
Black Death (Gilbert)	1954.02
Black Diamond (Holtzer)	1997.05
Black Eye (Steed)	1990.02
The Black Glass City (Philips)	1965.05
The Black Gold Murders (Ethan)	1959.08
The Black Iris (Little)	1953.03
Black Opal (Linklater)	1947.11
Black Orchids (Stout)	1942.05
The Black Path Of Fear (Woolrich)	1944.08
The Black Seraphim (Gilbert)	1984.02
The Black Tide (Innes)	1983.08
Black and Secret Midnight (Schunk)	1999.13
The Blackbird (Stark)	1969.11
The Blackbirder (Hughes)	1943.12
The Blackjack Hijack (Einstein)	1976.12
Blacklight (Knox)	1968.02
The Blank Wall (Holding)	1948.01
A Blast of Trumpets (Ashe)	1976.07
Bleak Spring (Cleary)	1993.08
Bleeding In The Eye Of A Brainstorm (Chesbro)	1995.02
Bleeding Maize and Blue (Holtzer)	1996.08
The Blessing Way (Hillerman)	1970.10
Blindsight (Stewart)	1987.03
Bliss Jumps The Gun (Sloan)	1999.06
The Blond Baboon (Wetering)	1978.08
The Blonde Cried Murder (Halliday)	1956.07
Blood Doesn't Tell (Barth)	1989.10
Blood Flies Upwards (Ferrars)	1977.11
Blood Money (Reagan)	1971.02
Blood Rain (Dibdin)	2000.01
Blood Sympathy (Hill)	1994.01
Blood Upon The Snow (Lawrence)	1945.02
Blood Will Tell (Christie)	1952.01
Blood of Your Sisters (Peel)	1997.06
Blood on the Black Market (Halliday)	1943.12
Bloodline (Boyle)	1995.03
Bloodlines (Hammond)	1998.03
Bloodtide (Knox)	1983.12
Bloody Bonsai (Abresch)	1998.10
The Bloody Book Of Law (Woods)	1984.12
Bloody Kin (Maron)	1985.02
Blue Bone (Woodhouse)	1973.14
Blue Murder (Rutland)	1943.01
Blueback (Knox)	1970.06
Bluebeard's Last Stand (Boyle)	1998.09
Bluefin Blues (Kemprecos)	1997.15
Blues For The Prince (Spicer)	1950.07
A Blurred Reality (Lewis)	1985.02
Bodies of Water (Borthwick)	1990.06
A Body For A Buddy (Stein)	1981.21
A Body For Bill (Shriber)	1943.02
Body Guard (Burns)	1991.12
The Body In The Basket (Bagby)	1954.12
The Body In The Bog (Page)	1996.12
The Body Shop (Berlinski)	1996.10
The Body in Cadiz Bay (Serafin)	1985.20
The Body in the Basement (Page)	1994.05
The Body in the Belfry (Page)	1990.02
The Body in the Billiard Room (Keating)	1987.15
The Body in the Library (Christie)	1942.03
The Bogus Buddha (Melville)	1990.05
The Bohemian Connection (Dunlap)	1985.07
Bolt (Francis)	1987.02
The Bombing Run (Stein)	1983.09
Bombship (Knox)	1980.21
The Bonded Dead (Chaber)	1971.07
Bones (Pronzini)	1985.11

Bones of Contention (Foley) — 1950.02
The Book Of Shadows (Grace) — 1996.18
The Book Of The Crime (Daly) — 1951.06
The Book Of The Dead (Daly) — 1944.09
The Book of the Lion (Daly) — 1948.07
Boomerang (Garve) — 1970.11
A Borderline Case (Williams) — 1960.08
Borderline Murder (Amos) — 1948.03
Born Guilty (Hill) — 1995.23
Born to be Hanged (Chaber) — 1973.16
Borrow The Night (Nielsen) — 1956.08
The Borrowed Alibi (Egan) — 1962.08
Borrower Of The Night (Peters) — 1973.18
The Boy Who Followed Ripley (Highsmith) — 1980.20
The Brandenburg Hotel (Winslow) — 1976.18
The Brass Rainbow (Collins) — 1969.06
Bravo for the Bride (Eyre) — 1995.04
Brazilian Sleigh Ride (Fish) — 1966.03
Break a Leg, Darling (Babson) — 1997.04
Brenda's Murder (Wells) — 1974.03
The Bric-A-Brac Man (Greenan) — 1977.06
Bridge Of Sand (Gruber) — 1963.10
The Bridge That Went Nowhere (Fish) — 1968.05
Brigade: the further adventures of Lestrade (Trow) — 1999.09
Brimstone (Duncan) — 1980.20
Broken Consort (Gollin) — 1990.08
Brothers of Silence (Gruber) — 1962.04
The Brownstone House (Foley) — 1974.15
The Buchan Papers (Jones) — 1997.10
Bullet Proof (Dean) — 1960.06
Bulrush Murders (Rothenberg) — 1991.11
Burden of Proof (Canning) — 1956.08
The Burglar In The Rye (Block) — 1999.01
The Burglar Who Painted Like Mondrian (Block) — 1998.04
Buried In Quilts (Frommer) — 1994.13
Buried In Stone (Wright) — 1996.14
Burn This (McCloy) — 1980.24
A Business Of Bodies (Forbes) — 1967.01
But I Wouldn't Want To Die There (Forbes) — 1972.13
The Buttercup Case (Crane) — 1959.11
Button Button (Bramhall) — 1944.09
By Hook or Crook (Gilbert) — 1947.02
By Reason Of (Henderson) — 1986.08
By-Line For Murder (Garve) — 1952.02
A Calculated Risk (Foley) — 1971.03
Call After Midnight (Eberhart) — 1965.02

Call It Accident (Foley) — 1966.02
Call the Witness (Sherry) — 1961.06
The Camelot Caper (Peters) — 1969.09
Canapes For The Kitties (Babson) — 1997.05
Candle For A Corpse (Granger) — 1996.15
The Cannibal Who Overate (Pentecost) — 1962.07
The Canvas Dagger (Reilly) — 1957.04
The Cape Murders (Weeks) — 1987.02
The Caper (Reagan) — 1969.10
The Captain (Shubin) — 1999.02
Captive (Gordons) — 1957.12
Cargo Of Eagles (Allingham) — 1968.08
Cargo Risk (Kirk) — 1981.06
Carmody's Run (Pronzini) — 1993.02
Carnage of the Realm (Goodrum) — 1979.12
Carriage of Justice (Hammond) — 1995.15
Casa Madrone (Eberhart) — 1980.12
Case Closed (Thomson) — 1977.12
The Case Of Robert Quarry (Garve) — 1972.11
The Case Of The Amorous Aunt (Gardner) — 1964.01
The Case Of The Angry Mourner (Gardner) — 1951.12
The Case Of The Backward Mule (Gardner) — 1946.08
The Case Of The Beautiful Beggar (Gardner) — 1965.09
The Case Of The Bigamous Spouse (Gardner) — 1961.11
The Case Of The Black-Eyed Blonde (Gardner) — 1944.12
The Case Of The Black-Eyed Blonde (Gardner) — 1947.12
The Case Of The Blonde Bonanza (Gardner) — 1962.07
The Case Of The Borrowed Brunette (Gardner) — 1947.01
The Case Of The Borrowed Brunette (Gardner) — 1947.12
The Case Of The Buried Clock (Gardner) — 1943.06
The Case Of The Calendar Girl (Gardner) — 1958.11
The Case Of The Careless Cupid (Gardner) — 1968.09
The Case Of The Crimson Kiss (Gardner) — 1971.05
The Case Of The Crooked Candle (Gardner) — 1944.07

<h1 style="text-align:center">The Detective Book Club 1942-2000 Title Index</h1>

The Case Of The Crying Swallow (Gardner)	1972.01
The Case Of The Daring Decoy (Gardner)	1957.11
The Case Of The Daring Divorce (Gardner)	1964.03
The Case Of The Deadly Toy (Gardner)	1959.01
The Case Of The Demure Defendant (Gardner)	1956.06
The Case Of The Drowning Duck (Gardner)	1942.07
The Case Of The Drowsy Mosquito (Gardner)	1943.11
The Case Of The Dubious Bridegroom (Gardner)	1949.03
The Case Of The Duplicate Daughter (Gardner)	1960.07
The Case Of The Empty Tin (Gardner)	1942.01
The Case Of The Fabulous Fake (Gardner)	1970.01
The Case Of The Fabulous Fake (Gardner)	1972.17
The Case Of The Fan-Dancer's Horse (Gardner)	1947.06
The Case Of The Fenced-In Woman (Gardner)	1973.01
The Case Of The Fiery Fingers (Gardner)	1951.07
The Case Of The Foot-Loose Doll (Gardner)	1958.05
The Case Of The Fugitive Nurse (Gardner)	1954.03
The Case Of The Gilded Lady (Gardner)	1956.11
The Case Of The Glamorous Ghost (Gardner)	1955.03
The Case Of The Golddigger's Purse (Gardner)	1945.07
The Case Of The Green-Eyed Sister (Gardner)	1954.01
The Case Of The Grinning Gorilla (Gardner)	1953.01
The Case Of The Half-Wakened Wife (Gardner)	1945.12
The Case Of The Half-Wakened Wife (Gardner)	1947.12
The Case Of The Hesitant Hostess (Gardner)	1953.07
The Case Of The Horrified Heir (Gardner)	1965.01
The Case Of The Ice-Cold Hands (Gardner)	1963.01
The Case Of The Irate Witness (Gardner)	1972.06
The Case Of The Irate Witness (Gardner)	1972.18
The Case Of The Lazy Lover (Gardner)	1947.10
The Case Of The Lonely Heiress (Gardner)	1948.05
The Case Of The Long-Legged Models (Gardner)	1958.01
The Case Of The Lucky Loser (Gardner)	1957.01
The Case Of The Mischievous Doll (Gardner)	1963.03
The Case Of The Missing Bronte (Barnard)	1983.09
The Case Of The Moth-Eaten Mink (Gardner)	1952.08
The Case Of The Mythical Monkeys (Gardner)	1959.07
The Case Of The Negligent Nymph (Gardner)	1950.01
The Case Of The Nervous Accomplice (Gardner)	1955.13
The Case Of The One-Eyed Witness (Gardner)	1951.01
The Case Of The One-Penny Orange (Cunningham)	1978.04
The Case Of The Phantom Fortune (Gardner)	1964.09
The Case Of The Postponed Murder (Gardner)	1973.07
The Case Of The Postponed Murder (Gardner)	1973.19
The Case Of The Queenly Contestant (Gardner)	1967.07
The Case Of The Reluctant Model (Gardner)	1962.01
The Case Of The Restless Redhead (Gardner)	1955.01
The Case Of The Runaway Corpse (Gardner)	1954.08
The Case Of The Russian Diplomat (Cunningham)	1978.13
The Case Of The Russian Diplomat (Cunningham)	1978.21

The Case Of The Screaming Woman
(Gardner) 1957.07
The Case Of The Shapely Shadow
(Gardner) 1961.01
The Case Of The Singing Skirt
(Gardner) 1959.11
The Case Of The Smoking Chimney
(Gardner) 1943.03
The Case Of The Spurious Spinster
(Gardner) 1961.05
The Case Of The Step-Daughter's
Secret (Gardner) 1963.09
The Case Of The Sun Bather's Diary
(Gardner) 1955.07
The Case Of The Terrified Typist
(Gardner) 1956.02
The Case Of The Troubled Trustee
(Gardner) 1965.03
The Case Of The Vagabond Virgin
(Gardner) 1948.08
The Case Of The Waylaid Wolf
(Gardner) 1960.01
The Case Of The Worried Waitress
(Gardner) 1966.09
A Case for Mr. Crook (Gilbert) 1952.11
The Case of the Careless Cupid
(Gardner) 1971.15
Castle In The Air (Westlake) 1980.16
Cat & Mouse (Gault) 1989.13
Cat And Mouse (Brand) 1951.01
The Cat And The Capricorn (Olsen) 1952.01
A Cat Of One's Own (Adamson) 1998.17
The Cat Who Could Read Backwards
(Braun) 1966.10
Cat in the Dark (Murphy) 1999.07
Cat-Eyed Trouble (Skinner) 1998.18
Catch A Falling Spy (Deighton) 1977.01
Catch Me, Kill Me (Hallahan) 1977.16
Catch Me, Kill Me (Hallahan) 1978.23
Catch the Saint (Charteris) 1976.01
Catching Fire (Smith) 1982.11
Catnapped (Gordons) 1975.04
Cats Prowl At Night (Fair) 1943.10
Cause and Effect (McInerny) 1987.13
Celebrity Trouble (Champion) 1997.17
Certain Sleep (Reilly) 1962.01
Chain of Death (McLarty) 1962.05
The Chameleon Course (Seaman) 1976.12
The Champagne Killer (Pentecost) 1973.03
The Chandler Policy (Disney) 1972.02

Change For The Worse
(Lemarchand) 1981.15
A Change of Heart (McCloy) 1973.09
Charisma (Bannister) 1994.15
Charlie Muffin, USA (Freemantle) 1980.18
Charlie's Bones (Thrasher) 1998.05
The Chase (Unekis) 1963.04
Cheating Death (Keating) 1994.02
A Checkmate for the Colonel
(Griswold) 1953.06
Cheer For The Dead (Colter) 1947.05
The Cheetah Chase (McQuillan) 1994.03
The Chickens In The Airshaft
(Franklin) 1972.15
The Chief Inspector's Daughter
(Radley) 1981.07
The Children Are Gone (Cavanaugh) 1966.07
The China Governess (Allingham) 1963.04
The Chinese Doll (Tucker) 1947.04
Choice Of Violence (Pentecost) 1961.11
A Chorus of Detectives (Paul) 1987.06
The Cinnamon Murder (Crane) 1946.09
Ciphered (Keech) 1980.11
Circles Of Confusion (Henry) 1999.12
Circus Day (Crane) 1986.15
City Called July (Engel) 1987.16
City of Fading Light (Cleary) 1985.16
The Clark Gable And Carole
Lombard Murder Case (Baxt) 1997.05
Cleveland Local (Roberts) 1997.14
The Clocks (Christie) 1964.11
Close Quarters (Curzon) 1996.06
A Clutch Of Coppers (Ashe) 1969.12
A Coat Of Varnish (Snow) 1980.05
A Coffin For Charley (Butler) 1994.04
Coffin For Christopher (Ames) 1954.11
The Coffin Tree (Butler) 1996.20
Coffin Underground (Butler) 1989.05
Coil Of Serpents (Stevenson) 1977.15
Cold Feet (Tucker) 1992.03
Cold Poison (Palmer) 1954.06
Cold Smoked (Beck) 1995.05
Collateral damage (Bowen) 1999.15
Collectors Item (Dean) 1953.05
Collision Bend (Roberts) 1996.21
Columbo and the Samurai Sword
(Magee) 1980.02
Columbo: The Game Show Killer
(Harrington) 1996.16
Columbo: The Helter Skelter
Murders (Harrington) 1994.12

Columbo: the Glitter Murder
  (Harrington) — 1997.11
Come Here And Die (York) — 1960.04
Come Out, Come Out
  (Malcolm-Smith) — 1965.11
The Come-On (Yorke) — 1979.12
A Common Death (Cooper) — 1991.02
The Company Of Saints (Anthony) — 1984.03
The Company She Kept (Eccles) — 1996.24
Compartment K (Reilly) — 1955.14
A Compelling Case (Underwood) — 1989.01
The Con (Boyle) — 1997.15
Conceal And Disguise (Kane) — 1967.01
Concrete Crime (Coles) — 1960.03
Condition Purple (Turnbull) — 1989.07
The Confession Of Brother Haluin
  (Peters) — 1989.02
A Conflict Of Interest (Williams) — 1972.02
Conflict of Interests (Ashford) — 1990.06
Conquest Before Autumn (Eden) — 1973.16
Conspiracy of Silence (Blizard) — 1954.09
A Conspiracy of Strangers (Martin) — 1986.11
The Conspirators (Haggard) — 1968.06
A Cool Day for Killing (Haggard) — 1969.04
Cop Cade (Ball) — 1979.05
The Copenhagen Connection
  (Peters) — 1982.16
Copper Peacock (Rendell) — 1992.02
Copper' Gold (Winslow) — 1978.12
The Copycat Killers (Pentecost) — 1984.02
The Coral Princess Murders (Crane) — 1954.14
A Corner Of Paradise (Holton) — 1977.07
Corpse Candle (Bagby) — 1968.02
The Corpse On The Dike (Wetering) — 1977.05
The Corpse That Came Back (Piper) — 1954.10
The Corpse With One Shoe (Scherf) — 1951.08
The Corpse With The Missing Watch
  (Walling) — 1950.04
The Corpse Without A Clue
  (Walling) — 1944.08
A Corpse by Any Other Name
  (Walling) — 1943.05
Corpse with the Flannel Nightgown
  (Scherf) — 1965.08
Corpses At Indian Stones (Wylie) — 1943.05
Cosi Fan Tutti (Dibdin) — 1999.18
The Counsellor Heart (Winslow) — 1980.24
The Count Of Nine (Fair) — 1958.07
Count The Cost (Ferrars) — 1957.11
Count on the Saint (Charteris) — 1981.01
Counterstroke (Garve) — 1978.18

Counterstroke (Wayland) — 1964.11
A Country Kind Of Death
  (McMullen) — 1975.16
The Country Of The Strangers
  (Wees) — 1960.03
Country and Fatal (Bagby) — 1980.21
Court Of Shadows (Jackson) — 1943.07
Cover-Up Stories (Babson) — 1988.14
Crackdown (Cornwell) — 1990.05
A Cracking of Spines (Roy Harley) — 1982.07
Craig's Spur (Madden) — 1963.07
A Credible Threat (Dawson) — 1996.16
A Crime Remembered (Ashford) — 1988.14
Crime Wind (Holbrook) — 1945.05
The Crime and the Crystal (Ferrars) — 1985.14
The Crime is Murder (Nielsen) — 1956.11
Crime on my Hands (Sanders) — 1945.01
The Crimshaw Memorandum (White) — 1967.04
The Croaker (Ashe) — 1973.11
The Croesus Conspiracy (Stein) — 1978.15
Crooked Wood (Underwood) — 1978.11
The Cross Bearer (Lewis) — 1995.06
Cross-check (Law) — 1997.12
The Crossfire Killings (Knox) — 1986.02
Crown Witness (Linscott) — 1995.18
The Crown in Darkness (Doherty) — 1988.02
Crows Can't Count (Fair) — 1946.05
The Cruise of a Deathtime (Babson) — 1985.12
Cry At Dusk (Ballard) — 1987.17
Cry For Help (Disney) — 1975.06
Cry Guilty (Woods) — 1981.13
Cry Guilty (Woods) — 1981.25
Cue For Murder (McCloy) — 1942.09
The Cup, The Blade Or The Gun
  (Eberhart) — 1961.09
Curiosity Didn't Kill The Cat (Wren) — 1974.07
The Curious Affair Of The Third Dog
  (Moyes) — 1974.02
Curly Smoke (Holtzer) — 1995.22
The Curse Of The Giant Hogweed
  (MacLeod) — 1985.15
The Curse Of The Pharaohs (Peters) — 1981.17
The Curse of the Bronze Lamp
  (Dickson) — 1945.09
Curses! (Elkins) — 1989.01
Curtain Fall (Dewhurst) — 1982.22
A Cut In Diamonds (Kirk) — 1986.09
Cut Thin to Win (Fair) — 1965.05
The D.A. Breaks A Seal (Gardner) — 1946.02
The D.A. Breaks An Egg (Gardner) — 1949.12
The D.A. Calls A Turn (Gardner) — 1944.02

The Detective Book Club 1942-2000 Title Index

The D.A. Cooks A Goose (Gardner) 1942.02
The D.A. Takes a Chance (Gardner) 1948.09
Daddy's Gone A-Hunting (Skinner) 1999.19
The Dame (Stark) 1969.02
The Damsel (Stark) 1967.08
Damsel in Distress (Dunn) 1997.17
Dance Of The Scarecrows (Sipherd) 1996.17
Dance Without Music (Cheyney) 1948.05
Dance on Blood (Linscott) 1998.05
The Dancing Savior (Hunter) 1999.03
Dancing in the Dark (Kaminsky) 1996.01
Danger Feeds My Fear (Strong) 1980.19
Danger Money (Eberhart) 1975.02
Danger Money (Eberhart) 1975.18
Danger Money (Eberhart) 1975.19
Danger Money (Eberhart) 1976.20
Danger: Hospital Zone (Curtiss) 1967.02
A Dangerous Funeral (McMullen) 1977.16
A Dangerous Liaison (Davey) 1987.03
Dangerous Passenger (Walsh) 1959.04
Dangerous To Know (Babson) 1981.22
Dangerous To Me (Foley) 1960.01
Dangerous by Nature (Coles) 1950.11
Dark Abyss (Knight) 1949.01
Dark Bahama (Cheyney) 1951.06
A Dark Coffin (Butler) 1996.22
The Dark Corner (Blizard) 1950.05
Dark Destination (Potts) 1955.11
Dark Duet (Cheyney) 1943.09
The Dark Fantastic (Masterson) 1959.07
The Dark Hill (Foley) 1975.05
Dark Horse (Shoemaker) 1996.02
Dark Interlude (Cheyney) 1947.08
The Dark Place (Elkins) 1983.16
Dark Prophecy (Alan) 1945.12
The Dark River (Clark) 1949.07
*The Dark Side of the Island
   (Hebden)* 1974.04
Dark Wanton (Cheyney) 1949.03
The Dark Wind (Hillerman) 1982.05
The Darker the Night (Brean) 1949.05
A Date With Danger (Vickers) 1944.09
*The Day Miss Bessie Lewis
   Disappeared (Disney)* 1972.16
The Day She Died (Reilly) 1963.01
Dead Aim (Wilcox) 1972.04
Dead Center (Wilcox) 1993.01
Dead Clever (Jeffries) 1989.03
The Dead Don't Speak (Erskine) 1955.02
Dead Drunk (Bagby) 1954.01
A Dead Ending (Philips) 1962.12

Dead Fall (Wilmer) 1954.04
Dead Giveaway (Brett) 1986.04
Dead Lagoon (Dibdin) 1994.08
Dead Lion (Bonett) 1949.07
*Dead Man's Fingers:A Chesapeake
   Bay mystery (Lee)* 1999.04
Dead Man's Folly (Christie) 1956.12
Dead Man's Mooring (Knox) 1988.01
Dead Man's Ransom (Peters) 1985.03
Dead Man's Shoes (Innes) 1954.12
Dead Man's Sweetheart (Linscott) 1997.04
Dead Matter (Frimmer) 1982.06
Dead Men Don't Dance (Chittenden) 1997.19
Dead Men's Plans (Eberhart) 1952.10
Dead Mr. Mozart (Barnard) 1995.17
Dead Of Winter (Cornish) 1959.07
Dead On Arrival (Thayer) 1960.11
Dead On Cue (Morice) 1985.11
The Dead Past (Piccirilli) 1997.18
Dead Reckoning (Thayer) 1954.13
The Dead Room (Resnicow) 1987.18
Dead Run (Foxx) 1975.17
The Dead Sea Cipher (Peters) 1970.10
The Dead Side Of The Mike (Brett) 1981.02
Dead South (Sullivan) 1996.12
Dead To Rites (Angus) 1979.05
*Dead Woman Of The Year
   (Pentecost)* 1968.03
Dead Yesterday (Fenisong) 1952.05
Dead and Dumb (Crispin) 1947.11
Dead at the Take-Off (Dent) 1946.06
Dead by Now (Erskine) 1954.06
The Dead of Winter (Gosling) 1996.01
Dead on Arrival (Simpson) 1987.10
Dead on Time (Keating) 1989.14
*Dead, She Was Beautiful
   (Masterson)* 1955.06
Deadeye (Llewellyn) 1991.03
Deadlier Than The Male (Holden) 1961.08
Deadline (Boyle) 1993.02
Deadline (Dewey) 1966.11
The Deadline (Franscell) 2000.03
Deadline at Dawn (Irish) 1944.03
Deadline: 2 a.m. (Pike) 1976.10
Deadly Contact (Dean) 1963.05
Deadly Delight (Stein) 1967.07
Deadly Duo (Allingham) 1949.10
The Deadly Friend (Pentecost) 1961.04
The Deadly Homecoming (George) 1973.04
The Deadly Isles (Vance) 1969.09
The Deadly Joke (Pentecost) 1971.11

Deadly Operation (Goldberg)	1999.08	*Death Mask (Pentecost)*	1981.05
Deadly Promise (Ballard)	1989.06	*Death Notice (Karl)*	1990.03
Deadly Purpose (Hansen)	1958.12	*The Death Of A Difficult Woman*	
Deadly Safari (McQuillan)	1990.03	*(Berry)*	1995.06
A Deadly Schedule (Hart)	1994.05	*Death Of A Don (Shaw)*	1982.02
A Deadly Shade of Gold		*Death Of A Garden Pest (Ripley)*	1996.18
(MacDonald)	1975.01	*Death Of A Hittite (Angus)*	1969.11
A Deadly Shade of Gold		*Death Of A Mystery Writer*	
(MacDonald)	1975.19	*(Barnard)*	1979.20
Deadly Trap (Pentecost)	1978.20	*Death Of An Ambassador (Coles)*	1957.09
Deadly is the Diamond (Eberhart)	1958.09	*Death Of An Englishman (Nabb)*	1983.06
Deal Me Out (Blazer)	1973.17	*Death Of An Intruder (Tyre)*	1953.03
Dear Miss Demeanor (Hess)	1987.13	*Death Of An Old Sinner (Davis)*	1957.07
Dearest Enemy (Woods)	1982.04	*The Death Of Cousin Rose*	
Death After Breakfast (Pentecost)	1978.08	*(Harrington)*	1996.14
Death Against The Clock (Gilbert)	1958.04	*A Death Of Distinction (Eccles)*	1998.21
Death And Letters (Daly)	1950.09	*Death Of Humpty Dumpty*	
Death And Mr. Potter (Foley)	1955.03	*(Alexander)*	1958.02
Death And The Little Brother		*Death On The Aisle (Lockridge)*	1942.04
(Knight)	1952.08	*Death On The Eno (Mackay)*	1982.02
Death And The Princess (Barnard)	1983.04	*Death On The Sixth Day (Farrell)*	1961.07
Death At The Door (Gilbert)	1945.03	*Death Paints a Portrait (Herber)*	1958.08
The Death At Yew Corner (Forrest)	1981.02	*Death Rings a Bell (Fitzsimmons)*	1942.08
Death Begs The Question (Eby)	1952.10	*Death Roll (Llewellyn)*	1989.04
Death Beside The Sea (Babson)	1983.09	*Death Row (Katz)*	1999.20
Death By Accident (Crider)	1998.02	*Death Scene (Suyker)*	1981.19
Death By Bequest (McMullen)	1978.04	*Death Sentence (Garfield)*	1976.03
Death By Sheer Torture (Barnard)	1982.08	*Death Sentence (Garfield)*	1976.20
Death Casts A Long Shadow		*Death Set to Music (Hebden)*	1983.13
(Gilbert)	1960.01	*Death Strikes At Heron House*	
The Death Ceremony (Melville)	1985.18	*(O'Neil)*	1944.08
Death Comes as the End (Christie)	1944.12	*Death Swap (Babson)*	1985.13
Death Drop (Gill)	1980.10	*Death Takes Time (Jeffries)*	1994.14
Death Echo (Tucker)	1993.03	*Death Takes a Bow (Lockridge)*	1943.08
A Death For A Dodo (Giroux)	1993.01	*Death Through The Looking Glass*	
Death Goes on Retreat (O'Marie)	1995.15	*(Forrest)*	1978.09
Death Goes to a Reunion (Knight)	1952.07	*Death Under Par (Law)*	1981.05
Death In A Cold Climate (Barnard)	1981.10	*Death Under the Lilacs (Forrest)*	1985.06
Death In A Sunny Place (Lockridge)	1972.10	*Death Undertow (Casley)*	1995.07
Death In Albert Park (Bruce)	1979.20	*Death Walks On Cat Feet (Olsen)*	1956.09
Death In Darkness (Whitney)	1978.06	*Death Warmed Over (Martin)*	1988.13
Death In The Channel (Anderson)	1977.02	*Death Warmed Up (Babson)*	1983.04
Death In The City (Anderson)	1983.02	*Death Watch (Hawkins)*	1958.09
A Death In The Life (Davis)	1976.17	*Death Wish (Garfield)*	1973.03
Death In The Limelight (Martin)	1946.04	*Death Won't Wait (Gilbert)*	1954.09
Death In The Morning (Radley)	1979.19	*Death and Taxes (Dewey)*	1967.10
Death Is Academic (Mackay)	1977.05	*Death and the Easter Bunny (Berry)*	1998.12
Death Keeps A Secret (Kelland)	1956.05	*Death at Deepwood Grange*	
Death Knocks Three Times (Gilbert)	1950.05	*(Underwood)*	1986.04
Death Lifts The Latch (Gilbert)	1946.03	*Death at the Table (Laurence)*	1997.18
Death Mask (Dentinger)	1988.02	*Death by FIre (Pentecost)*	1986.05

Death for a Dietician (Giroux) — 1989.13
Death for a Double (Giroux) — 1990.14
Death in Blue Folders (Maron) — 1985.22
Death in Good Company (Sprague) — 1998.03
Death in Lilac Time (Crane) — 1955.04
Death in Still Waters (Lee) — 1995.05
A Death in Town (Waugh) — 1989.05
Death in a Distant Land (Livingston) — 1988.09
A Death in the Family (Melville) — 1995.08
Death in the Greenhouse (Anderson) — 1983.10
Death in the Snow (Stern) — 1973.12
Death in the Willows (Forrest) — 1980.02
Death in the Wrong Room (Gilbert) — 1948.01
Death is a Dirty Trick (Philips) — 1981.01
Death of A Literary Widow (Barnard) — 1980.22
The Death of Me Yet (Masterson) — 1970.12
Death of a Butterfly (Maron) — 1984.06
Death of a DJ (Rubino) — 1995.16
Death of a Daimyo (Melville) — 1985.01
Death of a Doll (Lawrence) — 1947.03
Death of a Dutchman (Nabb) — 1983.15
Death of a Hawker (Wetering) — 1977.14
Death of a Heavenly Twin (Morice) — 1975.01
Death of a Prankster (Beaton) — 1993.04
Death of a Racehorse (Creasey) — 1962.08
Death of a Sunday Writer (Wright) — 1996.25
Death of a Wedding Guest (Morice) — 1976.14
Death of an Alaskan Princess (Smith) — 1988.03
Death of an Angel (O'Marie) — 1997.04
Death of an Expert Witness (James) — 1978.07
Death of an Expert Witness (James) — 1978.21
Death of an Expert Witness (James) — 1978.24
Death on the Mississippi (Forrest) — 1989.09
Death on the rocks (Wright) — 1999.15
Death squad London (Gerson) — 1989.04
Death's Clenched Fist (Sherburne) — 1982.18
Death's Gray Angel (Sherburne) — 1981.23
Death's Pale Horse (Sherburne) — 1980.14
Death's Savage Passion (Papazoglou) — 1986.13
The Death-Cap Dancers (Mitchell) — 1982.06
Death-Wish Green (Crane) — 1960.12
The Deaths Of Lora Karen (McDougald) — 1944.05
The Deception (Dale) — 1980.15
A Deceptive Clarity (Elkins) — 1987.09
Decoy (Maling) — 1970.02
The Deep Blue Good-By (MacDonald) — 1975.12
The Deep Blue Good-By (MacDonald) — 1976.21
Deepwater (Finer) — 1985.10
Deficit Ending (Martin) — 1990.10
The Delicate Ape (Hughes) — 1944.06
A Delicately Personal Matter (Werry) — 1986.06
Deliver Us From Wolves (Holton) — 1963.04
Depart This Life (Ferrars) — 1958.10
The Department Of Dead Ends (Vickers) — 1953.05
The Departure Of Mr. Gaudette (Disney) — 1964.12
Design For Murder (Quest) — 1981.14
Design for Dying (Morice) — 1988.17
Desire To Kill (Clarke) — 1982.19
Deveron Hall (Johnston) — 1977.08
The Devil to Play (Holton) — 1974.03
Devil's Due (Proctor) — 1961.04
The Devil's Hunt (Doherty) — 1998.06
Devil's Knell (Warner) — 1983.16
The Devil's Novice (Peters) — 1984.03
The Devil's Stronghold (Ford) — 1948.08
Devilweed (Knox) — 1966.08
Devious Murder (Bellairs) — 1981.06
The Diamond Bubble (Fish) — 1965.05
Diamond Cat (Babson) — 1995.21
Diamond in the Buff (Dunlap) — 1990.16
The Diamonds Of Loreta (Drummond) — 1980.10
Did She Fall Or Was She Pushed (Disney) — 1959.10
Die After Dark (Pentecost) — 1976.17
Die For Love (Peters) — 1984.04
A Die In The Country (Wells) — 1973.05
Die Laughing (Allen) — 1998.13
Die Like a Man (Delving) — 1970.12
Die Quickly, Dear Mother (Wells) — 1969.08
Die, Little Goose (Alexander) — 1956.05
Died in the Wool (Marsh) — 1945.07
Dig Me Later (Hagen) — 1949.08
Ding Dong Bell (Reilly) — 1958.12
Dinky Died (Wells) — 1970.10
A Dinner To Die For (Dunlap) — 1987.05
Dire Happenings at Scratch Ankle (Sibley) — 1993.02
Dirge for a Doge (Eyre) — 1997.06
Dirty Pool (Bagby) — 1967.02
Dishonor Among Thieves (Dean) — 1958.09
Displaced Person (Hilton) — 1988.04
Ditch Rider (Van Gieson) — 1998.25

The Detective Book Club 1942-2000 Title Index

Divided Treasure (Williams)	1988.04	*Dream Of Fair Woman (Armstrong)*	1966.06
Do Not Disturb (McCloy)	1943.07	*Drift Away (Tucker)*	1994.04
Do Not Fold, Spindle Or Mutilate		*Drink This (Dewhurst)*	1981.18
(Disney)	1971.06	*Drowned Hope (Westlake)*	1990.04
Do Not Murder Before Christmas		*Drowned Rat (Ferrars)*	1976.04
(Iams)	1950.03	*Drowning Pool (Cooper)*	1997.20
The Doctor Digs A Grave		*Dual Enigma (Underwood)*	1988.06
(Hathaway)	1998.21	*Duet of Death (Lawrence)*	1949.05
The Doctor and the Corpse (Murray)	1952.11	*The Duke Of Cleveland (Roberts)*	1995.13
Dog In The Manger (Curtiss)	1982.24	*Dupe (Cody)*	1982.03
Dogsbody, Inc. (Thrasher)	1999.18	*Dust Devils of the Purple Sage*	
Dolly Is Dead (Borthwick)	1995.20	*(Smith)*	1995.09
Don't Forget To Die (Chittenden)	1999.16	*Dusty Death (Thayer)*	1966.06
Don't Go Into The Woods Today		*Duty Elsewhere (Wainwright)*	1980.06
(Disney)	1974.12	*The Duveen Letter (Leather)*	1980.19
Don't Hang Me Too High		*Dying Echo (Knight)*	1949.05
(O'Sullivan)	1954.11	*A Dying Fall (Thomson)*	1985.04
Don't Look Back (Borgenicht)	1956.05	*Dying on the Vine (King)*	1998.08
Don't Open That Door (Curtiss)	1968.12	*Early Autumn (Parker)*	1981.01
Don't Turn Your Back on the Ocean		*An Easy Day for a Lady (Linscott)*	1995.23
(Dawson)	1994.15	*An Easy Way To Go (Coxe)*	1969.01
Done to Death (Woods)	1975.17	*Egypt's Choice (Broun)*	1964.02
The Doomsday Carrier (Canning)	1977.14	*El Rancho Rio (Eberhart)*	1971.01
The Door Fell Shut (Albrand)	1966.09	*Elope To Death (Ashe)*	1977.20
A Double Coffin (Butler)	1998.07	*The Elusive Mrs. Pollifax (Gilman)*	1972.04
Double Espresso (Bruno)	1998.23	*Elusive Quarry (Comfort)*	1995.05
Double Identity (Coxe)	1970.04	*Emily Dickinson Is Dead (Langton)*	1984.11
Double Image (Vickers)	1955.14	*The Empress of Coney Island*	
Double Jeopardy (Underwood)	1982.05	*(Gillespie)*	1986.07
The Double Man (Reilly)	1952.06	*The Empty Copper Sea (MacDonald)*	1978.14
Double Sin and Other Stories		*The Empty Copper Sea (MacDonald)*	1978.23
(Christie)	1961.12	*The Empty House (Gilbert)*	1979.14
The Double Take (Huggins)	1946.01	*Encore Murder (Babson)*	1990.05
Double or Quits (Fair)	1942.03	*Encounter with Evil (Dean)*	1961.05
Doubles In Death (Grew)	1953.09	*End Of A Party (Waugh)*	1965.06
Down For The Count (Kaminsky)	1985.03	*The End Of The Track (Garve)*	1956.09
Downbeat For A Dirge (Bird)	1952.12	*End-Game (Gilbert)*	1982.21
Drag Strip (Bartholomew)	1999.22	*Endless Night (Christie)*	1968.05
Drag The Dark (Davis)	1953.08	*The Enemy (Bagley)*	1978.12
Dragons At The Gate (Duncan)	1976.02	*Enemy in the House (Eberhart)*	1962.12
Dragons At The Party (Cleary)	1988.05	*Enough To Kill A Horse (Ferrars)*	1956.01
Dragonship (Kirk)	1977.12	*Enter a Gentlewoman (Woods)*	1982.20
Draw The Curtain Close (Dewey)	1948.02	*The Enthusiast (Hill)*	1979.12
Dread Journey (Hughes)	1945.09	*Episode Of The Wandering Knife*	
The Dreadful Lemon Sky		*(Rinehart)*	1951.02
(MacDonald)	1975.03	*Escapade (Satterthwait)*	1995.21
The Dreadful Lemon Sky		*Escape To Fear (Foley)*	1958.04
(MacDonald)	1976.21	*The Estate Of The Beckoning Lady*	
The Dreadful Lemon Sky		*(Allingham)*	1955.06
(MacDonald)	1976.23	*The Etruscan Bull (Gruber)*	1969.06
Dream Of A Falling Eagle (Chesbro)	1996.21	*The Etruscan Smile (Johnston)*	1977.13

The Etruscan Smile (Johnston)	*1977.23*
Eve of Destruction (Edwards)	*1998.18*
Even Cops' Daughters (Webb)	*1986.14*
Even Yuppies Die (Babson)	*1996.20*
Every Crooked Nanny (Trocheck)	*1992.03*
Every Inch A Lady (Fleming)	*1978.10*
Evidence of Things Seen (Daly)	*1943.09*
Evidence to Destroy (Yorke)	*1987.15*
Evil Breeding: A dog lover's mystery	
(Conant)	*1999.05*
Evil Mark (Miles)	*1986.07*
The Evil That Men Do (Pentecost)	*1966.10*
Evil Under The Sun (Christie)	*1942.01*
Evil at the Root (Crider)	*1990.09*
An Excellent Mystery (Peters)	*1986.09*
An Exchange Of Eagles (Sela)	*1977.18*
An Exchange Of Eagles (Sela)	*1977.22*
Exit Running (Spicer)	*1959.12*
Experiment with Death (Ferrars)	*1981.20*
Explosion (Disney)	*1948.05*
Extreme Odds (Hanson)	*1999.14*
An Eye For An Eye (Bayer)	*1945.08*
The Eye of the Needle (Walsh)	*1962.01*
Eyes That Watch You (Irish)	*1952.12*
The Eyewitness (Hebden)	*1967.11*
Face Down Among The Winchester	
Geese (Emerson)	*1999.06*
Face Down In The Marrow-Bone Pie	
(Emerson)	*1997.10*
Face Down Upon a Herbal	
(Emerson)	*1998.05*
Face Down in the Park (Foglia)	*1999.07*
The Face In The Shadows (Johnston)	*1971.14*
The Face Of Hate (DuBois)	*1949.03*
The Face Of The Enemy (Walsh)	*1967.04*
Faceless Enemy (Wees)	*1966.12*
Fade to Black (Staub)	*1998.14*
Fair Game (Hammond)	*1982.19*
The Fair Maid Of Bohemia	
(Marston)	*1997.07*
Faithful Unto Death (Graham)	*1998.09*
Falconer and the Face of God	
(Morson)	*1997.08*
Falconer and the Great Beast	
(Morson)	*1999.05*
Falconer's Judgement (Morson)	*1996.19*
Fall From Grace (Canning)	*1981.12*
Fall From Grace (Wright)	*1991.10*
Fall Guy For Murder (Goldman)	*1943.08*
Fallen Into the Pit (Peters)	*1994.06*
False Scent (Marsh)	*1960.05*
Family Affair (Eberhart)	*1981.16*
Family Business (Lewin)	*1995.09*
Family Fortune (Eberhart)	*1976.17*
Family Fortune (Eberhart)	*1977.23*
Family Fortune (Eberhart)	*1977.25*
Family Skeletons (MacPherson)	*1997.06*
The Famous McGarry Stories	
(Taylor)	*1958.05*
The Fantastic Saint (Charteris)	*1983.05*
The Faraway Drums (Cleary)	*1982.16*
The Farmhouse (Reilly)	*1947.08*
The Fatal Amateur (Mathews)	*1959.05*
Fatal Charm (Morice)	*1989.14*
Fatal Finish (D'Alton)	*1983.02*
Fatal Harvest (Amos)	*1958.03*
Fatal In My Fashion (McGerr)	*1954.14*
Fatal Lady (Foley)	*1964.04*
Fatal Purchase (Rowe)	*1945.06*
Fate Worse than Death (Radley)	*1986.08*
Fear Comes To Chalfont (Crofts)	*1942.07*
The Fear In Yesterday's Rings	
(Chesbro)	*1991.05*
Fear of a Stranger (Foley)	*1967.07*
Fellowship Of Fear (Elkins)	*1983.07*
The Fence (Nelson)	*1953.07*
The Ferguson Affair (Macdonald)	*1961.02*
Festival (Anderson)	*1980.07*
A Few Dying Words (Gosling)	*1994.07*
The Fifth Caller (Nielsen)	*1959.04*
The Fifth Man (Coles)	*1946.01*
Figure in the Dusk (Creasey)	*1953.12*
Figurehead (Knox)	*1969.03*
Filmi, Filmi, Inspector Ghote	
(Keating)	*1977.17*
Final Appearance (Nolan)	*1943.04*
Final Closing (Lee)	*1997.09*
Final Curtain (Ballard)	*1992.01*
Final Cut (Wright)	*1991.05*
Final Moments (Page)	*1987.04*
Find the Woman (Disney)	*1963.02*
A Fine And Private Place (Queen)	*1971.09*
A Fine And Private Place (Queen)	*1971.15*
A Fine And Private Place (Queen)	*1972.17*
A Fine And Private Place (Queen)	*1973.19*
A Fine Italian Hand (Wright)	*1993.01*
The Finger (Stein)	*1973.07*
The Fingerprint (Gilbert)	*1965.06*
Fire Horse (Shoemaker)	*1995.10*
Fire Storm (Duncan)	*1979.03*
Fire Will Freeze (Millar)	*1944.04*
Firestorm (Peel)	*1984.01*

First Gravedigger (Paul) 1981.11
First Hit of the Season (Dentinger) 1984.15
The First Mrs. Winston (Foley) 1973.01
Fish or Cut Bait (Fair) 1963.05
The Five Bells And Bladebone
  (Grimes) 1987.05
Five Bullets (Thayer) 1944.11
Five Passengers From Lisbon
  (Eberhart) 1946.07
Five Pieces Of Jade (Ball) 1972.13
Five Roads To Death (Philips) 1978.03
The Five-Day Nightmare (Brown) 1962.10
A Fix Life This (Constantine) 1976.07
Flash Point (Craig) 1987.16
Flesh And Blood (Cook) 1989.01
Fletch Reflected (McDonald) 1994.08
Flight Into Fear (Kyle) 1972.14
Flight Into Terror (White) 1955.12
A Flight from Paris (Webster) 1987.06
Flight of the Witch (Peters) 1991.04
Flowers For His Funeral (Granger) 1995.02
Flowers by Request (Holton) 1964.04
The Fly On The Wall (Hillerman) 1972.03
Flyaway (Bagley) 1979.17
The Flying Red horse (Crane) 1949.11
Folio On Florence White (Oursler) 1942.06
Follow Me (Reilly) 1960.09
The Foo Dog (Wells) 1972.01
A Fool And His Honey (Harris) 1999.01
A Fool for Murder (Babson) 1984.08
Fool's Gold (Wood) 1986.19
Fools Die on Friday (Fair) 1947.08
Footnote to Murder (Taylor) 1983.15
The Foretelling (Crane) 1982.22
Found: A Body (Struthers) 1999.13
Four Lost Ladies (Palmer) 1950.01
Four Past Four (Vickers) 1945.10
The Fourteen Dilemma (Pentecost) 1976.08
The Fourth Postman (Rice) 1948.10
Fowl Play (DuBois) 1951.12
The Frazer Acquittal (Ransome) 1955.08
The Fred Astaire and Ginger Rogers
  Murder Case (Baxt) 1996.06
Free Fall in Crimson (MacDonald) 1981.09
Freezing (Evans) 1998.09
The Frenchman (Johnston) 1976.11
The Frenchman (Johnston) 1976.22
Frequent Hearses (Crispin) 1982.11
The Friday Harbor Murders (Weeks) 1988.06
The Frightened Fiancee (Coxe) 1951.02
The Frightened Murderer (Rutledge) 1957.08

The Frightened Wife (Rinehart) 1953.11
Frobisher's Savage (Tourney) 1994.09
Frog In The Throat (Ferrars) 1981.04
Frogskin and Muttonfat (Caverly) 1996.08
Full Circle (Wilcox) 1995.11
Full House (Singer) 1986.10
A Funeral Of Gondolas (Holme) 1983.11
Funerals Are Fatal (Christie) 1953.03
Funny, Jonas, You Don't Look Dead
  (McMullen) 1977.02
Fury's Children (Shubin) 1999.08
Fuzz (McBain) 1968.10
The Garb of Truth (Stuart) 1984.01
The Garbage Collector (Stein) 1984.13
The Garden Club Mystery
  (Landrum) 1998.24
The Garden Plot (Borthwick) 1997.10
Gemini Trip (Law) 1978.02
Genealogy of Murder (Martin) 1996.02
Gentle Albatross (Foote-Smith) 1976.18
The Gentle Assassin (Richards) 1965.03
Gentleman Traitor (Williams) 1976.09
Gently Between The Tides (Hunter) 1983.10
The Genuine Article (Guthrie Jr.) 1977.20
Getting Away With Murder?
  (Morice) 1984.04
Ghost Of A Chance (Roos) 1947.07
The Ghost Writer (Carter) 1975.13
The Ghostway (Hillerman) 1985.05
Gideon's Art (Marric) 1972.05
Gideon's Art (Marric) 1972.18
Gideon's Drive (Marric) 1977.04
Gideon's Fog (Marric) 1975.05
Gideon's Fog (Marric) 1975.20
Gideon's Force (Marric) 1985.06
Gideon's Law (Marric) 1986.03
Gideon's Men (Marric) 1973.01
Gideon's Press (Marric) 1974.01
Gideon's Way (Marric) 1986.17
The Gift Horse (Gruber) 1943.01
Girl From Nowhere (Foley) 1949.06
The Girl From The Mimosa Club
  (Ford) 1957.06
Girl Missing (Sherry) 1962.09
Girl On The Run (Waugh) 1966.04
Girl Watcher's Funeral (Pentecost) 1969.09
The Girl Who Cried Wolf (Waugh) 1959.02
The Girl Who Wasn't There (Dewey) 1960.06
The Girl Who Wouldn't Talk
  (Vickers) 1959.09

The Detective Book Club 1942-2000 Title Index

The Girl With Six Fingers (Pentecost) 1969.06

The Girl With the Frightened Eyes (Lariar) 1945.12

Girl on a High Wire (Foley) 1970.01

Give 'Em The Ax (Fair) 1944.10

A Glancing Light (Elkins) 1991.05

The Glass Factory (Wishnia) 2000.02

Glitterbug (Kenrick) 1991.12

Go Down, Death (Hays) 1946.06

Go Gently, Gaijin (Melville) 1988.08

Go West, Inspector Ghote (Keating) 1981.13

Go, Lovely Rose (Potts) 1954.08

Go-Between (Maling) 1971.03

The Goblin Market (McCloy) 1944.03

God in Concord (Langton) 1992.02

A Going Concern (Aird) 1994.12

Going Wrong (Rendell) 1991.06

The Gold Frame (Resnicow) 1985.01

The Gold Gamble (Resnicow) 1988.06

The Gold Gap (Gruber) 1968.04

Gold In Every Grave (Nelson) 1951.11

The Golden Creep (Bagby) 1982.21

The Golden Deed (Garve) 1960.07

The Golden Sabre (Cleary) 1982.04

The Golden Soak (Innes) 1973.14

The Golden Trap (Pentecost) 1967.09

The Golden Years Caper (Carson) 1971.04

Good Behavior (Westlake) 1986.09

Good Cop, Bad Cop (D'Amato) 1998.10

The Good Detective (Keating) 1995.12

Good Luck To The Corpse (Murray) 1952.04

Good Night, Sweet Prince (Berry) 1990.15

Good Spies Don't Grow On Trees (Lovell) 1986.18

Good and Dead (Langton) 1986.21

Gospel (James) 1999.25

The Gospel Makers (Fraser) 1996.03

The Gourmet Detective (King) 1996.17

Grave Danger (Roos) 1966.03

Grave Doubt (Baker) 1973.08

A Grave Undertaking (White) 1962.02

Graveyard Plots (Pronzini) 1985.16

The Gravy Train (Masterson) 1971.11

The Great Mail Robbery (Kelland) 1951.10

The Great Yant Mystery (Cunningham) 1943.12

The Greek Affair (Gruber) 1964.10

The Green Ace (Palmer) 1951.05

Green Frontier (Hilton) 1982.15

The Green Hell Treasure (Fish) 1971.06

The Green Ripper (MacDonald) 1979.21

The Green Stone (Blanc) 1962.02

The Gremlin's Grampa (Pike) 1972.07

The Grey Beginning (Michaels) 1984.12

Grim City (Hensley) 1994.04

A Gross Carriage Of Justice (Fish) 1979.13

Grow Young And Die (O'Farrell) 1952.08

The Grub-And-Stakers Quilt A Bee (Craig) 1985.08

The Grub-and-Stakers Move A Mountain (Craig) 1981.10

Guaranteed To Fade (Bagby) 1979.03

The Guardian (Hough Jr.) 1975.11

Guilt Is Where You Find It (Thayer) 1957.05

Guilty Conscience (Underwood) 1994.10

The Gun in Daniel Websters Bust (Scherf) 1949.10

Gunner Kelly (Price) 1984.15

A Haiku for Hanae (Melville) 1989.09

Hail, Hail, The Gang's All Here (McBain) 1971.08

Half Past Nun (Quill) 1997.09

Hallowe'en Party (Christie) 1970.03

A Hammer In His Hand (Masterson) 1960.04

Hand Of Fate (Underwood) 1982.16

A Handy Death (Rothblatt) 1973.18

Hang The Consequences (Meek) 1985.09

Hang the Little Man (Creasey) 1965.02

Hanged For A Sheep (Gatenby) 1973.08

Hanged For A Sheep (Lockridge) 1942.09

Hanged Man's House (Ferrars) 1974.18

The Hanging Tree (Knox) 1984.05

Hangman's Row (Stein) 1982.13

The Hangman's Tree (Disney) 1949.08

Hangover House (Rohmer) 1949.12

Happy Holiday (O'Finn) 1951.04

Happy Never After (Trocheck) 1995.19

Hard Detective (Keating) 2000.01

Hard Tack (D'Amato) 1991.02

Hark, Hark, The Watchdogs Bark (Wells) 1976.04

Harm's Way (Aird) 1984.06

The Hatchet Man (Marshall) 1977.09

The Hatter's Phantoms (Simenon) 1976.19

Hawk Watch (Bird) 1954.09

He Didn't Mind Danger (Gilbert) 1949.09

He Never Came Back (McCloy) 1954.13

He Who Whispers (Carr) 1946.05

He Wouldn't Kill Patience (Dickson) 1944.04

Headhunt (Brennan) 1991.09

Headlong For Murder (Mace) 1943.06

The Detective Book Club 1942-2000 Title Index

Heart Trouble (Trocheck)	*1996.04*
Heartbreaker (Ferrigno)	*1999.09*
Heir Apparent (Withers)	*1961.07*
The Heir Hunters (Ballinger)	*1966.08*
Hellspout (Knox)	*1977.04*
Helpline (Sultan)	*1999.21*
A Herald Of Doom (Ashe)	*1975.03*
Here Lies... (Disney)	*1963.12*
The Hermit Of Eyton Forest (Peters)	*1988.07*
The Hidden And The Hunted (Swiggett)	*1950.11*
The Hidden Hour (Ransome)	*1966.07*
The Hidden Man (Underwood)	*1985.06*
Hide Her From Every Eye (Pentecost)	*1966.04*
The Hiding Place (Keith)	*1965.07*
High Rendezvous (Knight)	*1954.07*
High Stakes (Francis)	*1976.08*
High Stakes (Francis)	*1976.22*
High Stakes (Francis)	*1976.24*
High Stand (Innes)	*1988.08*
High Tide (Hubbard)	*1970.12*
The High Wire (Haggard)	*1964.02*
Hijacked (Harper)	*1971.01*
Hildegarde Withers Makes The Scene (Palmer)	*1969.12*
Hire a Hangman (Wilcox)	*1991.06*
The Historical Society Murder Mystery (Landrum)	*1996.18*
Hit and Run (Creasey)	*1959.12*
A Hobby Of Murder (Ferrars)	*1995.13*
The Hochman Miniatures (Fish)	*1967.10*
The Hollow (Christie)	*1946.10*
The Hollow Needle (Coxe)	*1949.02*
Hollow Vengeance (Morice)	*1982.20*
The Holm Oaks (Hubbard)	*1966.06*
Holy Treasure! (Williams)	*1989.07*
Home and Murder (Stein)	*1962.08*
Home to Roost (Garve)	*1977.03*
The Homicidal Horse (Pentecost)	*1980.08*
Homicide House (Frome)	*1950.07*
Honest Money (Gardner)	*1991.07*
Honest Reliable Corpse (Bagby)	*1969.05*
Honeymoon With Death (Pentecost)	*1975.15*
Honolulu Story (Ford)	*1946.08*
The Honourable Detective (Ashford)	*1988.09*
Hoodwink (Pronzini)	*1981.21*
Hook, Line And Murder (Elkjer)	*1998.11*
Hopscotch (Garfield)	*1975.06*
The Horn Of Roland (Peters)	*1975.02*
The Hornet's Nest (Fischer)	*1944.05*
Horror on the Ruby X (Crane)	*1956.10*
Hosanna Shout (Irvine)	*1995.10*
The Hospitality Of The House (Disney)	*1964.05*
Hostage To Death (Ashford)	*1978.09*
Hot Red Money (Kendrick)	*1959.11*
The Hot Rock (Westlake)	*1970.11*
Hot Summer Killing (Philips)	*1969.03*
Hotshots (Gieson)	*1996.23*
The Hour Before Midnight (Johnston)	*1978.11*
The Hour Before Midnight (Johnston)	*1979.22*
The House In The Forest (Cumberland)	*1951.04*
The House On The Left Bank (Johnston)	*1975.03*
The House That Died (Gill)	*1955.07*
A House by the side of the road (Gleiter)	*1998.12*
House of Storm (Eberhart)	*1949.09*
The House on K Street (White)	*1965.12*
The House on Plymouth Street and Other Stories (Curtiss)	*1985.14*
The House that Jack Built (Dewhurst)	*1984.07*
How Like An Angel (Millar)	*1962.10*
How Still My Love (Siegel)	*1958.03*
How To Live Dangerously (Fleming)	*1975.08*
A Howling In The Woods (Johnston)	*1969.01*
Humans (Westlake)	*1992.01*
The Hundreth Door (Foley)	*1951.03*
Hunt With the Hounds (Eberhart)	*1950.10*
Hunter Of The Blood (Masterson)	*1977.08*
The Hunting Season (Mayo)	*1985.09*
Hush-A-Bye Murder (Alexander)	*1957.09*
I Came to a Castle (Johnston)	*1970.02*
I Came to the Highlands (Johnston)	*1974.10*
I Could Murder Her (Lorac)	*1952.04*
I Found Him Dead (Gallagher)	*1947.11*
I Gave At The Office (Westlake)	*1971.09*
I Met Murder (Ferrars)	*1986.10*
I Want to Go Home (Lockridge)	*1948.06*
I'll Sing You Two-O (Fraser)	*1996.26*
I, Martha Adams (Winslow)	*1984.13*
I, Said the Demon! (Baxt)	*1969.07*
Iced (Robitaille)	*1995.10*
The Iciest Sin (Keating)	*1990.13*
An Ideal Crime (Ashford)	*1986.10*
If She Should Die (Rydell)	*1961.03*
If Two of Them are Dead (Forbes)	*1968.09*

The Detective Book Club 1942-2000 Title Index

If You Want To See Your Wife Again... (Craig) — 1972.05
In At The Kill (Ferrars) — 1979.13
In Colt Blood (Jaffe) — 1998.15
In Connection With Kilshaw (Driscoll) — 1974.08
In Her Garden (Godden) — 1981.11
In The Enemy Camp (Duncan) — 1985.23
In The Frame (Francis) — 1977.11
In The Frame (Francis) — 1977.24
In The Time Of The Poisoned Queen (Dukthas) — 1998.02
In the Teeth of Adversity (Babson) — 1990.06
In the dark (McKinney) — 1999.10
In-Laws and Outlaws (Paul) — 1990.01
Incident In Iceland (Webster) — 1979.19
Incident at 125th Street (Brown) — 1970.06
An Incident at Bloodtide (Chesbro) — 1993.06
Incident at Hendon (Letton) — 1968.04
Incident at Parga (Livingston) — 1988.03
The Indigo Necklace (Crane) — 1945.03
Inherited Murder (Martin) — 1994.01
Innocent Blood (James) — 1980.17
The Innocent Bottle (Gilbert) — 1949.04
Innocent Bystander (Frost) — 1955.13
The Innocent Mrs. Duff (Holding) — 1946.04
The Inside Man (Coxe) — 1974.12
The Inside-Out Heist (Reagan) — 1971.05
Inspector Ghote Breaks An Egg (Keating) — 1971.14
Inspector Ghote Draws The Line (Keating) — 1979.14
Inspector Ghote Goes By Train (Keating) — 1972.15
Inspector Ghote Trusts The Heart (Keating) — 1973.13
Inspector Maigret And The Burglar's Wife (Simenon) — 1956.04
Inspector Maigret And The Dead Girl (Simenon) — 1956.01
Inspector Saito's Small Satori (Van De Wetering) — 1985.03
Inspector West Takes Charge (Creasey) — 1973.06
Inspector West at Home (Creasey) — 1974.03
Intelligence (Goldberg) — 2000.03
Interface for Murder (Biggle Jr.) — 1987.01
Intrigue For Empire (Knight) — 1944.10
Invisible Green (Sladek) — 1979.15
Invitation To Murder (Ford) — 1954.12
Invitation To Murder (Shriber) — 1944.02
Invitation To Vengeance (Knight) — 1961.01
Invitation to Violence (White) — 1958.03
Irish Tenure (McInerny) — 1999.22
The Iron Cobweb (Curtiss) — 1953.04
The Iron Sanctuary (MacLeod) — 1968.06
Is There a Traitor in the House? (McGerr) — 1965.01
Isle of Snakes (Fish) — 1963.06
It's Her Own Funeral (Carnac) — 1952.10
It's Murder, Mr Potter (Foley) — 1961.04
It's Raining Violence (Du Bois) — 1950.03
Italian Fever (Martin) — 1999.11
The Jackal's Head (Peters) — 1968.11
Jade for a Lady (Chaber) — 1962.07
The Japanese Corpse (Wetering) — 1978.01
The Japanese Corpse (Wetering) — 1978.22
Jet Stream (Ferguson) — 1974.06
Jewels for a Shroud (Steiguer) — 1950.10
Jigsaw (McBain) — 1970.07
Jimmy The Kid (Westlake) — 1974.15
Jink (McMahon) — 1971.12
The Judas Freak (Pentecost) — 1974.16
The Judas Goat (Parker) — 1978.17
The Judas Goat (Parker) — 1978.22
The Judge And His Hangman (Durrenmatt) — 1955.10
Judgement Deferred (Ashford) — 1994.11
A Judgement In Stone (Rendell) — 1978.09
Judgement On Deltchev (Ambler) — 1951.08
Judicial Body (Scherf) — 1957.10
Juggernaut (Bagley) — 1987.07
The Juror (Underwood) — 1975.16
Jury Of One (Eberhart) — 1960.08
Just a Corpse at Twilight (Van de Wetering) — 1994.12
Justice Has No Sword (Franklin) — 1953.12
Keep the Baby, Faith (DeGrave) — 1986.20
Keeper Of The Children (Hallahan) — 1979.04
The Kentish Manor Murders (Symons) — 1988.10
Kept Women Can't Quit (Fair) — 1960.11
The Key (McClintick) — 1987.08
The Key Man (Kelland) — 1952.09
A Key To The Morgue (Martin) — 1959.09
The Kid Who Came Home With A Corpse (Stone) — 1972.14
The Kidnaped Child (Ashe) — 1971.15
The Kidnaped Child (Ashe) — 1972.17
The Kidnapped Child (Ashe) — 1971.08
The Kidnapping Of The President (Templeton) — 1975.07

The Detective Book Club 1942-2000 Title Index

Kiet and the Golden Peacock (Alexander)	1990.02	The Lake of Darkness (Rendell)	1980.13
Kill Once, Kill Twice (Hunt)	1957.01	Lame Dog Murder (Creasey)	1973.02
Kill Or Cure (Ferrars)	1957.03	Lament For The Bride (Reilly)	1952.01
Kill With Care (Nelson)	1954.02	The Last Act Of All (Templeton)	1996.17
Kill and Kill Again (Pentecost)	1987.09	Last Flight (Land)	1975.13
Kill or Cure (Kittredge)	1995.14	The Last Gamble (Foley)	1957.02
Killed In Fringe Time (DeAndrea)	1996.03	The Last Judgement (Clarke)	1985.12
Killed In The Act (DeAndrea)	1982.07	The Last Kabbalist Of Lisbon (Zimler)	1998.04
Killed On The Ice (DeAndrea)	1984.03	Last Man Standing (Wright)	1991.01
Killed With A Passion (DeAndrea)	1983.11	The Last One Kills (Masterson)	1969.10
Killed in Paradise (DeAndrea)	1988.11	Last Respects (Aird)	1983.03
Killer Among Us (Martin)	1959.02	The Last Sherlock Holmes Story (Dibdin)	1978.20
Killer Loose! (Holden)	1953.06	The Last Sherlock Holmes Story (Dibdin)	1978.23
A Killer in the Street (Nielsen)	1967.06		
Killer's Ink (Karl)	1988.02	The Last Straw (Disney)	1955.02
Killer's Wake (Cornwell)	1989.11	Last Walk Home (Page)	1983.13
Killer.app (D'Amato)	1996.19	Last Will And Testament (Ferrars)	1979.03
A Killing In Antiques (Knox)	1981.24	Last Will And Testament (Ferrars)	1979.22
A Killing In The Market (Ball)	1978.10	The Last of the Honeywells (Gillespie)	1988.12
A Killing Kindness (Hill)	1981.15		
Killing No Murder (Shaw)	1981.14	The Late Bill Smith (Garve)	1971.12
Killing Orders (Paretsky)	1985.07	The Late Clara Beame (Caldwell)	1963.09
The Killing Strike (Creasey)	1961.05	The Late Miss Trimming (Carnac)	1957.07
Killing Thyme (Abresch)	1999.17	The Laughing Hangman (Marston)	1996.24
Killing Words (Ramsey)	1994.09	Laughter In The Alehouse (Kane)	1968.08
Killing me softly (Eccles)	1999.23	The Laughter Trap (Philips)	1964.12
Killing the Goose (Lockridge)	1944.03	Lautrec (Zollinger)	1990.12
Killing the Lawyers (Hill)	1997.11	The Lazarus Hotel (Bannister)	1997.13
Kimono for a Corpse (Melville)	1988.12	The Leather Duke (Gruber)	1949.08
The Kingsford Mark (Canning)	1976.13	The Leavenworth Irregulars (Blankenship)	1974.05
The Kinsmen (Haggard)	1975.05		
The Kiwi Target (Ball)	1989.06	A Legacy From Tenerife (Webster)	1984.11
A Knife For The Juggler (Coles)	1965.04	Legacy Of Fear (Weston)	1951.01
Knockdown (Francis)	1975.11	Leisure Dying (O'Donnell)	1976.16
Knockdown (Francis)	1975.18	Leisure Dying (O'Donnell)	1976.23
The Koberg Link (Maling)	1980.05	Lemon Garden (Rossiter)	1991.09
Labyrinth (Pronzini)	1980.12	Lemons Never Lie (Stark)	1971.10
Ladies Won't Wait (Cheyney)	1951.10	Lend Me Your Ears (Stein)	1977.06
The Lady Finger (Malcolm-Smith)	1962.11	The Leper of Saint Giles (Peters)	1982.24
Lady Killer (Coxe)	1949.06	Less Than Meets the Eye (Berlinski)	1994.16
Lady Killer (Holding)	1942.04	The Lester Affair (Garve)	1974.07
Lady Left (Westbrook)	1991.02	Lestrade And The Hallowed House (Trow)	1999.16
The Lady Of The Labyrinth (Llewellyn)	1990.11		
Lady To Kill (Dent)	1947.01	Lestrade and the Brother of Death (Trow)	1999.17
A Lady in a Million (Shane)	1943.09		
Lady, Be Careful (Reeve)	1950.02	Lestrade and the Deadly Game (Trow)	1999.02
Lady, Beware (Cheyney)	1950.12		
The Lafitte Case (Peters)	1997.12	Lestrade and the Leviathan (Trow)	1999.04
The Lake Effect (Roberts)	1994.13	Let The Dead Past (Strange)	1953.05

Let Us Prey (McInerny) 1982.14
Let the Tiger Die (Coles) 1947.10
Lethal Lady (King) 1948.04
Letter From The Dead (Clarke) 1981.19
Letter Of Intent (Curtiss) 1971.09
The Letter of The Law (Berry) 1987.08
Lew Archer Private Investigator
  (Macdonald) 1977.21
Libation By Death (Yeager) 1998.06
Lie Down With Dogs (Gleiter) 1996.14
Lieberman's Law (Kaminsky) 1996.04
The Lies That Bind (Gieson) 1993.03
A Life For A Death (Ashe) 1973.15
Light Through Glass (Lemarchand) 1986.11
The Light in the Swamp (Johnston) 1971.04
The Lighthouse (Pronzini) 1986.12
The Limbo connection (Quinn) 1978.02
The Limping Goose (Gruber) 1954.14
Line Up For Murder (Babson) 1982.08
Lion In The Valley (Peters) 1986.17
Lion In Wait (Gardiner) 1963.08
The Listening Walls (Millar) 1959.09
The Little Brothers (Davis) 1974.02
Little Green Man in Ireland
  (Branham) 1998.14
Little Hercules (Gruber) 1966.02
The Little Lie (Potts) 1969.04
A Little Sin (Hardy) 1958.10
Live Bait (Knox) 1979.18
The Lock and the Key (Gruber) 1948.10
The Locked Room (Sjowall) 1974.02
The Locked Room (Sjowall) 1974.19
Lockestep (Barnao) 1987.01
The Lolita Man (James) 1999.11
London Blood (Hall) 1997.14
The London Deal (Crisp) 1979.05
The Lonely Target (Pentecost) 1960.02
The Lonesome Badger (Gruber) 1954.05
Long Body (McCloy) 1956.01
The Long Divorce (Crispin) 1951.12
A Long Finish (Dibdin) 1999.12
The Long Fuse (White) 1974.16
The Long Journey Home (Gilbert) 1985.08
A Long Line Of Dead Men (Block) 1994.14
A Long Way Down (Fenwick) 1959.03
Look Back on Murder (Gray) 1986.13
Look Behind You, Lady (Erskine) 1952.12
Look Three Ways At Murder
  (Creasey) 1965.08
The Looking Glass Murder (Gilbert) 1967.08
Loophole (Maling) 1971.13

Loose connection (Meek) 1989.04
The Lord Mayor of Death (Babson) 1980.03
The Loss Of The Culion (Ashford) 1982.03
The Lost Caesar (Fenisong) 1945.10
The Lost Victim (Waters) 1974.04
The Love Talker (Peters) 1980.20
Love of Money (Taylor) 1986.14
The Love-Death Thing (Dewey) 1970.01
A Lovely Day To Die   (Fremlin) 1984.09
Low Treason (Tourney) 1983.06
The Luck Runs Out (MacLeod) 1980.03
Lucky Devil (Maling) 1978.11
Lucky To Be Alive? (Cromie) 1979.09
The Lunatic Fringe (DeAndrea) 1981.07
Mad Dogs and Scotsmen
  (Hammond) 1996.16
Maid To A Murder (Vickers) 1950.08
Maigret And The Apparition
  (Simenon) 1976.14
Maigret And The Apparition
  (Simenon) 1977.25
Maigret And The Loner (Simenon) 1975.09
Maigret And The Loner (Simenon) 1975.18
Maigret And The Nahour Case
  (Simenon) 1983.08
Maigret And The Toy Village
  (Simenon) 1980.04
Maigret At The Coroners (Simenon) 1981.25
Maigret Has Doubts (Simenon) 1982.17
Maigret In Exile (Simenon) 1979.10
Maigret Loses His Temper
  (Simenon) 1974.10
Maigret Rents a Room (Simenon) 1961.06
Maigret Sets a Trap (Simenon) 1972.08
Maigret and the Black Sheep
  (Simenon) 1976.07
Maigret and the Black Sheep
  (Simenon) 1976.24
Maigret and the Bum (Simenon) 1974.04
Maigret and the Bum (Simenon) 1974.19
Maigret and the Headless Corpse
  (Simenon) 1968.07
Maigret and the Hotel Majestic
  (Simenon) 1978.07
Maigret and the Hotel Majestic
  (Simenon) 1978.21
Maigret and the Informer (Simenon) 1973.10
Maigret and the Informer (Simenon) 1973.20
Maigret and the Man on the Bench
  (Simenon) 1976.01

The Detective Book Club 1942-2000 Title Index

*Maigret and the Millionaires
(Simenon)* 1975.01
*Maigret and the Millionaires
(Simenon)* 1975.19
Maigret and the Spinster (Simenon) 1977.22
Maigret and the Spinster (Simenon) 1977.14
Maigret at the Coroner's (Simenon) 1981.05
Maigret in New York (Simenon) 1955.04
Maigret in Vichy (Simenon) 1969.05
Maigret on the Defensive (Simenon) 1982.01
Maigret's Dead Man (Simenon) 1964.06
Maigret's Pickpocket (Simenon) 1968.11
Maigret's Pipe (Simenon) 1979.01
Maigret's Pipe (Simenon) 1979.22
Maigret's Rival (Simenon) 1980.13
Majic Man (Collins) 1999.11
Make No Bones (Elkins) 1992.02
The Malabang Pearl (Archer) 1965.03
Malice Domestic (Foley) 1968.07
Malice Domestic (Hardy) 1957.03
Malice Prepense (Wilhelm) 1996.05
The Malignant Heart (Sibley) 1958.06
Mamista (Deighton) 1991.08
*The Mamur Zapt and the Girl in the
Nile (Pearce)* 1994.16
*Mamur Zapt and the Spoils of Egypt
(Pearce)* 1995.16
The Man In My Grave (Tucker) 1956.08
The Man In The Cage (Vance) 1960.11
The Man In The Green Hat (Coles) 1955.03
A Man In The Middle (Chaber) 1968.01
Man In The Middle (Heal) 1980.22
Man In The Net (Quentin) 1956.12
The Man In The Shadow (Foley) 1953.02
Man Missing (Eberhart) 1954.04
The Man Nobody Saw (Cheyney) 1949.11
*The Man Who Cried All The Way
Home (Hitchens)* 1967.04
*The Man Who Followed Women
(Hitchens)* 1960.05
*The Man Who Looked Back
(Fleming)* 1952.09
*The Man Who Lost His Shadow
(Denham)* 1980.07
*The Man Who Wasn't There
(Wainwright)* 1989.07
*The Man Who Would Do Anything
(Ross)* 1963.07
*The Man With A Load Of Mischief
(Grimes)* 1981.22

*The Man With Fifty Complaints
(McMullen)* 1979.01
The Man With The Cane (Potts) 1957.10
*The Man With The President's Mind
(Allbeury)* 1978.16
*The Man With Two Clocks
(Masterson)* 1974.11
*The Man With the Lumpy Nose
(Lariar)* 1944.07
*The Man With the President's Mind
(Allbeury)* 1978.24
The Man in Gray (Crane) 1958.08
The Man of Gold (Hervey) 1985.20
*The Man on a Nylon String
(Masterson)* 1963.06
Manifesto For the Dead (Stansberry) 2000.01
Manila Bay (Marshall) 1986.12
Mankiller (Wilcox) 1981.04
Manmade For Murder (Burton) 1997.15
The Manuscript Murders (Lewis) 1982.18
Manuscript for Murder (Stern) 1971.02
Maracaibo Mission (Mason) 1966.01
The Marble Orchard (Nolan) 1995.15
Mark One: The Dummy (Ball) 1974.17
Mark Three For Murder (Hansen) 1957.02
*The Marshal And The Madwoman
(Nabb)* 1989.12
The Marshal at Villa Torrini (Nabb) 1994.11
Mary's Grave (McClintick) 1987.10
The Mask Of Alexander (Albrand) 1955.08
Mask Of The Jaguar (North) 1981.07
Mask Of Treason (Stevenson) 1980.06
Masks of Rome (Llewellyn) 1988.15
Masquerade (Satterthwait) 1998.12
The Master Key (Togawa) 1985.07
Masterpiece of Murder (Kruger) 1996.06
A Matter Of Confidence (Williams) 1973.08
The Maya Stone Murders (Shuman) 1989.10
Mayday From Malaga (Kirk) 1983.16
A Maze Of Murders (Jeffries) 1998.13
*McGarr At The Dublin Horse Show
(Gill)* 1980.07
*McGarr On The Cliffs Of Moher
(Gill)* 1978.16
*McGarr and the Politician's Wife
(Gill)* 1977.19
The Median Line (Haggard) 1981.20
Medusa (Innes) 1988.13
Meet A Dark Stranger (Huff) 1974.11
Meet In Darkness (Ransome) 1964.08
Melora (Eberhart) 1959.08

The Detective Book Club 1942-2000 Title Index

Memories Can Be Murder (Shelton)	*1999.08*
Memory Boy (Canning)	*1982.09*
The Men In Her Death (Ransome)	*1956.09*
The Men in Her Death (Morice)	*1981.20*
The Menace Within (Curtiss)	*1979.09*
Menaces, Menaces (Underwood)	*1976.16*
The Merchant Of Murder (Dean)	*1959.01*
The Merry Devils (Marston)	*1990.07*
Merry Go Round (Stern)	*1969.04*
Message from Hong Kong (Eberhart)	*1969.03*
Method In Madness (Disney)	*1957.06*
Midnight Clear (Trocheck)	*1998.14*
Midnight Ferry to Venice (Healey)	*1982.15*
The Midnight Man (Kane)	*1966.09*
The Mighty Blockhead (Gruber)	*1942.02*
The Mind Readers (Allingham)	*1965.12*
The Mind of Mr. Mosley (Greenwood)	*1987.07*
The Mirror of Hell (Holton)	*1972.09*
The Mischief Makers (Haggard)	*1982.21*
Miss Seeton Draws The Line (Carvic)	*1970.08*
Missing From Her Home (Gilbert)	*1969.08*
The Missing Heiress (Carey)	*1952.09*
The Missing Link (Boyle)	*1997.07*
Missing Marlene (Marshall)	*1999.13*
The Missing Mr. Mosley (Greenwood)	*1985.09*
The Missing Widow (Gilbert)	*1948.06*
Missing Woman (Lewin)	*1981.23*
Missing, Presumed Dead (Keith)	*1961.11*
Mistletoe from Purple Sage (Smith)	*1998.03*
The Misty Curtain (Cores)	*1964.10*
Mom Meets Her Maker (Yaffe)	*1990.07*
Money Burns (Maxwell)	*1991.09*
Money For The Taking (Disney)	*1968.03*
The Money Men (Haggard)	*1982.05*
Money Trail (Jovanovich)	*1990.14*
Monk's-Hood (Peters)	*1981.16*
Montezuma's Revenge (Harrison)	*1973.02*
The Moon Gate (Estes)	*1954.10*
Moondrop to Murder (Hilton)	*1986.08*
Morbid Kitchen (Melville)	*1996.09*
More Tales Of The Black Widowers (Asimov)	*1977.01*
More Work for the Undertaker (Allingham)	*1949.04*
Mortal Stakes (Parker)	*1976.03*
Mortal Stakes (Parker)	*1976.23*
Most Cunning Workmen (Lewis)	*1985.10*
Most Deadly Hate (Woods)	*1986.15*
Mother of the Bride (Westfall)	*1998.22*
The Motive (Carmichael)	*1977.15*
Motive For Murder (Fraser)	*1997.09*
Motto For Murder (Mace)	*1943.11*
Mountain Massacres (Champion)	*1997.16*
The Mourning Tree (Johnston)	*1972.05*
A Mouthful of Sand (Meek)	*1989.08*
The Mozart Score (Leather)	*1979.20*
Mr. Crook Lifts The Mask (Gilbert)	*1971.01*
Mr. Donaghue Investigates (Shone)	*1995.24*
Mrs. Craggs: Crimes Cleaned Up (Keating)	*1986.02*
Mrs. Mallory investigates (Holt)	*1990.03*
Mrs. Malory and the Only Good Lawyer (Holt)	*1998.25*
Mrs. Pollifax And The Hong Kong Buddha (Gilman)	*1985.11*
Mrs. Pollifax On Safari (Gilman)	*1977.07*
Mrs. Pollifax On The China Station (Gilman)	*1983.17*
Mrs. Pollifax Pursued (Gilman)	*1995.17*
Mrs. Pollifax and the Lion Killer (Gilman)	*1996.07*
A Multitude Of Sins (Wren)	*1975.15*
The Mummy Case (Peters)	*1985.12*
Murder & Sullivan (Frommer)	*1997.16*
Murder After A Fashion (Dean)	*1961.02*
Murder Anonymous (Gilbert)	*1969.02*
A Murder Arranged (Philips)	*1978.18*
Murder As The Curtain Rises (Philips)	*1981.24*
Murder At Drury Lane (Hall)	*1993.04*
Murder Begets Murder (Jeffries)	*1980.03*
Murder Benign (Hunt)	*1996.05*
Murder By Proxy (Morice)	*1978.18*
Murder By The Waters (Hall)	*1995.13*
Murder California Style (Breen)	*1987.04*
Murder Clear, Track Fast (Philips)	*1961.08*
Murder Comes Home (Gilbert)	*1951.07*
Murder Comes To Eden (Ford)	*1955.10*
Murder Crossed (Boylan)	*1996.03*
The Murder Game (Allen)	*1993.04*
Murder Goes Round and Round (Pentecost)	*1988.14*
Murder In Bright Red (Crane)	*1954.02*
Murder In Hawaii (Allen)	*1999.14*
Murder In Luxury (Pentecost)	*1981.12*
Murder In Mimicry (Morice)	*1977.11*
Murder In Paradise (Davey)	*1982.19*
Murder In The Family (Bradley)	*1951.10*

Murder In The Mist (Scott)   1998.04
Murder In The Queen's Armes
   (Elkins)   1985.18
The Murder In The Stork Club
   (Caspary)   1946.07
Murder In The Title (Brett)   1983.17
Murder In Waiting (Eberhart)   1973.13
Murder In the Town (Richart)   1947.07
A Murder Is Announced (Christie)   1950.09
Murder Is My Business (Halliday)   1945.05
Murder Is Suspected (Alding)   1979.09
Murder Is The Pay-Off (Ford)   1951.04
Murder Makes An Entrance
   (Kelland)   1955.09
Murder Most Familiar (Bremner)   1954.04
Murder Most Fouled Up (Wells)   1968.11
Murder Most Fowl (Crider)   1994.15
Murder Must Wait (Upfield)   1953.09
The Murder Of Miranda (Millar)   1979.10
The Murder Of The Dainty-Footed
   Model (Hewens)   1968.03
The Murder Of Whistler's Brother
   (Alexander)   1957.04
Murder Off The Record (Bingham)   1958.01
Murder On Angler's Island (Reilly)   1945.04
Murder On Broadway (Koch)   1996.08
Murder On Martha's Vineyard
   (Roos)   1981.17
Murder On The Lusitania (Allen)   1999.25
Murder On The Purple Water
   (Crane)   1947.09
Murder On Tour (Clark)   1989.02
Murder On Trial (Underwood)   1957.12
Murder Out Of School (Ross)   1960.07
Murder Out of Wedlock (Pentecost)   1984.08
Murder Round The Clock
   (Pentecost)   1985.13
Murder Steps Out (Reeve)   1951.05
Murder Sweet and Sour (Pentecost)   1985.14
Murder Through the Looking Glass
   (Garve)   1952.07
Murder Twice Told (Hamilton)   1950.12
Murder Under Blue Skies (Scott)   1998.15
Murder Under The Mistletoe
   (Jordan)   1989.08
Murder Uptown (Hill)   1992.03
Murder Wears A Mummer's Mask
   (Halliday)   1943.04
Murder Will Out (Vickers)   1954.05
Murder Will Out (Yeager)   1995.04
Murder With Malice (Underwood)   1977.10

Murder With Mushrooms (Ashe)   1974.09
Murder Within Murder (Lockridge)   1946.02
Murder and Chips (Mantell)   1982.14
Murder at San Simeon (Hall)   1988.16
Murder at Wittenham Park (Heber)   1997.01
Murder at the MLA (Jones)   1993.09
Murder at the Movies (Eddenden)   1996.09
Murder at the PTA Luncheon
   (Wolzien)   1988.04
Murder by the Day (Johns)   1953.07
Murder in C Major (Frommer)   1986.04
Murder in Cowboy Bronze
   (McCormick)   1985.02
Murder in High Places (Pentecost)   1983.14
Murder in Mendocino (Kittredge)   1987.10
Murder in Montparnasse (Engel)   1999.15
Murder in Ordinary Time (O'Marie)   1992.04
Murder in Two Flats (Vickers)   1952.05
Murder in Vegas (Allen)   1991.10
Murder in a Cathedral (Ruth
   Dudley)   1997.11
Murder in a Mummy Case (Beck)   1986.16
Murder in the Mountains
   (Chinchinian)   1997.12
Murder in the White House (Truman)   1980.21
Murder is Served (Lockridge)   1949.01
Murder is Where You Find It
   (Hansen)   1956.06
Murder of a Nymph (Neville)   1950.10
Murder of the Well-Beloved (Neville)   1954.01
Murder on Mike (Jeffers)   1985.21
Murder on Safari (Waugh)   1987.11
Murder on a Mystery Tour (Babson)   1987.18
Murder on the Atlantic (Allen)   1995.16
Murder on the Flying Scotsman
   (Dunn)   1997.03
Murder on the Iditarod Trail (Henry)   1991.06
Murder with Love (Lord)   1944.01
Murder's A Waiting Game (Gilbert)   1972.13
Murder's Out Of Tune (Woods)   1985.15
Murder's Web (Dunn)   1950.06
Murder, London - New York
   (Creasey)   1962.03
Murder, London-Australia (Creasey)   1966.03
Murder, Murder, Little Star
   (Babson)   1980.14
Murder: One Two Three (Creasey)   1960.12
The Murderer is a Fox (Queen)   1945.09
Murders Anonymous (Ferrars)   1978.17
Mute Witness (Pike)   1964.01
My Brother's Killer (Potts)   1976.05

My Brother's Killer (York)	*1959.04*
My Late Wives (Dickson)	*1946.08*
My Life Is Done (Woods)	*1976.16*
My Name Is Norval (White)	*1980.11*
My Neighbor's Wife (Disney)	*1958.01*
My face among strangers (Shubin)	*1999.10*
The Mysterious Suspect (Rhode)	*1953.10*
Mysteriouser an Mysteriouser	
* (Bagby)*	*1965.09*
Mystery In The Woodshed (Gilbert)	*1942.07*
The Mystery Lady (Clarke)	*1986.05*
Naked Villainy (Woods)	*1987.12*
Name Your Poison (Reilly)	*1942.06*
The Name's Death, Remember Me?	
* (Forbes)*	*1970.03*
The Nameless Corpse (Kelland)	*1957.08*
Natural Enemy (Langton)	*1982.10*
The Neapolitan Streak (Holme)	*1981.03*
The Neat Little Corpse (Murray)	*1950.06*
Necessary Evil (Roos)	*1965.08*
Necessity (Garfield)	*1984.09*
Nemesis (Christie)	*1972.01*
Nemesis (Christie)	*1973.19*
Never Pick Up Hitch-Hikers!	
* (Peters)*	*1977.01*
Never Say Die (Foote-Smith)	*1977.09*
Never Say Die (Shriber)	*1951.03*
Next of Kin (Eberhart)	*1982.20*
A Nice Little Business (Dewhurst)	*1988.01*
A Nice Little Killing (Gilbert)	*1974.09*
Night Before the Wedding (Gordons)	*1969.05*
Night Cover (Lewin)	*1976.15*
Night Drop (Davis)	*1955.14*
The Night Hunters (Miles)	*1973.13*
Night Man (Ullman)	*1951.07*
Night Of The Kill (James)	*1961.09*
The Night They Murdered Chelsea	
* (Hinxman)*	*1985.19*
Night Train To Paris (Coles)	*1952.03*
Night Walk (Daly)	*1948.02*
Night of Clear Choice (Disney)	*1967.08*
Night or Error (Bagley)	*1987.12*
The Night, The Woman (Ransome)	*1963.05*
Nightfall (Goodis)	*1948.04*
Nightmare In Pink (MacDonald)	*1976.04*
Nightmare In Pink (MacDonald)	*1976.21*
Nightmare Time (Pentecost)	*1986.17*
Nightwatch (Palmer)	*1996.11*
Nine Lives To Murder (Babson)	*1993.08*
Nine O'Clock Tide (Eberhart)	*1978.04*
Nine O'Clock Tide (Eberhart)	*1978.24*
Nipped In The Bud (Palmer)	*1952.02*
No Birds Sing (Bannister)	*1996.23*
No Dust In The Attic (Gilbert)	*1963.09*
No Forwarding Address (Bowers)	*1991.11*
No Hiding Place (Foley)	*1969.08*
No Honeymoon For Death (Kruger)	*1995.12*
No Next Of Kin (Disney)	*1960.03*
No Offense Intended (Seranella)	*1998.17*
No Peace For The Wicked (Ferrars)	*1966.10*
No Place for Murder (Coxe)	*1976.01*
No Tears For Shirley Minton (Lowe)	*1956.03*
No Tears for the Dead (Foley)	*1948.07*
No Vacation for Maigret (Simenon)	*1953.12*
Nobody Here By That Name	
* (MacKenzie)*	*1988.08*
Nobody Roots For Goliath	
* (Champion)*	*1998.16*
Nobody's Perfect (Westlake)	*1977.20*
Nobody's Sorry He Got Killed	
* (Goldstein)*	*1976.05*
None of Maigret's Business	
* (Simenon)*	*1958.08*
North Star (Innes)	*1975.08*
A Nose for It (Stein)	*1981.09*
Not Exactly A Brahmin (Dunlap)	*1985.23*
Not Me Inspector (Reilly)	*1959.12*
Not Quite Dead Enough (Stout)	*1944.12*
The Notch On The Knife (Haggard)	*1973.18*
Nothing Can Rescue Me (Daly)	*1943.04*
Nothing's Certain But Death (Wren)	*1978.13*
A Nun In The Closet (Gilman)	*1975.11*
The Nun's Tale (Robb)	*1995.09*
Nursery Tea and Poison (Morice)	*1976.06*
Nursery Tea and Poison (Morice)	*1976.20*
The Obituary Club (Pentecost)	*1958.12*
An Obscure Grave (Woods)	*1985.05*
The October Cabaret (Quest)	*1979.19*
Odds On Miss Seeton (Carvic)	*1976.10*
Of Missing Persons (Goodis)	*1950.09*
Oh, Bury Me Not (Wren)	*1977.08*
Old Bones (Elkins)	*1988.05*
The Old Fox Deceiv'd (Grimes)	*1982.23*
The Old House Of Fear (Kirk)	*1961.10*
Old Saxon Blood (Tourney)	*1988.15*
Old Students Never Die (Ross)	*1962.04*
The Olmec Head (Westheimer)	*1974.15*
Omega-Minus (Allbeury)	*1975.10*
Ominous Star (Foley)	*1971.13*
On the Inside (Wood)	*1990.04*
Once A Widow (Roberts)	*1957.11*
One Angel Less (Roden)	*1945.06*

One False Move (Roos)   1966.11
One Fearful Yellow Eye (MacDonald)   1977.23
One Fearful Yellow Eye (MacDonald)   1978.01
One For My Dame (Webb)   1961.10
One O'Clock At The Gotham (Foley)   1974.12
One Of Us Must Die (Clarke)   1981.06
The One That Got Away (McCloy)   1946.01
One of Those Things (Cheyney)   1950.03
One-Man Jury (Ransome)   1965.02
Only Couples Need Apply (Disney)   1973.10
The Only Game (Ruell)   1993.09
The Only Good Lawyer (Healy)   1998.17
Only Half a Hoax (Taylor)   1984.10
Only the Rich Die Young (Pentecost)   1964.06
Open Season (Thielen)   1959.03
Operation Apricot (Haddad)   1978.06
Orchids To Murder (Footner)   1945.03
Ordeal by Innocence (Christie)   1959.05
Original Sin (James)   1995.17
The Orion Line (Luard)   1977.02
Oscar Mooney's Head (Huntsberry)   1961.06
The Other (Tryon)   1971.14
The Other Devil's Name (Ferrars)   1986.18
The Other Maritha (Leonard)   1972.09
Out For The Kill (Gilbert)   1961.01
Out Of Control (Kendrick)   1945.08
Out Of The Dark (Curtiss)   1964.09
Out Of The Depths (Holton)   1966.12
Out of the Past (Wentworth)   1953.06
Outcasts (Hensley)   1981.11
The Outsiders (Martin)   1945.06
Ovation by Death (Yeager)   1996.19
Overdue For Death (Ross)   1947.04
A Pact With Satan (Holton)   1960.09
Paint, Gold and Blood (Gilbert)   1989.09
The Painted Tent (Canning)   1974.14
Painted for the Kill (Cores)   1943.08
A Pair for the Queen (Comfort)   1998.15
The Pale Door (Roberts)   1955.02
The Pale Horse (Christie)   1962.11
A Palm For Mrs. Pollifax (Gilman)   1973.15
The Panama Paradox (Wolfe)   1978.05
Pangolin (Driscoll)   1979.08
Panic In Paradise (Amos)   1952.02
Paper Chase (Cook)   1990.07
Parrot Blues (Van Gieson)   1995.04
Parsley, Sage, Rosemary And Crime (Myers)   1995.07
Partnerships Can Kill (Shelton)   1997.08

The Party Killer (Pentecost)   1985.16
Pass The Gravy (Fair)   1959.03
Passage to Danger (Lanham)   1962.06
Passenger To Nowhere (Gilbert)   1966.11
Passing Strange (Aird)   1981.10
Passport For A Renegade (Bennett)   1955.11
Past Mischief (Curzon)   1996.15
Pattern For Murder (Shriber)   1945.02
Pattern for Terror (Pentecost)   1990.08
The Pavilion (Lawrence)   1946.02
Payoff For The Banker (Lockridge)   1945.04
Pearlhanger (Gash)   1985.13
Pearls Before Swine (Allingham)   1945.07
Peking Duck (Simon)   1979.16
Pel And The Faceless Corpse (Hebden)   1982.23
Pel and the Pirates (Hebden)   1987.06
Pennies From Hell (Alexander)   1960.12
The People From The Sea (Johnston)   1980.01
People Of Darkness (Hillerman)   1981.02
The People on the Hill (Johnston)   1971.05
Pepper Pike (Roberts)   1988.15
Perfect Murder (Hitt)   1991.04
A Person Shouldn't Die Like That (Goldstein)   1972.11
Peter's Pence (Cleary)   1974.05
The Phantom Cottage (Johnston)   1970.06
Phantom Lady (Irish)   1942.06
The Philomel Foundation (Gollin)   1980.06
Phoenix No More (Gage)   1979.06
The Phone Calls (O'Donnell)   1972.06
Picture Miss Seeton (Carvic)   1969.01
A Picture of Her Tombstone (Lipinski)   1996.11
Pictures in the Dark (Stuart)   1986.01
Pillar Of Fire (Irvine)   1995.18
A Pinch Of Poison (Lockridge)   1942.01
A Pinch Of Snuff (Underwood)   1974.14
The Pink Umbrella (Crane)   1943.10
The Pinned Man (Griswold)   1955.07
A Pint of Murder (Craig)   1980.23
Place For A Poisoner (Lorac)   1949.06
A Plague Of Demons (Ashe)   1977.07
A Plague Of Violence (Pentecost)   1971.06
Plague of Kinfolks (Sibley)   1995.03
Play Like You're Dead (Masterson)   1967.11
Poetic Justice (Taylor)   1988.07
Poison Flowers (Cooper)   1991.11
Poison In The Pen (Wentworth)   1955.09
The Poisoned Orchard (Curtiss)   1980.15
Police Blotter (Pike)   1965.12

Police Chief (Ball) — 1977.18
Police Chief (Ball) — 1977.21
Police Chief (Ball) — 1977.24
Policeman's Dread (Creasey) — 1964.07
Pool Of Tears (Wainwright) — 1978.06
Poor Butterfly (Kaminsky) — 1990.12
Poor Harriet (Fenwick) — 1957.09
Port Of Seven Strangers (Knight) — 1945.11
Port of Light (Serafin) — 1987.11
Poseidon's Gold (Davis) — 1994.16
Postmark Murder (Eberhart) — 1956.04
Postscript to Murder (Meek) — 1997.16
Potomac Fever (Horrock) — 1999.16
The Powder Barrel (Haggard) — 1966.01
The Power House (Haggard) — 1967.06
The Power Killers (Philips) — 1974.11
Power Plays (Wilcox) — 1979.21
Prelude To Murder (Gilbert) — 1959.08
A Presence In An Empty Room (Johnston) — 1980.09
Presumption of Guilt (Kelly) — 1998.18
Pretty Maids all in a Row (Fraser) — 1987.04
The Pretty Pink Shroud (Ferrars) — 1978.01
A Pretty Place for Murder (Hart) — 1988.16
The Price Of Silence (Pentecost) — 1984.11
The Price of Failure (Ashford) — 1998.19
A Pride Of Dolphins (Hebden) — 1975.06
Primrose Convention (Bannister) — 1998.06
The Prince Lost To Time (Dukthas) — 1995.18
The Prince Of Darkness (Doherty) — 1993.07
Print-Out (Gillespie) — 1983.07
Prisoner's Friend (Garve) — 1962.10
Prisoner's Plea (Waugh) — 1964.01
A Problem In Prague (Webster) — 1982.07
A Problem in Angels (Holton) — 1970.03
Proceed To Judgement (Woods) — 1980.08
Proof (Francis) — 1985.17
The Protectors (Haggard) — 1973.04
The Protege (Armstrong) — 1970.05
Publish and Be Killed (Morice) — 1986.12
The Pumpkin Seed Massacre (Slater) — 1999.17
Punch With Care (Taylor) — 1947.01
Pure Poison (Waugh) — 1967.02
Purple Place for Dying (MacDonald) — 1977.03
Pursuit (Fish) — 1979.07
Pursuit Of Arms (Hammond) — 1986.19
Pursuit of Fear (Beechcroft) — 1990.15
Pushing Murder (Boylan) — 1993.05
Put Out The Light (Foley) — 1976.19
Put Out the Light (Woods) — 1985.18
Quaker Indictment (Allen) — 1998.11
The Quallsford Inheritance (Biggle Jr.) — 1986.13
The Quarry (Pike) — 1964.09
Quarry (Pronzini) — 1992.01
The Queen Against Karl Mullen (Gilbert) — 1991.07
Quest of the Bogeyman (Lockridge) — 1964.03
A Question Of Inheritance (Bell) — 1981.18
A Question Of Murder (Gilbert) — 1955.10
A Question Of Principle (Ashford) — 1987.02
A Question Of Quarry (Bagby) — 1981.16
Questionable Remains (Connor) — 1997.17
R.S.V.P. Murder (Eberhart) — 1965.11
A Rabble Of Rebels (Ashe) — 1972.15
Race for the Golden Tide (Gordons) — 1983.18
A Rage of Innocents (Mitchell) — 1998.20
The Raggedy Man (O'Donnell) — 1995.19
Rainbow's End (Peters) — 1980.04
Rally to Kill (Knox) — 1975.17
The Random Factor (LaRosa) — 1978.19
Random Killer (Pentecost) — 1979.17
Ransom (Cleary) — 1973.10
The Ransomed Madonna (White) — 1964.08
The Rat Began To Gnaw The Rope (Grafton) — 1943.07
Raven After Dark (Mackenzie) — 1980.04
Raven And The Kamikaze (Mackenzie) — 1978.02
Raven And The Ratcatcher (MacKenzie) — 1977.09
Raven Rock (Ballard) — 1986.01
Raven Settles a Score (MacKenzie) — 1979.01
Raven and the Paperhangers (MacKenzie) — 1981.08
Raven's Longest Night (Mackenzie) — 1984.02
Raven's Revenge (Mackenzie) — 1982.12
Raven's Shadow (MacKenzie) — 1985.05
Reach Of Fear (Mathews) — 1958.10
Reardon (Pike) — 1970.09
A Recipe For Murder (Ashford) — 1980.22
Reckless Lady (Foley) — 1973.16
Recoil (Garfield) — 1977.13
Recoil (Garfield) — 1977.24
Red Right Returning (St. Edmunds) — 1996.24
Reel Murder (Babson) — 1987.09
Reflex (Francis) — 1981.13
Reflex (Francis) — 1981.25
Reincarnation in Venice (Ehrlich) — 1979.11
Reincarnation in Venice (Ehrlich) — 1979.23
Relative To Death (Forbes) — 1965.10

The Detective Book Club 1942-2000 Title Index

Relatively Dangerous (Jeffries)	*1987.13*
Relentless (Garfield)	*1972.12*
The Reluctant Ronin (Melville)	*1988.10*
A Remarkable Case Of Burglary	
(Keating)	*1976.15*
The Rembrandt Panel (Banks)	*1980.23*
Remember To Kill Me (Pentecost)	*1984.12*
Rendezvous In Black (Woolrich)	*1948.08*
Repent at Leisure (Foley)	*1962.12*
Requiem For A Blonde (Roos)	*1959.02*
Requiem For A Postman (Press)	*1992.04*
Reservations For Death (Kendrick)	*1957.05*
Rest You Merry (MacLeod)	*1979.06*
The Resurrection Man (Walsh)	*1966.05*
Revenge of the Gypsy Queen (Neri)	*1999.05*
The Rheingold Route (Maling)	*1979.10*
Riddle of St. Leonard's (Robb)	*1997.13*
Riddle of a Lady (Gilbert)	*1956.11*
Ring for a Noose (Gilbert)	*1964.04*
Ringed With Fire (Campbell)	*1942.08*
The Rio Casino Intrigue (Mason)	*1942.03*
Ripley's Game (Highsmith)	*1974.08*
Ripoff (Maling)	*1976.11*
Road Block (Waugh)	*1960.10*
The Roaring Boy (Marston)	*1995.20*
Roast Eggs (Clark)	*1982.06*
Robak's Witch (Hensley)	*1997.19*
Robbed Blind (Hart)	*1990.09*
The Robineau Look (Knight)	*1955.05*
The Rockefeller Gift (Winslow)	*1981.24*
The Rockford Files: Devils On My	
Doorstep (Kaminsky)	*1998.21*
The Rockford Files: The Green	
Bottle (Kaminsky)	*1996.25*
The Rocksburg Railroad Murders	
(Constantine)	*1973.11*
Rogue's Wager (Briody)	*1998.10*
The Rolling Heads (Stein)	*1979.11*
The Romanov Succession (Garfield)	*1975.02*
Rook Takes Knight (Palmer)	*1968.12*
A Room At The Hotel Ambre	
(Armstrong)	*1956.03*
Root Of All Evil (Ferrars)	*1984.09*
Root Of Evil (Goldthwaite)	*1948.04*
Rosa's Dilemma (Underwood)	*1990.10*
The Rose Window (Blanc)	*1967.05*
Roses, Roses (James)	*1999.18*
Rotten Apples (Cooper)	*1995.14*
Rub-A-Dub-Dub (Fish)	*1971.13*
Rumpole a La Carte (Mortimer)	*1991.03*
Run For Your Life (Foley)	*1957.04*
Run Scared (Eberhart)	*1963.11*
Run To Evil (Egan)	*1963.11*
Run, Fool, Run (Gruber)	*1966.12*
Run, Sara, Run (Worboys)	*1981.14*
A Rush For The Ultimate (Keating)	*1983.01*
SS-GB (Deighton)	*1979.14*
Sabotage (John)	*1973.17*
A Sad Song Singing (Dewey)	*1964.02*
The Sad, Sudden Death Of My Fair	
Lady (Forbes)	*1971.07*
Sadie When She Died (McBain)	*1972.16*
The Safe House (Cleary)	*1975.12*
Safely to the Grave (Yorke)	*1986.20*
The Saint And The People Importers	
(Charteris)	*1972.07*
The Saint And The Templar Treasure	
(Charteris)	*1979.21*
The Saint In Trouble (Charteris)	*1979.08*
The Saint In Trouble (Charteris)	*1979.23*
Saint Peter's Fair (Peters)	*1982.12*
The Saint in Pursuit (Charteris)	*1971.03*
Salt Is Leaving (Priestley)	*1975.07*
Salvage Job (Kirk)	*1979.04*
Salvage for the Saint (Charteris)	*1983.18*
Saratoga Backtalk (Dobyns)	*1994.06*
Saratoga Fleshpot (Dobyns)	*1995.21*
Saratoga Hexameter (Dobyns)	*1990.04*
Saratoga Snapper (Dobyns)	*1986.18*
Saratoga Swimmer (Dobyns)	*1982.03*
The Satan Sampler (Canning)	*1980.09*
Satan's Fire (Doherty)	*1996.26*
Saturday Of Glory (Serafin)	*1982.10*
Saturnalia: SPQR V (Roberts)	*2000.02*
A Savage Place (Parker)	*1981.21*
A Savage State Of Grace	
(MacKenzie)	*1988.05*
Savings And Loam (McInerny)	*1990.11*
Saxon's Ghost (Fisher)	*1969.12*
Sayonara, Sweet Amaryllis (Melville)	*1985.19*
Scandal At High Chimneys (Carr)	*1959.10*
The Scapegoat (Orum)	*1976.06*
Scared To Death (Foley)	*1967.03*
Scared To Death (Morice)	*1978.08*
The Scarlet Feather (Gruber)	*1948.06*
Scarlet Night (Davis)	*1980.16*
Scattershot (Pronzini)	*1982.12*
The Scene Of The Crime (Creasey)	*1963.12*
The Scent Of Fear (Yorke)	*1981.15*
Schroeder's Game (Maling)	*1977.15*
The Sea Kings' Daughter (Michaels)	*1976.09*
Sea Trials (Morton)	*2000.02*

The Detective Book Club 1942-2000 Title Index

Seafire (Knox)	1972.03		*Shell Game (Powell)*	1950.08
Search Committee (McInerny)	1991.04		*The Shelton Conspiracy (Foley)*	1967.11
Search For A Sultan (Coles)	1961.09		*Sherbourne's Folly (Barry)*	1979.06
Search for a Scientist (Leonard)	1948.01		*The Sheriff Of Bombay (Keating)*	1984.13
Seasons of Death (Wren)	1981.09		*Sherlock Holmes and the Case Of*	
Second Shot in the Dark (Roome)	1991.10		*The Raleigh Legacy (Greenwood)*	1986.14
The Second Sickle (Curtiss)	1950.04		*Sherlock Holmes and the Case of*	
The Second Sorrowful Mystery			*Sabina Hall (Greenwood)*	1988.11
(Harrington)	1999.04		*Sherlock Holmes and the Thistle of*	
A Secret Dying (Lewis)	1993.06		*Scotland (Greenwood)*	1989.06
The Secret Of The Doubting Saint			*Sherlock in Love (Naslund)*	1993.03
(Holton)	1961.12		*The Sherman Letter (Palmer)*	1995.08
The Secret Servant (Lyall)	1981.03		*Shills Can't Cash Chips (Fair)*	1962.03
Secrets in Stone (Shone)	1996.02		*Ship Shapely (Boyle)*	1999.25
See How They Run (Green)	1976.10		*Shoot A Sitting Duck (Alexander)*	1956.03
Seeds Of Murder (York)	1958.07		*A Shoot in Cleveland (Roberts)*	1998.22
Seeing is Believing (Ferrars)	1996.07		*Short Break in Venice (Inchbald)*	1984.10
The Senator Must Die (Koch)	1998.01		*The Shortest Journey (Holt)*	1994.07
Send for the Saint (Charteris)	1978.13		*Shotgun (McBain)*	1969.11
Sensational Music Club Mystery			*Should Auld Acquaintance (Disney)*	1962.03
(Landrum)	1995.03		*A Show Of Hands (Crossman)*	1997.02
A Sense Of Loyalty (Ashford)	1985.15		*Shred of Evidence (McGown)*	1996.09
A Sensitive Case (Wright)	1990.11		*A Shroud for Delilah (Fraser)*	1986.06
Serious Intent (Yorke)	1996.10		*The Shrunken Head (Fish)*	1964.03
Serpent Amongst the Lilies (Doherty)	1990.01		*The Shudders (Abbot)*	1943.02
Seven Chose Murder (Vickers)	1959.01		*The Shy Tulip Murders (Rothenberg)*	1996.11
The Seventh Sense (MacGregor)	1999.19		*Sight Of Death (York)*	1958.11
Shadow For A Lady (Linklater)	1947.05		*The Silent Partner (Knight)*	1951.05
A Shadow In The Wild (Masterson)	1957.06		*The Silent Speaker (Stout)*	1946.10
Shadow Of A Doubt (Thomson)	1982.18		*The Silent Witness (Coxe)*	1973.06
A Shadow Of Himself (Delving)	1972.06		*The Silver Castle (Quest)*	1978.15
The Shadow Of The Palms (Law)	1980.12		*The Silver Dolphin (Johnston)*	1979.07
A Shadow of Death (Ashe)	1976.11		*The Silver Dolphin (Johnston)*	1979.23
A Shadow of Death (Ashe)	1976.22		*The Silver Leopard (Reilly)*	1947.06
Shadow on the Window (Bagby)	1955.12		*Simon Said (Shaber)*	1997.03
Shadows In Their Blood (Babson)	1993.07		*The Sin File (Ransome)*	1966.02
Shadows On The Sceptered Isle			*Sing Me A Murder (Nielsen)*	1961.02
(Stang)	1980.15		*Singapore (Ball)*	1986.03
The Shadowy Third (Page)	1947.02		*Singapore Transfer (Warga)*	1991.08
Shake Hands Forever (Rendell)	1976.02		*Singing In The Shrouds (Marsh)*	1958.06
The Shaman Laughs (Doss)	1995.07		*Sinister Errand (Cheyney)*	1945.11
Shannon Terror (DuBois)	1964.08		*The Sinister Strangers (Kelland)*	1961.12
Shape of Fear (Hamilton)	1986.20		*Sink Or Swim (Hammond)*	1997.02
The Shape of Fear (Pentecost)	1965.01		*The Sitting Duck (Bagby)*	1982.08
Shark River (Powell)	1949.12		*Situation Tragedy (Brett)*	1981.23
A Sharp Rise in Crime (Creasey)	1979.11		*The Six Iron Spiders (Taylor)*	1942.05
She Died A Lady (Dickson)	1943.03		*Six Murders in the Suburbs (Vickers)*	1955.01
She Walks Alone (McCloy)	1948.09		*Six Silver Handles (Homes)*	1944.06
She Was Only the Sheriff's Daughter			*Six Who Ran (Chaber)*	1964.12
(Forbes)	1970.07		*Skeleton In Search Of A Closet*	
Shed Light on Death (Taylor)	1985.20		*(Ferrars)*	1983.01

Skinwalkers (Hillerman)	1987.14
The Skull Beneath The Skin (James)	1983.05
Slam the Big Door (MacDonald)	1987.15
Slay-Ride (Francis)	1974.07
Slayground (Stark)	1972.02
The Sleep Is Deep (Nelson)	1953.01
Sleep Without Morning (Foley)	1972.10
The Sleepers Of Erin (Gash)	1983.12
Sleeping Dogs (Ross)	1978.17
The Sleeping Sphinx (Carr)	1947.03
The Sleepless Men (Nisot)	1959.06
Slickensides: A Derbyshire Mystery (Hilton)	1987.08
The Slippery Step (Foley)	1977.13
Slow Down The World (Ashford)	1977.05
The Slow Gallows (Masterson)	1979.13
Small Towns Can Be Murder (Shelton)	1998.16
Smiling the Boy Fell Dead (Delving)	1967.05
Smokescreen (Francis)	1973.09
Smokescreen (Francis)	1973.20
Smooth Justice (Underwood)	1980.01
Snake Oil (Roberts)	1990.09
Snares Of The Enemy (King)	1986.19
The Snatch (Champion)	1998.23
The Sniper (Pentecost)	1965.07
Snowtrap (Peel)	1985.21
So Many Steps to Death (Christie)	1955.04
So Soon Done For (Babson)	1988.07
So Young a Body (Bunce)	1950.02
Soft Money (Wishnia)	1999.21
The Sole Survivor and The Kynsard Affair (Vickers)	1951.08
Solomons Seal (Innes)	1981.08
Solved (Gorman)	1991.12
Some Die Eloquent (Aird)	1980.10
Some Must Watch (Ransome)	1961.03
Some Run Crooked (Hilton)	1978.19
Some Slips Don't Show (Fair)	1957.10
Some Women Won't Wait (Fair)	1953.10
Someone At The Door (Crane)	1985.08
Someone Else's Grave (Smith)	1984.14
Someone in the House (Michaels)	1982.01
Something About Midnight (Olsen)	1950.05
Something For The Birds (Drachman)	1958.07
Something Of The Night (McMullen)	1981.04
Something To Hide (MacDonald)	1953.02
Something Wicked (Ferrars)	1984.05
Somewhere In The House (Daly)	1946.03
The Song of a Dark Angel (Doherty)	1995.22
Sorrow's Crown (Piccirilli)	1999.14
A Sort of Samurai (Melville)	1982.15
Sound An Alarm (Holden)	1954.05
A Sound of Lightning (Cleary)	1976.14
Sour Grapes (Cooper)	1998.24
Soviet Sources (Cullen)	1990.12
Sow Death, Reap Death (Pentecost)	1982.04
The Spanish Prisoner (Gruber)	1970.05
Speak No Evil (Warner)	1985.21
Spend Game (Gash)	1981.17
The Spider-Orchid (Fremlin)	1978.12
Spin Your Web Lady (Lockridge)	1949.04
Spit In The Ocean (Singer)	1987.17
A Splinter Of Glass (Creasey)	1972.14
The Spoilers (Bagley)	1970.07
The Spreewald Collection (Mackenzie)	1975.10
A Sprig Of Sea Lavender (Anderson)	1979.02
Spy On The Run (Lovell)	1982.22
Spy Sinker (Deighton)	1990.13
Spy Story (Deighton)	1974.18
The Spy Who Barked In The Night (Lovell)	1986.15
The Spy Who Got His Feet Wet (Lovell)	1985.22
Spy in Chancery (Doherty)	1989.10
St Peter's Finger (Mitchell)	1987.14
Staircase Four (Reilly)	1949.07
The Stairway (Curtiss)	1957.12
The Stalking Man (Tucker)	1949.10
Stamped for Murder (Benson)	1952.05
Starr Bright Will Be With You Soon (Smith)	1999.20
The Stars are Dark (Cheyney)	1944.01
A Stench Of Poppies (Drummond)	1979.02
Still No Answer (Thayer)	1958.05
Sting In The Tail (Hammond)	1995.20
A Stir Of Echoes (Matheson)	1958.06
Stitches in Time (Michaels)	1995.23
Stolen Goods (Kelland)	1950.11
Stone Dead (Smith)	1998.08
Stormtide (Knox)	1973.11
Straight (Francis)	1990.14
The Strange Bedfellow (Berckman)	1956.07
A Strange Place For A Murder (Barroll)	1979.15
A Stranger In My Grave (Millar)	1961.03
Strangler (Maness)	1998.24
Strangler's Serenade (Irish)	1951.06
Stream Sinister (Knight)	1945.04
Street Of The Five Moons (Peters)	1978.14

The Detective Book Club 1942-2000 Title Index

Streets of Fire (Cook)	1989.11	They're Going To Kill Me (Amos)	1956.02
Strictly A Loser (Sherry)	1965.10	Thicker Than Water (York)	1962.06
Student Body (Borthwick)	1987.16	Thicker Than Water (Zimmerman)	1991.01
The Substitute Victim (Pentecost)	1984.04	A Thief For Two (Woods)	1978.03
Such Pretty Toys (Dean)	1982.23	A Thief Of Time (Hillerman)	1989.12
Sudden Squall (Nolan)	1955.06	A Thief in the Night (Walsh)	1963.01
Sudden Vengeance (Crispin)	1950.06	Thin Air (Hammond)	1994.13
Suddenly One Night (Roos)	1971.04	The Thing At The Door (Slesar)	1974.14
Suffer A Witch (Foley)	1965.04	Thinner Than Water (Ferrars)	1982.17
Summer Of The Dragon (Peters)	1979.18	The Third Bullet and Other Stories	
Summer Will End (Yeager)	1996.22	(Carr)	1954.08
Sunk Without a Trace (Devine)	1980.02	The Third Figure (Wilcox)	1968.08
Sweetfeed (Healy)	1997.13	The Third Identity (Gatenby)	1980.09
Sweetwater Ranch (Norman)	1991.03	The Thirteen Trumpeters (Meynell)	1979.02
Switchback (Wilcox)	1993.05	Thirteenth Night (Gordon)	1999.20
T as in Trapped (Treat)	1948.03	The Thirteenth Trick (Braddon)	1974.06
Take A Body (Creasey)	1972.12	This Way Out (Radley)	1990.15
Taking Lives (Pye)	1999.12	This Woman Wanted (Foley)	1971.08
A Talent For Destruction (Radley)	1983.06	Three For The Money	
Talking God (Hillerman)	1989.11	(McConnaughey)	1954.07
Tanner on Ice (Block)	1998.25	Three Minutes To Midnight (Davis)	1972.07
A Tapestry of Murders (Doherty)	1996.07	Three Of Diamonds (Knight)	1953.11
Target For Tragedy (Philips)	1983.01	Three's A Crowd (Disney)	1971.10
The Tarnished Angel (Pentecost)	1963.03	Three, Three, The Rivals (Fraser)	1995.06
A Taste Of Sangria (Keith)	1968.10	A Three-Pipe Problem (Symons)	1975.14
A Taste Of Treason (Maling)	1983.17	The Three-Time Losers (Bagby)	1958.04
A Taste for Burning (Bannister)	1995.08	The Threepersons Hunt (Garfield)	1974.10
The Taurus Trip (Dewey)	1971.02	Through A Glass, Darkly (Mccloy)	1950.08
Teacher's Blood (Ross)	1964.05	Thunderball (Fleming)	1961.08
Tell Her It's Murder (Reilly)	1954.11	Thursday's Folly (Philips)	1967.12
Tell Them What's-Her-Name Called		Thy Brother Death (Ferrars)	1993.08
(Davis)	1975.04	Tiger On My Back (Gordons)	1960.05
Temple Dogs (Duncan)	1977.16	Tight as a Tick (Kelner)	1998.19
Ten Lords A Leaping (Edwards)	1996.12	Till Death Do Us Part (Carr)	1944.10
Tenant For The Tomb (Gilbert)	1971.10	A Time For The Death Of A King	
The Tenth Life (Lockridge)	1977.22	(Doherty)	1995.11
The Tenth Life (Lockridge)	1978.03	The Time of Murder at Mayerling	
The Tenth Point (Walsh)	1965.04	(Dukthas)	1996.22
The Terrible Tide (Craig)	1983.14	Time of Terror (Pentecost)	1975.08
Terror's Cradle (Kyle)	1975.04	Tinsley's Bones (Wilde)	1942.05
The Terrorists (Sjowall)	1977.03	To Cache A Millionaire (Scherf)	1972.11
The Terrorists (Sjowall)	1977.25	To Catch a Thief (Sanders)	1943.06
The Theft of the Magna Carta		To Die A Little (Jobson)	1979.16
(Creasey)	1973.12	To Hide A Rogue (Walsh)	1964.07
Then Came Violence (Ball)	1980.11	To Live and Die in Dixie (Trocheck)	1993.05
There Must Be Some Mistake		To Save His Life (Roos)	1968.09
(Babson)	1987.17	To the Tune of Murder (Ballard)	1952.07
There is a Tide (Christie)	1948.03	Tomorrow Is Another Day	
There's Always A Payoff (Hansen)	1960.02	(Kaminsky)	1995.11
They Never Say When (Cheyney)	1945.02	Tomorrow's Silence (Goller)	1980.18
They Stay for Death (Woods)	1980.17	Too Busy to Die (Roden)	1945.01

Too Clever By Half (Jeffries)   1990.13
Too Close to the Edge (Dunlap)   1987.12
Too Late For Tears (Huggins)   1947.09
Too Long Endured (Thayer)   1951.02
Too Many Suspects (Rhode)   1945.08
Too Many Women (Stout)   1948.02
Too Much Poison (Rowe)   1945.01
Too Old to Die (Travis)   1969.02
Too Sane a Murder (Martin)   1984.06
The Tooth And The Nail (Ballinger)   1955.09
Top Banana (James)   1999.21
Top Of The Heap (Fair)   1952.03
Touch And Go (Meek)   1993.07
A Touch Of Jonah (Holton)   1968.12
A Touch of Mortality (Granger)   1997.18
A Tough One to Lose (Kenrick)   1972.16
Tourist Trap (Stratton)   1976.09
Tourists Are for Trapping (Babson)   1990.16
A Tournament Of Murders (Doherty)   1997.19
The Tower (Hubbard)   1967.10
The Toy (Booton)   1976.02
Tracked in the Whites (Eslick)   1998.08
A Trail Of Ashes (Babson)   1985.17
Traps Need Fresh Bait (Fair)   1967.05
The Trash Stealer (Potts)   1968.06
A Travesty (Westlake)   1977.10
Treasure Up In Smoke (Williams)   1978.15
Treble Exposure (Morice)   1988.12
Trial and Terror (Treat)   1949.09
Trick Or Treat (Disney)   1955.13
Triple Crown (Breen)   1986.07
Trojan Gold (Peters)   1987.18
The Trouble At Turkey Hill (Knight)   1946.04
Trouble For Tallon (Ball)   1981.12
Trouble In Paradise (Fish)   1975.09
The Trouble With A Bad Fit (Crespi)   1996.23
The Trouble With Tycoons (Taylor)   1967.12
Trouble in Burma (Mason)   1962.09
Troubled Journey (Lockridge)   1970.04
Troubled Waters (Lemarchand)   1983.02
The Troublemaker (Potts)   1973.06
Trust Me On This (Westlake)   1988.17
Try Anything Once (Fair)   1962.09
Tumbleweed (Wetering)   1976.18
The Tunnel (Byrne)   1977.19
Turkey Tracks (Brown)   1995.24
Turkish Rondo (Stevenson)   1982.01
Turkish White (Arrighi)   1977.19
The Turquoise Lament (MacDonald)   1974.01
The Turquoise Lament (MacDonald)   1974.19

Twelve Deaths of Christmas
   (Babson)   1980.23
Twice Bitten (Hammond)   1999.03
Twice Shy (Francis)   1982.13
Twice in a Blue Moon (Moyes)   1993.09
The Twilight Man (Gruber)   1967.06
Twist Of The Knife (Canning)   1955.05
The Twisted People (Philips)   1965.11
Two Clues (Gardner)   1947.04
Two Little Rich Girls (Eberhart)   1972.03
Two Little Rich Girls (Eberhart)   1972.18
Two Little Rich Girls (Eberhart)   1973.20
Two Ways To Die (Thayer)   1959.10
Two-Thirds Of A Ghost (McCloy)   1957.03
Unappointed Rounds (Disney)   1957.01
Uncertain Death (Gilbert)   1963.02
The Unconscious Witness (Freeman)   1942.04
The Under Dog And Other Stories
   (Christie)   1952.03
Under Orion (Law)   1978.19
Under The Wolf's Head (Cameron)   1999.06
Under a Monsoon Cloud (Keating)   1986.21
Undercover Cat (Gordons)   1963.10
Undercurrent (Pronzini)   1973.14
The Underground Man (Macdonald)   1971.07
The Undertaker Wind (Masterson)   1973.15
Undue Influence (Borgenicht)   1989.05
The Unexpected Mrs. Pollifax
   (Gilman)   1966.05
Unfair Exchange (Babson)   1986.21
The Uninvited Corpse (Underwood)   1987.05
The Unknown Quantity (Eberhart)   1953.08
Unlucky Seven (Boyle)   1997.01
Unnatural Causes (Noguchi)   1988.11
The Unquiet Sleep (Haggard)   1963.03
Unseemly End (Jeffries)   1982.14
The Unsuspected (Armstrong)   1946.05
Untidy Murder (Lockridge)   1947.10
Until Death Do Us Part (McMullen)   1983.04
Unwanted Company (Seranella)   2000.03
Up For Grabs (Fair)   1964.05
Up To The Hilt (Rowe)   1945.11
The Urgent Hangman (Cheyney)   1952.06
Utter Death (Hymers)   1954.03
Valentine murder (Meier)   1999.10
The Valley Of Smugglers (Upfield)   1960.10
Valse Macabre (Knight)   1952.11
Vanish In An Instant (Millar)   1953.02
Vanished (Carleton)   1955.05
Vanishing Point (Canning)   1983.05
The Vanishing Violinist (Frommer)   1999.24

The Detective Book Club 1942-2000 Title Index

The Vatican Rip (Gash)	1982.09	*Wavecrest (Knox)*	1985.23
Veiled Antiquity (MacPherson)	1998.20	*We Haven't Seen Her Lately*	
Veiled Murder (Campbell)	1950.01	*(Ferrars)*	1956.10
Vendetta's Victim (Matthews)	1998.16	*We The Bereaved (Clarke)*	1983.07
Venetian Blind (Haggard)	1960.06	*Weave a Wicked Web (Kruger)*	1967.09
The Venice Train (Simenon)	1974.13	*Wedding Treasure (Williams)*	1985.22
Venus in Copper (Davis)	1992.04	*The Weird World Of Wes Beattie*	
Verdict Suspended (Nielsen)	1964.07	*(Harris)*	1963.10
Verdict in Blood (Bowen)	1999.19	*Welcome To The Grave (McMullen)*	1979.08
The Verona Passamezzo (Gollin)	1985.04	*The Well-Dressed Skeleton*	
A Very Quiet Place (Garve)	1968.04	*(Williams)*	1962.11
A Very Welcome Death (Mathews)	1961.10	*West On 66 (Cobb)*	1999.01
Victim Of Circumstance		*What Crime Is It? (Gardiner)*	1956.12
(Underwood)	1980.16	*What Did Hattie See? (Roos)*	1970.09
The Vienna Elephant (Leather)	1978.05	*What Rhymes With Murder? (Iams)*	1950.07
Violence (Woolrich)	1958.11	*What, Me, Mr. Mosley?*	
The Virgin In The Ice (Peters)	1983.12	*(Greenwood)*	1988.17
Visa To Limbo (Haggard)	1980.08	*Whatever Goes Up (Millhauser)*	1945.05
The Visitor (Gilbert)	1967.12	*Whatever Happened To Baby Jane?*	
The Voice (Gilbert)	1966.04	*(Farrell)*	1960.10
Voice Out of Darkness (Curtiss)	1948.09	*When The Killing Starts (Wood)*	1989.12
Vortex (Cleary)	1978.14	*Where Agents Fear to Tread (Lewis)*	1984.14
Vow of Adoration (Black)	1998.19	*Where Are The Children? (Clark)*	1975.09
A Vow of Devotion (Black)	1995.24	*Where Dead Soldiers Walk (Biggle*	
A Vow of Fidelity (Black)	1996.13	*Jr.)*	1994.11
Vow of Poverty (Black)	1996.05	*Where Helen Lies (Foley)*	1976.13
The Wager (Fish)	1974.13	*Where Nobody Dies (Wheat)*	1986.06
The Waikiki Widow (Sheridan)	1954.03	*Where There's Smoke (Kelland)*	1959.05
Wait For Death (Ashe)	1972.10	*Where There's Smoke (McKinney)*	1999.22
Wait for What Will Come (Michaels)	1978.20	*Which Doctor? (Candy)*	1954.07
Wait for What Will Come (Michaels)	1978.22	*Whiff of Sulphur (Linscott)*	1987.03
The Waiting Game (Wayland)	1965.09	*While Drowning In The Desert*	
Waiting for the End of the World		*(Winslow)*	1996.15
(Taylor)	1984.14	*The Whip (Mason)*	1948.07
Wake For A Lady (Roden)	1946.07	*Whisper Murder! (Kelsey)*	1946.03
Wake The Sleeping Wolf (Foley)	1952.06	*Whispering Caverns (Winter)*	1975.07
Wake Up To Murder (Allen)	1997.20	*The Whispering Death (Vickers)*	1947.02
Wake Up, Darlin' Corey (Wren)	1984.08	*The Whispering Master (Gruber)*	1947.09
Walk A Wicked Mile (Hansen)	1955.08	*The Whispering Wall (Carlon)*	1997.08
Walk-In (Scott)	1977.06	*The White Dress (Eberhart)*	1946.10
The Walker In Shadows (Michaels)	1980.05	*The White Lie Assignment (Driscoll)*	1975.15
Walking Dead Man (Pentecost)	1973.12	*The White Pavilion (Johnston)*	1974.01
Walking Shadow (Offord)	1960.02	*Whitewater (Knox)*	1974.17
Wanted For Murder (Rutledge)	1956.04	*Whitewater VJ (McBriarty)*	1987.11
Wanton's web (Matthews)	1999.09	*Who Benefits? (Thayer)*	1955.12
Warning Bell (Ransome)	1960.04	*Who Lies Here? (Peters)*	1965.10
The Wasp (Curtiss)	1963.07	*Who Saw Him Die? (Radley)*	1989.13
The Watch Sinister (Blizard)	1951.09	*Who Saw Maggie Brown? (Roos)*	1968.01
The Watcher (Smith)	1980.14	*Who'd Hire Brett (Brett)*	1981.19
The Watcher (Wilcox)	1978.07	*Whoever Has the Heart (Melville)*	1994.10
The Watchers (Siller)	1969.10	*Whoever I Am (Dewhurst)*	1983.11

The Detective Book Club 1942-2000 Title Index

Why Me *(Westlake)*	1983.08
Why Murder? *(Philips)*	1979.18
Why She Cries, I Do Not Know *(Masterson)*	1973.04
Wicked Designs *(O'Donnell)*	1980.24
A Wicked Slice *(Elkins)*	1989.02
Widow's Mite *(Holding)*	1953.04
The Widow's Woods *(Ballard)*	1991.07
Widows Wear Weeds *(Fair)*	1966.05
The Wife That Died Twice *(Bohle)*	1962.06
The Wilby Conspiracy *(Driscoll)*	1973.05
Wild Midnight Falls *(Chaber)*	1968.10
Wild Night *(Foley)*	1966.08
Wilderness *(Parker)*	1980.01
Williamsburg Forgeries *(Ballinger)*	1989.03
Win, Lose or Die *(Gardner)*	1989.14
Windfall *(Bagley)*	1982.24
Winifred *(Disney)*	1976.08
Winning Can Be Murder *(Crider)*	1996.10
Winter Chill *(Cleary)*	1996.20
Winter Garden Mystery *(Dunn)*	1995.14
The Winter Spy *(Henissart)*	1977.12
The Witch Hill Murder *(Winslow)*	1978.05
Witch Miss Seaton *(Carvic)*	1971.11
Witchrock *(Knox)*	1978.10
With Intent To Kill *(Pentecost)*	1982.17
With Murder For Some *(Huston)*	1953.08
With This Ring *(Eberhart)*	1942.02
Without A Trace *(Ransome)*	1962.05
Witness At Large *(Eberhart)*	1967.03
Witness Before the Fact *(Ferrars)*	1980.13
The Witness for the Prosecution *(Christie)*	1949.01
The Wizard's Daughter *(Michaels)*	1981.08
Wolf In Man's Clothing *(Eberhart)*	1943.02
A Wolf by the Ears *(Lewis)*	1973.09
The Woman In Black *(Ford)*	1947.07
The Woman In Red *(Gilbert)*	1943.10
The Woman On The Roof *(Eberhart)*	1968.01
Woman With a Gun *(Coxe)*	1972.09
Woman in Red *(Gosling)*	1984.10
A Word After Dying *(Granger)*	1998.07
Working Murder *(Boylan)*	1989.03
Worm of Doubt *(Meek)*	1988.03
The Wrong Body *(Gilbert)*	1951.11
The Wrong Way Down *(Daly)*	1946.09
Wychford Murders *(Gosling)*	1986.16
Wycliffe And The House Of Fear *(Burley)*	1995.12
Wycliffe And The Scapegoat *(Burley)*	1979.16
Wycliffe In Paul's Court *(Burley)*	1981.03
Wycliffe and the Beales *(Burley)*	1984.15
Wycliffe and the Dunes Mystery *(Burley)*	1994.10
Wycliffe and the Quiet Virgin *(Burley)*	1986.11
Wycliffe's Wild Goose Chase *(Burley)*	1983.03
X Marks the Dot *(Stafford)*	1944.01
The Xavier Affair *(Fish)*	1969.07
The Year of the Monkey *(Berry)*	1988.18
The Yellow Gold of Tiryns *(Osborne)*	1970.04
The Yellow Villa *(Blanc)*	1964.06
The Yellow Violet *(Crane)*	1943.01
Yesterday's Enemy *(Haggard)*	1977.10
You Can Die Laughing *(Fair)*	1957.05
You Only Hang Once *(Roden)*	1944.04
You Who Know *(Freeling)*	1994.06
You Won't Let Me Finnish *(Fleming)*	1974.05
You'll Be Sorry! *(Rogers)*	1945.10
You're Never Too Old To Die *(Goldstein)*	1974.17
The Young Can Die Protesting *(Wells)*	1970.02
Young Mrs. Cavendish And The Kaiser's Men *(Beck)*	1988.01
Your Eyelids Are Growing Heavy *(Paul)*	1981.18
The Z-Papers *(Simmons)*	1976.15
Zanzibar Intrigue *(Mason)*	1963.12
Zen and the city of angels *(Cosin)*	1999.23
Zurich/AZ900 *(Albrand)*	1974.18
The hireling's tale *(Bannister)*	1999.23